D1558440

BEGINNING MATH CONCEPTS FOR GAME DEVELOPERS

JOHN P. FLYNT
BORIS MELTREGER

THOMSON

COURSE TECHNOLOGY

Professional ■ Technical ■ Reference

Educational facilities, companies, and organizations interested in multiple copies or licensing of this book should contact the Publisher for quantity discount information. Training manuals, CD-ROMs, and portions of this book are also available individually or can be tailored for specific needs.

ISBN-10: 1-59863-290-6
ISBN-13: 978-1-59863-290-3
Library of Congress Catalog Card Number: 2006927124
Printed in the United States of America
07 08 09 10 11 PH 10 9 8 7 6 5 4 3 2 1

Publisher and General Manager, Thomson Course Technology PTR:
Stacy L. Hiquet

Associate Director of Marketing:
Sarah O'Donnell

Manager of Editorial Services:
Heather Talbot

Marketing Manager:
Heather Hurley

Senior Acquisitions Editor:
Emi Smith

Project Editor:
Jenny Davidson

Technical Reviewer:
Marcia Flynt

PTR Editorial Services Coordinator:
Erin Johnson

Interior Layout Tech:
Interactive Composition Corporation

Cover Designer:
Mike Tanamachi

CD-ROM Producer:
Brandon Penticuff

Indexer:
Kevin Broccoli

Proofreader:
Kim Benbow

Thomson Course Technology PTR,
a division of Thomson Learning Inc.
25 Thomson Place
Boston, MA 02210
http://www.courseptr.com

This book is dedicated to its readers.

ACKNOWLEDGMENTS

John To Emi Smith and Stacy Hiquet for arranging for the publication. To Jenny Davidson, for watching over the schedule and making it happen. Thanks to Marcia for the tremendous technical editing effort. You have made this book possible. To Boris for creating Visual Formula and Visual Code and working on a tight schedule. And to Janet for being an inspiration. Amy, thank you for working problems. Also, thanks to Adrian Flynt, Beth Walker, Brent Jones, and Kevin Claver for moral support and to Professor Michael Main for talk about Cartesian concerns.

Boris Thanks to my wife Janet and son Leonid for creative advice about how to present math and for testing Visual Formula. Also, to John and Marcia for involving me in this exciting project.

ABOUT THE AUTHORS

John P. Flynt, Ph.D., has taught at colleges and universities, and has authored courses and curricula for several college-level game development programs. His academic background includes work in information technology, the social sciences, and the humanities. Among his works are *In the Mind of a Game, Perl Power!, Java Programming for the Absolute Beginner, UnrealScript Game Programming All in One, Software Engineering for Game Developers,* and *Simulation and Event Modeling for Game Developers* (with co-author Ben Vinson). Flynt coauthored another book with Boris Meltreger, *Beginning Pre-Calculus for Game Developers.* John lives in the foothills near Boulder, Colorado.

Boris Meltreger received an advanced degree (Candidate of Technical Science) in Russia. He has extensive experience in R&D for sonar, optical computing, and laser therapy equipment. He has authored 18 inventions and many technical articles, research reports, and manuals. For the past few years, Boris has been with Rogue Wave Software, specializing in software libraries for C++ and C#. His dedication to the study of mathematics goes back to high school, where he specialized in physics and math as a student in renowned School 239 in St. Petersburg. Boris lives in Aurora, Colorado.

CONTENTS

INTRODUCTION

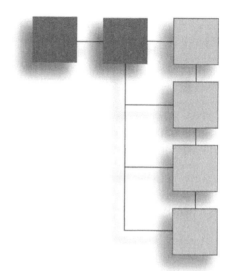

About This Book

You can benefit from reading this book if you are interested in exploring approaches to supplementing your beginning game development and math studies with programming activities that combine game development with basic math. This book caters to students of pre-calculus and calculus, and beginning and intermediate programmers who have an interest in learning to program with C#. It does not teach you the fundamentals of programming, but the programming examples it provides are all explained fully and will aid you in learning how to program if you are working with C# for the first time. This book provides hands-on activities in which you put basic math equations to work to generate sets of numbers that allow you to create graphs or drive animations. By the time you reach Chapter 10, you have in hand an application you have developed from the ground up that should allow you to endlessly explore game development scenarios for 2D games. In fact, Chapter 2 provides the basics of several game development projects that have been used many times in classrooms.

On the accompanying CD, you will find Visual Formula and Visual Code, along with an appendix of installation and usage instructions. You can use these applications to test-drive the equations you use in the Code Lab application that you work with throughout the book. After testing your equations, you can generate bodies of data that you can then put to work to guide objects as they move in the animated space the Code Lab provides.

Who Should Read This Book

This book in part represents the result of a conversation that took place between one of the authors and a professor of computer science at a leading university. You can gain a sense of whether it is suitable for you if you consider that the conversation concerned whether it would be helpful for beginning game development students and math students to have at hand a book that would teach them how to build their own program for creating a Cartesian coordinate system and then turning this into a game. This book follows that scenario.

Rest assured that every program is explained in intricate detail, so if you are a beginner, you stand an excellent chance of being able to progress through the book without much difficulty. For math students, the book is intended to provide you with a set of software projects you can explore as you exercise math skills you acquire in pre-calculus and calculus classes. The software you work with allows you to program equations, generate data using them, and then use the data you generate to create static graphs of animated games.

If you are an intermediate or advanced programmer, it is hoped that you will find this book to be a starting point for efforts you might undertake to review math skills by putting them to work in the context the Code Lab provides to enhance its functionality and create games using it. You can review the construction of Code Lab from the ground up in the first eight chapters of the book. The final two chapters of the book provide you with C# projects that you can use as a starting point for advanced development efforts.

For readers who want to learn C# and already possess knowledge of another programming language, especially Java or VB, this book provides you with a set of projects that you can use to explore and learn C# without having to begin from the very beginning. By the end of the book, you should have a solid grasp of what C# is about, and yet along the way, you will not have had to review all the language features in detail.

The Chapters

Chapter 1 provides you with an overview of how to use the book. This book is about how to use math to generate data that can drive games. The data you generate complement and provide an alternative to beginning games that are based on isolated user interactions. This book emphasizes that patterns of data can be used to drive games. You find in this chapter a directive to complete a short tutorial on getting started with C#. To complete this work, you must first download the free version of C# Express. You can find directions in Appendix A.

Chapter 2 provides a review of basic math and how functions work. The review serves to refresh a few notions about what you do with a function and how you can employ it to generate data that you can use in a game. This chapter also gets you started with the Code Lab application and discusses at length many characteristics and uses of C#.

Chapter 3 involves you in working with functions to generate a few simple bodies of data. It also extends your work with C# by helping you work with such things as exception handling.

Chapter 4 takes you on a journey in which you expand the Code Lab in fairly extensive ways. You review the use of the `DataForm`, `CoordSystem`, `CartForm`, and `Functions` classes. You explore how a collection can serve as a pipeline for data between forms. In this chapter, you lay the groundwork for the Cartesian plotting system that you develop using the `CartForm` and `CoordSystem` classes.

Chapter 5 marks the end of the two-chapter excursion that allows you to build your own Cartesian coordinate system. In this chapter, you plan and create a grid with axes, and attend to the development of methods to plot points, lines, and curves. You deal with issues of translating the world space of the Microsoft form into the world space of your Cartesian system. The actions you undertake in this respect are directly applicable to the types of actions you perform when you translate world to local space in a game. You also work with scaling issues and learn about the C# Graphics class.

Chapter 6 furnishes you with opportunities to further your work in two central ways. The first involves generating data and drawing graphs for varying equations. The second involves pursing a theme that is central to the book. This theme concentrates on composing complex events from simple events. In this instance, the simple events are isolated functions. The complex events are composed functions. You make use of the `List` collection to store data from different functions, and from this emerges the ability to create composite patterns. This chapter focuses on the conceptual foundations. In later chapters, you attend to programming details.

Chapter 7 offers a concentrated review of quadratic equations and equations involving absolute values. It also reviews discontinuous equations. Equations of this type represent fundamental patterns, so in this respect, the work you perform in this class complements the work you perform in previous chapters, where you work extensively with linear equations. The goal is to provide you with a few tools to develop different types of patterns. At the same time, you find a fairly comprehensive math review.

Chapter 8 ventures into limits and provides the farthest point of progress you find into the realm of calculus. If you have taken a calculus course and want to use equations based on calculus, you can do so easily enough at this point, but to make the book so that it conforms to the notion of "beginning math concepts," the formal presentation of math stops with limits. Your programming in this chapter involves some new and interesting turns. You explore how to store data from different equations in the collection and then retrieve it according to values that limits define. What you accomplish using limits you can extend to any number of contexts.

Chapter 9 provides what might constitute the beginning point for many readers. Here you begin work on an application context suitable for a game that incorporates animated features. You learn about eliminating flicker in panels, and you develop the AniForm class to accommodate animation. Through four iterations of the AniForm class, you incorporate data to create successively more complex patterns of behavior for an animated object.

Chapter 10 finishes off your work with what amounts to two extensive revisions of the AniForm class. In the first revision, you replace the Cartesian grid with a star-filled background. You replace your animated point with a blinking object. You create complex events that allow you to explore how a body of data becomes a node and how programmatic interactions between nodes become transitions in event contexts.

Appendix A provides you with instructions about how to obtain and install Visual C# Express.

Appendix B shows you how to install Visual Formula and work with it.

Appendix C, which is on the CD only, provides you with information about how to obtain supplemental software from Microsoft.

The CD

On the CD you'll find all the projects for the book. You'll find a separate C# project for Chapters 2 through 10. The projects are ready to go. Click on the *.sln file and go to work!

In addition, you'll find supplementary software. This includes Visual Formula, which Appendix B documents. Visual Formula allows you to easily set up almost any equations you care to name in the areas of algebra and trigonometry and generate a graphical representation of it. In this way, you can quickly review a given equation before you write a C# program for it in the Code Lab.

You also get a copy of Visual Code. Documentation for Visual Code is on the CD. Visual Code offers several features similar to Visual Formula, but it is designed to allow you to write C# code to implement equations. You program math equations in C# and then compile them to test them. You can work simultaneously with up to 12 equations during any given test session. You can generate both tabular and graphical output. You can save your work and screen shots of the data and graphs you work with. You can take screenshots of problems you want to work with and have them visible as you work. Generally, Visual Code represents a polished, greatly enhanced, and professionally produced version of the Code Lab that you develop in the book.

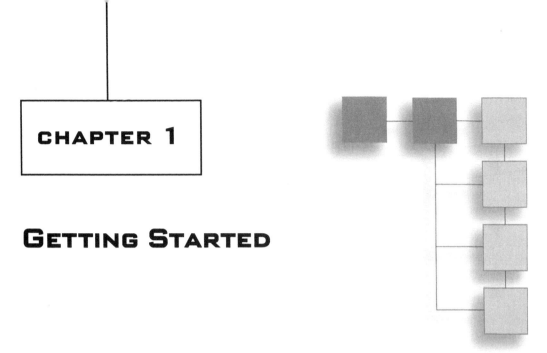

CHAPTER 1

GETTING STARTED

In this chapter, you explore some of the fundamental themes of this book. The book does not so much teach you math as offers you some avenues for extending the ways that you learn and use math as you develop computer games. The games this book concern remain simple, the type of game you develop if you are first exploring game development. However, what you explore in simple terms can be extended to more complex applications. What applies to learning applies to the creation and use of mathematical data. While you develop isolated bodies of data using isolated functions, you can also compose functions you develop in isolation into complex functions. The Code Lab application fosters such activity. It provides you with a number of classes and contexts of development that allow you to generate tables of data and then to use this data to create stationary and animated events. In addition to working with the Code Lab application and functional approaches to creating events in games, you also use data that extends into the realm of metadata. Metadata is data about data. Among the topics explored in this chapter are the following:

- Understanding how to develop a game

- Different ways of generating the events that are involved in a game

- How to view the development of a game as an extensible activity

- The concept of data as a node of intelligence

- The uses of functional composition and decomposition

- Getting started with the C# development environment

Game Contexts

Many good books on beginning game development follow what might be viewed as a standard path. As Figure 1.1 illustrates, through largely empirical, hands-on exploration, you develop a basic game that you interact with using event processing from the keyboard or the mouse. You might develop a pong, galactic battle, or battleship game. You use the arrow keys or the mouse to trigger events. If the sprites in the game move automatically, they do so because you embed or call set functions in the main game loop. In fact, the events of the game are often the result of fixed methods that at most use a random number generator to vary things slightly (such as the position of a target). Generally, you work in a context in which you invoke only a few types of events. These events tend to be specifically programmed responses to the click of the mouse or the press of a key. All interaction is framed in immediate context and is generated through isolated events.

The isolated-event model provides an excellent and rewarding approach for beginning game developers because it allows you to develop a game in a fairly free-form way. After you have put in place your basic game loop and figured out how to process keyboard or mouse input, you can then begin expanding on a basic

The code contains algorithms that create
relatively isolated events. Within
the game loop, the program detects
user-generated actions and responds to them.

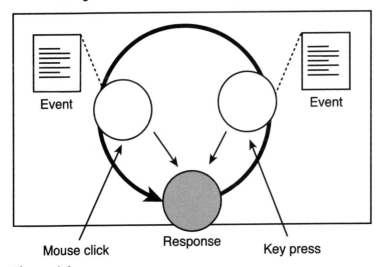

Figure 1.1
Isolated responses to events depend on isolated event scenarios.

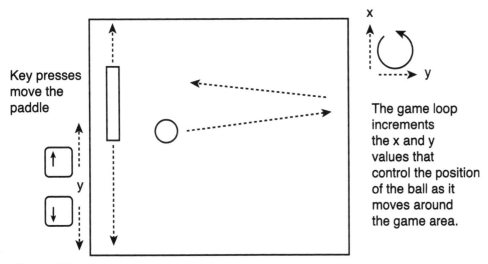

Figure 1.2
Action occurs in a context characterized by user input and programmed responses to the input.

game scenario by making the events you have programmed into the game loop more complex. Figure 1.2 summarizes the context of a paddle or pong game. The following list traces activities you might undertake as you develop such a game:

- **Timer and loop.** Create a timer or a thread and program a statement that allows an infinite (game) loop to execute.

- **Graphics.** Figure out how to position a graphical object (ball or paddle) in the client, window, or screen area.

- **Animation.** Make an object, such as a ball, move according to values that the game loop generates.

- **Nodes.** Make a second object, like a paddle, that moves up and down with the up and down arrow keys.

- **Collision.** Figure out how to detect collisions so that when one object crosses the path of the other, you can know it via values you store in a variable.

- **Intelligence.** Record the collision by incrementing a given value so that you can keep track of the number of collisions.

- **Response.** Display the collisions as a score.

- **Rules.** Set up a timer so that the duration of the actions is limited.

444 tion

- **Game.** Add an algorithm that allows the player a given amount of time to make so many scores. If the player scores the stipulated number of times during the time allowed, the player wins. Otherwise, the player loses.

The pong game Figure 1.2 illustrates captures the heart of many beginning game development activities because it contains the essential features of many computer games. You can summarize these as follows:

- **Sustained interaction.** The application (or game) begins to execute at the player's command and continues to operate indefinitely as the player interacts with it.

- **Player input.** The application accepts a narrow, well-defined range of input from the player.

- **Game response.** The application responds to the narrow range of input in precise ways.

- **A rule (or set of rules) that structure the activity.** The acceptance of and response to input take place according to a logic that the game prescribes.

Extending the Game

Many of the themes dealt with in this book constitute the practical outcome of exploring the possibilities of a game you have begun to develop. A simple game becomes a complex game because you combined simple activities to create complex activities. There are two general paths you follow in this respect. They can be placed under the headings of *extensivity* and *extensibility*. The next couple of sections explore these concepts in greater detail. While the discussions of these two headings slightly digress from the central themes of this chapter, it remains important to keep it in mind when you consider the general notion that to create complex types of interaction in a game, you combine simpler forms of interactions. Later in this chapter, the discussions of functional composition and data nodes extend this theme.

Extensivity

Extensivity relates to the art or culture of the game you create. It encompasses what you see and feel and what you do. A culture is a context of activity that extends to anything you find relevant and meaningful. Extensivity means that the more you work with it, the more you figure out how to add new and interesting things to your game. For example, with a pong or paddle game, when the ball hits the bat, you decide to add a crack or beep. When you win the game, you decide to add a marquee with "Winner" flashing in big letters. As you improve in your skills, you add functionality that allows you to see speeds at which the ball moves: slow, medium, or fast. The list goes on. At some point, you make it so the ball changes to a different color each time you hit it.

In each instance, what you add to the game reflects your experiences as a player. You might have to struggle to develop the programming or artistic skills necessary to add the features you want to add, but you do so willingly. You are pursuing and completing a vision. What you bring to this experience might depend on any number of factors. It might be that you play another game and like a feature of that game. It might be that something just seems to make sense at a given point. Extensivity is driven by your sense of what makes the game complete.

Extensibility

Extensibility relates to software engineering. In software engineering parlance, when software is extensible, you can add features to it without breaking it. As an analogy, consider one of the projects in which someone builds a house of cards or toothpicks. It is easy to imagine a situation in which the addition of a single card or toothpick brings the whole structure tumbling down. This is the opposite of extensibility. Extensibility means that when you want to add to a part of the structure, you can do so with relative ease.

In a game, extensibility results in part from your growing awareness, as a developer, of what you have developed. In formal engineering contexts, extensibility results from the architectural principles regulating the development project. In either case, as you program the game, you write methods or create classes that allow you to do more with less.

For example, to consider once again the pong game, extensibility characterizes a situation in which, after you create a method that allows you to move the paddle up and down, you then create another version of this method. The second version takes little work and makes it possible for you to vary the rate at which the paddle moves as you press the arrow keys. As another example, after you create a way to track the score, you can then proceed to divide or multiply the score in different ways. Or as a final example, after you figure out how to put one background into the game, you can vary the backgrounds so that different stadiums are represented. When a game is extensible, it allows you to proceed existing functionally to more easily implement new functionality.

Note

More information on event models, extensivity, and other such topics is available in *Simulation and Event Modeling for Game Developers*, by John Flynt and Ben Vinson (Thomson Course Technology, 2005) or *In the Mind of a Game*, by John Flynt (Thomson Course Technology, 2005). For a discussion of the formal aspects of software engineering, see John Flynt's, *Software Engineering for Game Developers* (Thomson Course Technology, 2004).

Heuristics

The scenario that emerges with the development of a game proves endlessly interesting, culturally and technically, because it allows you to learn in a multitude of ways as you develop your game. Whether your forte is art, programming, music, math, or almost anything else, when you develop a game on a computer, you enter into a place in which you can incorporate what you learn into the game and, as you do so, learn new ways to learn.

This is at the heart of the notions of *heuristics*. Heuristics is a word derived from the ancient Greek term for "to find," and so it is in essence, a way of finding or discovering. Game development provides heuristics that make it possible to learn how to learn as you learn. Every tool you develop becomes a tool with which you can develop more tools. Every path you follow leads to other paths.

What applies to game development applies to math, of course. It also applies to every branch of science. Generally, any valid science or technology provides a fairly endless context for the work of heuristics because such activities consistently incorporate tested knowledge and experimentally established data. What you learn or discover one day remains valid the next. Likewise, what you learn or discover in one area of exploration or development proves potentially applicable in all other areas.

This book tries to bring into play as much as possible the heuristics of game development to allow you to improvise some ways to increase your capacity to explore math. The mathematical topics it deals with tend to be limited to algebra and beginning calculus, but it is hoped that what begins in this simple way can be taken in many directions and to many levels. The pattern the book follows is that of the pong game. You begin simple and allow extensivity and extensibility to do their work.

Alternative Models

Figure 1.3 provides both an extension of and alternative to the approach to game development the previous sections have presented. It is still the case that heuristics and the actions of extensivity and extensibility come into play, but the model used for the game (the game architecture) takes a different path.

From this approach, you still put in place a basic game loop. You still write methods that address given events. What differs, however, is that you withhold the effort you usually undertake right at the start to connect the game with input you provide from the keyboard or mouse. Certainly, at some point along the line, you want to add these capabilities, but in this context, the emphasis is on substituting input from sets of data that you generate using math equations for the input that you usually garner from the player.

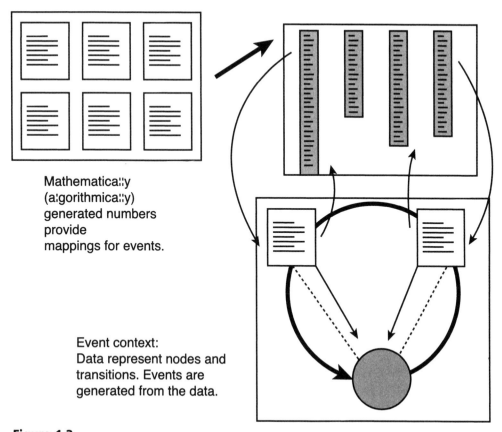

Mathematically
(algorithmically)
generated numbers
provide
mappings for events.

Event context:
Data represent nodes and
transitions. Events are
generated from the data.

Figure 1.3
The program provides mapped scenarios that bring forward paths of activities from mathematically (or algorithmically) generated data.

That constitutes the first major difference. The second major difference is that you generate events based on how you apply programs to the data. Initially, the responses are those of generating graphs to represent the data. This type of activity might seem fairly restricted if you value a game as a medium through which actions invoke immediate, isolated responses. In this context, the action you see results from maps of data you provide to the game before the game begins to execute. You design and generate the data, but the gratification of seeing it do something is delayed.

Generating data mathematically and then finding ways to incorporate such data in the play of a game shifts player interaction to a different context. Now, instead of clicking a mouse button, you write a linear equation. You generate data using the equation. You then click a button and see what your application or game does with it. After a time, you add event processing to your application or game so that when you click a button, you see events unfold in a more complex way, one that makes use of the data you provide in ways that prove far more complex.

The uses are more complex than those you usually work with when you write a game. They are more complex because they respond to events on more than a basic, one-to-one stimulus-response basis. As you discover in later chapters, for example, you might use a thousand pieces of data to generate a few events. It is like clicking the mouse a thousand times.

In Figure 1.3, at the top right you see icons that represent files of data. They might also represent database tables. On the top left, you see icons that represent functions that generate the data. The game then uses the data to generate events. To make this possible, you write methods (or functions) that use the data in specific *event contexts*. As this chapter and Chapter 10 discuss in greater detail, an event context includes nodes (data that "makes sense" to other data) and transitions (ways that data makes sense to other data).

A Framework for Exploration

In this book, instead of storing your data in a file or a database, you use a temporary object known as a *collection*. A collection is an object you create with C#. It is like an array. It allows you to store a huge amount of data, and as implemented in this book, it allows you to pass your data around between different windows and use it in different ways. When you work with C#, the type

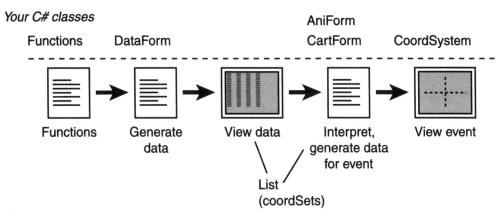

Figure 1.4
The path differs but reaches the same destination.

of collection you use is known as a *list*. (This is one among several objects known as collections.)

Figure 1.4 illustrates this activity. As you develop the Code Lab application, you write methods for mathematical functions and put them in a class called, as you might guess, Functions. You then move to another class, called DataForm, where you make use of the functions to generate data. As you generate the data, you see it and store it. Initially you see it in the form as a table of values. The DataForm class allows you to generate this table. The purpose of seeing the data in a tabular form is to allow you to study it on an empirical basis, to see the numbers your function generates.

Next you move to a graphical representation of the numbers. In this area, the book provides two primary pathways. The first involves a static graph. The second involves animation. To develop static graphs, you use the CartForm class. This class and its accompanying Cartesian grid allow you to plot data. Another path leads to animation. You accomplish this by creating a class called AniForm, which allows you to author game-like animations.

Behind the scenes is a general class called CoordSystem. You spend two chapters developing the basics of this class. It allows you explore a topic that proves essential to the development of games. One is to create code that translates one framework of space into another. In this case, you move in three realms. You begin with the raw data from your functions. You then venture into the world space of the window Microsoft C# provides. Then you move to the space of the graphical representation you are trying to create.

Nodes and Values

Artificial intelligence and schemes of relating information that use neuron synapses as models lie far outside the scope of this book. However, in one respect, you perform a few tasks in this book that help you relate to how such advanced forms of guiding the activity of games tends to emerge. Toward this end, you develop a customized form of data called Values. This data item might just as well have been called DataNode or NeuralNode, but such names seemed far too pretentious for the current context. As it is, the Values object contains and organizes information that ... *well* ... possesses *value,* and that seemed to be an appropriate occasion for its naming.

As Figure 1.5 shows, the Values object allows you to store two types of information. The first two fields, represented by X and Y, store information about coordinates in a Cartesian plane.

The second two fields serve in a different capacity. They store information about information. Such information, among other things, allows you to know about or make decisions about the first fields.

Given these two forms of data, a Values object provides you with a data object that has built into it the capacity to furnish an intelligent response to your uses of the basic data it contains. Granted, you have to write a program that fosters the

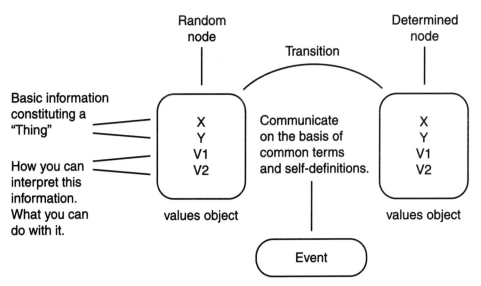

Figure 1.5
The Values object gives you a way to explore data that creates its own event contexts.

intelligence, but if you give some thought to the meaning of such data, you can understand fairly readily that the implications are extensive.

From a mathematical perspective, you can approach data from two general directions. If you remember a film called *A Beautiful Mind,* you recall that the mathematician at one point followed pigeons around the quadrangle of a college to collect data on their movements. He then returned to his dorm room to write mathematical equations that recreated the patterns. Another approach is to write mathematical equations and then observe the patterns that result. One approach is inductive (drawing a generalization from data); the other approach is deductive (explaining data from a generalization).

From the data you gather, you can create math equations that generalize or summarize how the data emerges. On the other hand, to explore the manifestations or behaviors of a given equation, you write a program that generates data using the equation. Both are completely acceptable paths of exploration.

This is in part the reason the Code Lab application consists of several separate classes. Some allow you to make generalizations. Others allow you to observe data. Working with the different classes allows you to isolate your activities in different ways. You can create functions and see the bodies of data you can create with them. You can then work from the data and create events in the form of graphical images of different forms of animated behavior.

The Values object caters to this activity because it provides a data type that can store information about itself. Even if the discussion is far from such topics, it remains that such an object is in some ways comparable to a neural node. The concept of a node is that a given item of data might be both a raw number and at the same time a number that has meaning in a given way because it is part of a larger pattern (see Figure 1.6). That is the purpose of setting up the Values object so that it possesses X, Y, V1, and V2 elements.

You can view the X and Y fields as raw data. You can view the V1 and V2 fields as metadata fields. Such fields store data about data. The uses you make of the Values object change as you work through different problems. The examples the book provides serve as places to begin. One pattern of use is one of successively evaluating a starter set of data and then storing the results of the evaluation in metadata fields the Values object furnishes.

Much more might be said on this topic, and thousands of books at this point do, in fact carry the conversation forward. In this setting, however, it is enough to

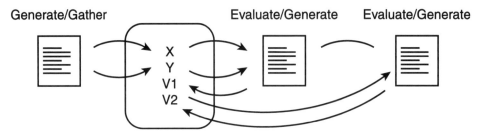

Figure 1.6
A node is a group of data that can tell you something about itself.

emphasize that if you want to expand the use of the Values object, then the Code Lab application should provide plenty of avenues for doing so.

Note

You implement the Values data type in Chapter 4, and you expand it to its intelligent version later on. Since you work with fairly large groups of Values objects, in Chapters 2 and 3, you work your way gradually into the notion of a collection.

Mathematics and Functionality

The emphasis on generating mathematical data and then using it in a context that ultimately leads you to activities that are clearly oriented toward game development does not in itself constitute a formalized, systematic study of mathematics. In this respect, then, the discussions of math focus on *concepts*. Among other things, a concept is a framework of awareness. It is not necessarily accompanied by problems and practices that allow you to solidify a skill. In this respect, you find that a few central themes emerge.

The discussion of functions emphasizes linear and quadratic equations and restricts itself largely to what you find in the study of algebra. To make use of this discussion, you can either draw from the methods that are provided in the Functions class or program your own methods to generate bodies of data that you can work with in a ready way to create events. You can display the events in stationary or animated forms. The book at first emphasizes stationary graphing. Then it moves to animation.

Figure 1.7 pulls together a few key concepts you use as you work with the Code Lab application. The first is that you can view complex events as resulting from

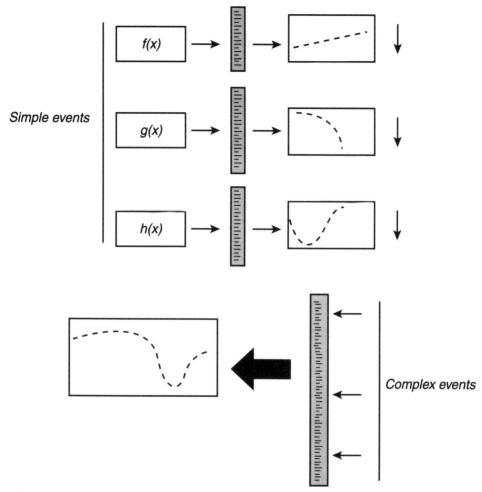

Figure 1.7
Composition of simple events allows you to create more complex events.

the combination of simple events. In this instance, you use functions to generate relatively small tables of data. Each such table of data generates an isolated image. You can then combine the data in these isolated tables to form a large table. The large table allows you to generate a composed, complex image.

As you might expect, the general term for using functionally generated data in this way is functional composition. The uses of such composition extend into every imaginable area of human knowledge.

When you combine functionally generated data, you compose functions. When you begin with a body of data and attempt to discover patterns in it that you can

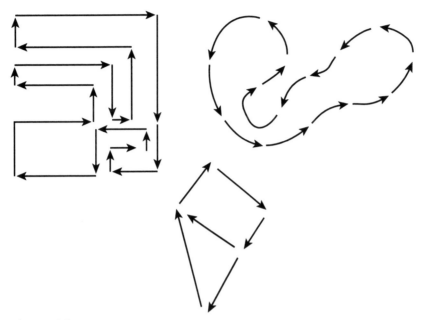

Figure 1.8
Composed patterns are both functional and synthetic.

regenerate functionally, you involve yourself in functional decomposition. The one is the reflection of the other. You can use functional decomposition, for example, to confirm or test the results of functional composition.

In the contexts of mathematics and game development, when you seek to create a complex event, you begin by analyzing the event you want to create to discover its functional components. You then work on creating the components in isolation, testing them, and combining them. The line compositions in Figure 1.8 depict curves and vectors. Through the course of this book, you work with equations and can generate such entities.

The implication for game development of using functional compositions to create complex events is that the events allow players to enter into a more complex world when they play your game.

Development Strategies

In this book, you make use of the Visual C# Express development environment. As of the writing of this book, you can freely obtain the Visual C# Express development environment if you download it from a site Microsoft provides.

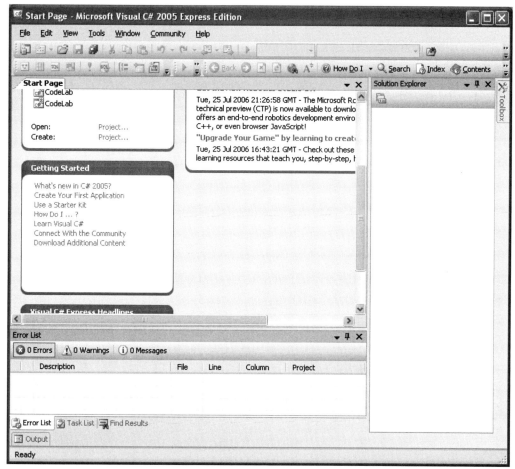

Figure 1.9
Find the tutorial for Create Your First Application.

You can find instructions for accessing and retrieving the development software in Appendix A.

If you have not before worked with the Visual C# Express integrated development environment (IDE), you can work through a tutorial. The tutorial provides a safe way to experiment with the IDE and to develop a simple application. You find this tutorial listed on the start page of the IDE (see Figure 1.9). The start page appears when you open the IDE for the first time. As Figure 1.10 illustrates, it is listed under Getting Started on the left side of the page in the rounded panel. It is called "Create Your First Application." If the Getting Started panel is not visible, then use the scroll bar to scroll to it.

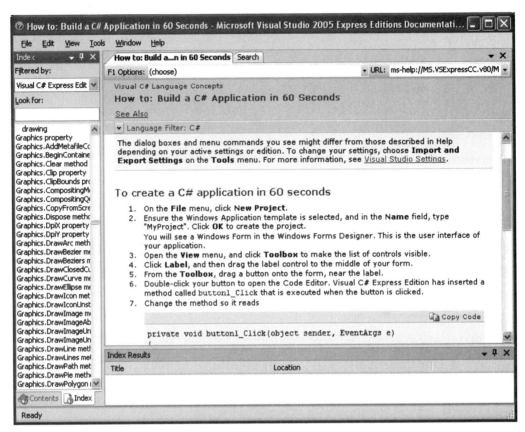

Figure 1.10
If you are new to the C# IDE, explore it by completing the tutorial.

When you click the Create Your First Application link, the IDE accesses the tutorial and loads it into the Help window of your application. Figure 1.10 shows what you see. On the left you see the index of all the topics in the Help library. In the main frame of the Help window, you see the tutorial. This proves an invaluable toolkit. Your IDE remains open on your desktop, and you can work back and forth as you complete the tutorial. At the same time, if you want to begin a random exploration of the thousands of components you can work with as you program with C#, the list on the side is ready at hand.

Conclusion

This chapter has provided a summary review of some of the topics you explore in depth in chapters to come. At the center of much that follows in this book is the notion that you can use math to generate data that you then use to create the events of your game. The most elementary types of games tend to use events that are isolated to immediate, specific contexts. Developing more sophisticated games depends on the ability to create complex events that draw together what might amount to thousands of pieces of information. Mathematically generated sets of data can be part of such activity. The goal here is not to immerse you in complex schemes of artificial intelligence or data collection but to provide you with conceptual tools that allow you to see how data from a set of functions can be collected to create a complex event. The whole course of this book involves developing and exploring this theme.

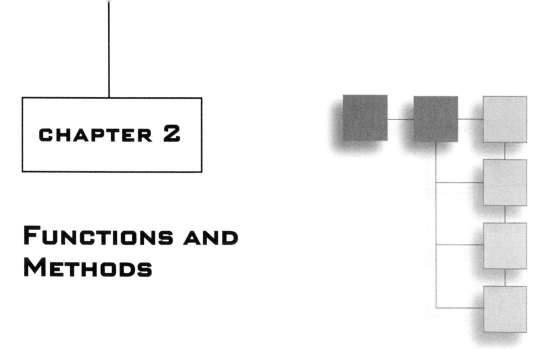

CHAPTER 2

FUNCTIONS AND METHODS

In this chapter, you engage in a few investigations that encompass mathematical functions and the use of such functions in methods you create using C#. Key concepts in this respect are values you establish as a range and the use of a function to generate values for a domain. To explore this notion, you develop methods in the DataForm class and the Functions class. The methods you implement allow you to make the click of a button initiate an event that creates a table of range and domain values that show the relationship between the burning of carbon and the addition of carbon dioxide to the atmosphere. Along the way, you investigate several features of classes, including how classes work within namespaces, how to declare a constant field, and how to define methods within classes. Additional topics include the following:

- How relationships in science and other areas lead to functions

- Exploring the notion that a function embodies an equation

- Picturing the work of a function in terms of domains and ranges

- Exploring the methods in the DataForm class that process input from the button and generate a table

- Examining the full implementation of the Functions class

- Implementing a function and then making changes to reduce the amount of code in it

Patterns

When you write a computer program, you can use the term "function" to refer to lines of code that perform the same action over and over again. As Figure 2.1 illustrates, you provide a function with input, and the function returns or delivers output. The input consists of data of a fairly specific type. Likewise, the output values also consist of a fairly specific type of data.

The notion of a function proves primary, both in programming and in mathematics, because in many ways it represents the most essential result of applying math to the real world. Math involves many aspects of detecting patterns in the behavior of the universe (which encompasses abstract or creative thought). A big part of that activity encompasses finding regular approaches to describing in a quantitative manner the phenomena you encounter as you interact with the universe.

One of the most essential aspects of the development of mathematics since long before the time of Pythagoras has been that mathematicians have represented mathematical concepts in visual or tactile ways. Representation of a mathematical concept might begin with drawing triangles and circles in sand, but it also entails what you see when you type characters using a word processor or play the latest version of a computer game. In both instances, a functional mathematical relationship allows someone to create a tangible event that unfolds in a uniform, predictable way.

In general, when you can reduce your understanding of a concept to a form that allows you to repeat your thought in a consistent, predictable way, you arrive at the basis of understanding that characterizes science and mathematics. Science

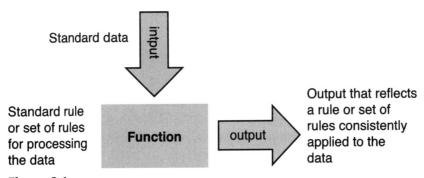

Figure 2.1
A function represents a set way of processing data and generating a result.

might be viewed more as an activity of discovering and creating patterns. Mathematics emphasizes the definition of quantities. The modern world has emerged with the reduction of events to abstract, often quantitative relationships. A function is a way to describe or represent a relationship.

Rules, Domains, and Ranges

A function embodies the application of some type of rule or set of rules for relating two or more occurrences. For example, if you address the amount of carbon dioxide (CO_2) in the atmosphere, you can relate this to the amount of burned carbon. Fossil fuel and biomass (forests, grass, and so on) count as carbon. People burn carbon as they drive their cars, heat their homes, or produce electricity. Forest fires produce carbon dioxide, as do wildfires in grasslands. One quantity relates to another.

When you relate two events in an empirical or scientific manner, you say that one thing is a function of another. For example, as Figure 2.2 illustrates, the quantity of CO_2 that enters the atmosphere can be measured by its weight. You can weigh the carbon burned and the CO_2 in the atmosphere. You can then

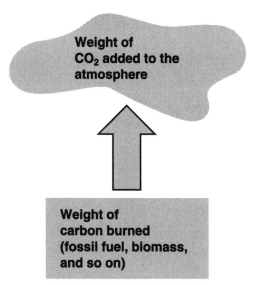

Figure 2.2
The amount of CO_2 is a function of the amount of burned carbon.

conclude that the weight of the CO_2 added to the atmosphere is a function of the weight of the burned carbon.

When you establish a function, you usually try to assert that one thing depends in a specific way on another. The level of CO_2 depends specifically on burned carbon. When you can express this dependency using quantities, then you have at hand a reliable and convenient way to test your assertion.

Generally, the assertion itself is a rule or a hypothesis. Expressed mathematically, it is an equation. It is a formal statement that allows you to assert how one thing depends on another.

When you work an equation that establishes a relationship on a mathematical basis, you assert that a relation exists between two groups of numbers. With respect to the conversion of carbon to CO_2, the two groups of numbers establish first, the different quantities of carbon and, second, different quantities of CO_2.

Accordingly, if you allow **D** to designate the set of real numbers, you establish a function for the set of real numbers (**D**). The function is a rule (f). The function makes it so that for any number (x) in the set **D**, you can generate another number. The number you generate is unique, and you can express it as $f(x)$, which is usually read "the function of x" or "f of x."

Figure 2.3 summarizes this activity. If **D** designates the domain of the function, $f(x)$ designates the range. The numbers you generate using the function constitute the range of values of the function.

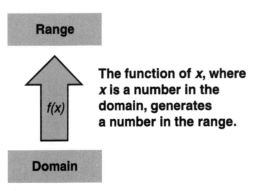

Figure 2.3
A function draws from a domain and generates unique values that constitute a range.

Table 2.1 Carbon Burned and CO_2 Levels

Carbon Burned*	1	2	3	4	5	6	7	8
CO_2	3.67	7.23	11.01	14.68	18.35	22.02	25.69	29.36

Consider, for example, that if you burn a billion tons of carbon, then you produce 3.67 billion tons of CO_2. The relationship this establishes can be expressed in this equation, where x designates the amount of carbon and y designates the amount of CO_2. Given this basis of understanding, if during a given year people worldwide burn 7 billion tons of carbon, then 25.69 billion tons of CO_2 enters the atmosphere. You can formulate an equation to express this relationship as follows:

$$y = 3.67(x)$$

If x equals 7, then the function of 7 reads in this way:

$$f(7) = 25.69$$

If you explore the several domain values for the tons of carbon burned and find the functions of these values as the tons of CO_2 entering the atmosphere, you end up with the data represented in Table 2.1.

When you create a function, the function is unique if each value of x is unique. For each value of x, in other words, the function generates a distinct value. To verify the uniqueness of the values that the function generates, you can inspect the data in Table 2.1, comparing the figures in the top row with those in the bottom, and then the figures in each row. Such an approach proves tedious after a while, however. Figure 2.3 represents a more convenient approach. This is the graphical approach.

To employ the graphical approach, you chart domain and range values along the x and y axes of a Cartesian coordinate system. You then plot the values using coordinate pairs. Each pair consists of a domain (x) and its corresponding range (y) value. Figure 2.4 illustrates the results of graphing the functional relationship between the amount of carbon burned in billions of tons and the amount of

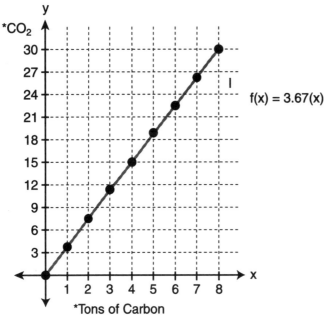

Figure 2.4
A function shows the amount of carbon burned (fossil fuel and other biomass) related to the amount of CO_2 churned into the atmosphere.
(*Billions of tons)

CO_2, again in billions of tons, that is then put into the Earth's atmosphere. Using such a graph, you can easily trace the unique value each application of the function generates.

Variations on Graphs of Functions

In some cases, as when you work with functions that involve absolute values and exponents, you generate graphical representations that vary from the single line evident in Figure 2.4. Instead, you find graphs that reveal reflected lines and curves. With a function involving an absolute value or the exponent of 2, you end up with lines or curves that are reflected or mirrored across the *y* axis.

Figure 2.5 illustrates the graphs that result from functions that involve absolute values and the square of a number. Even with such representations, it remains that for each *x* value, a unique relationship with the *y* value results.

One way to test a function is to apply the horizontal line rule. This rule involves drawing horizontal lines at any point along the *x* axis of the Cartesian plane on which you have plotted the values of a function. If the line crosses the line or curve at only one point, then you are dealing with a valid function.

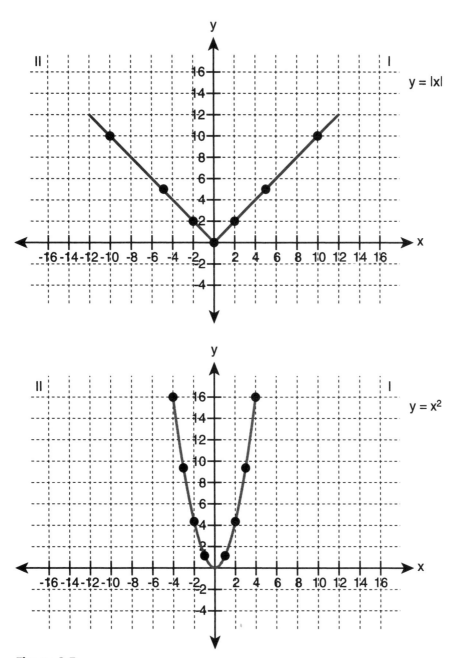

Figure 2.5
The graphs of functions involving absolute values and roots represent unique relationships between the *x* and *y* values.

Lab Work for the CO_2 Table

Open the folder in the BCGDCode directory named Chapter 2. In the CodeLab folder, open the CodeLab.sln file. Figure 2.6 illustrates the Microsoft Visual Studio C# IDE as it might appear when you first open the CodeLab project. If you do not see the Solution Explorer pane, select View > Solution Explorer from the top menu. To view the Code Lab form, click DataForm.cs.

Click on the DataForm.cs listing in the Solution Explorer to verify that the Code Lab form is in focus. (It is in focus when you see the eight small squares around the client area, as shown in Figure 2.6.) Then double-click in the client area of the

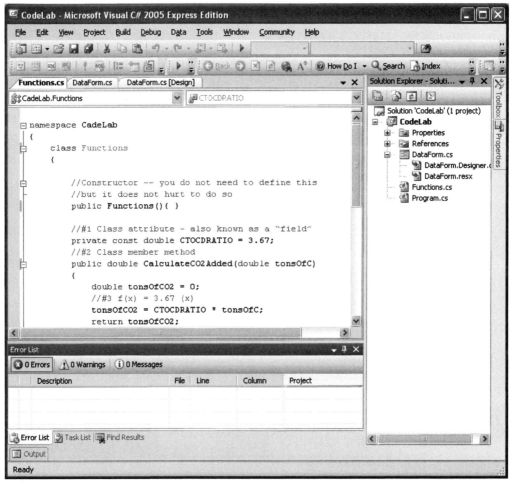

Figure 2.6
Double-click in the white client area of the Calculus Lab form to open the code file for the form.

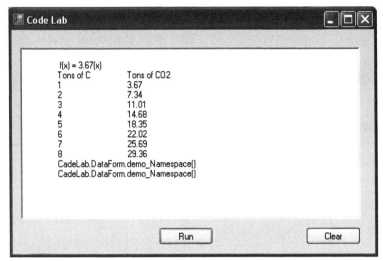

Figure 2.7
Click the Run button to execute the `calculateCO2Added()` method.

Code Lab form. The code for the DataForm.cs file opens for you. The next section discusses the code in detail.

Note

When you open the project in Microsoft Studio, what you see depends on your individual project settings. To adjust the what you see, select View from the main menu. From there, you can select configuration options.

To test the Code Lab application, press F5. The Microsoft Visual Studio C# IDE goes into the background, and you see the Code Lab application.

Click the Run button. You see the table Figure 2.7 illustrates. To clear the client area, click the Clear button. Then click the Run button again to see the table generated once again.

To close the Code Lab application and return to the Microsoft Visual Studio C# IDE, click the red X control button on the upper right of the title bar.

Note

If you find that the Microsoft Visual Studio C# IDE does not respond when you try to change the code in your Code Lab project, it is likely that the application is in "debug" mode. This means that you have pressed F5, so the application has compiled and is running. To return to development mode, press Shift + F5 or select Debug > Stop Debugging from the top-level menu.

Generating a Table

If you scroll through the CodeLab.DataForm.cs file, you find two methods, `runButton_Click()` and `performCCalculation()`. These two methods do not themselves contain code that performs calculations. The `runButton_Click()` method responds to your click of the Run button. When you click on the Run button in the Code Lab window, the application executes any statements you include within the opening and closing braces of the `runButton_Click()` method. In this instance, the one action it performs involves calling the `performCCalculation()` method, which generates the table Figure 2.7 illustrates.

```
//CodeLab.DataForm.cs
    private void runButton_Click(object sender, EventArgs e)
    {
        //#1 Call the display function
        performCCalculation();
    }
    //Lines left out ...
    //#2 Generates a table of values

    private void performCCalculation()
    {
        //#3 Create an instance of the Functions class
        Functions functions = new CodeLab.Functions();
        //#4 Set up domain and range variables
        double tonsOfC = 1;
        double tonsOfCO2 = 0;
        //Write the output to the table
        displayArea.AppendText("\n\t f(x) = 3.67(x)");
        displayArea.AppendText("\n\tTons of C \tTons of CO2");
        //#5 Repeat the calculation 8 times.

        for (int ctr = 0; ctr < 8; ctr++)
        {
            //#6 Apply the function
            tonsOfCO2 = functions.calculateCO2Added(tonsOfC);
            //Write lines in the table
            displayArea.AppendText("\n\t" + tonsOfC +
                                    "\t\t" + tonsOfCO2);
            tonsOfC++;
        }
    }//end method
```

To understand the code in the CodeLab.DataForm.cs file, first locate comment #1 in the `runButton_Click()` method. As mentioned previously, you trigger the `runButton_Click()` method when you click the Run button. When you click the button, you cause the program to execute statements the method contains. In this case, the focus of activity rests on the method directly following comment #1. This is the `performCCalculation()` method.

Calling a Method from the Functions Class

To call the method, you create a statement that consists of the name of the method. Opening and closing parentheses at the end of the name identify it as a called function. Since the method has no arguments, you include nothing within the parentheses. To show that the call to the function is a statement, you close the line with a semicolon.

At comment #2, you define the `performCCalculation()` method. This method creates a table of values. It also calls another, specialized method, `calculateCO2Added()`. To call the `calculateCO2Added()` method, you must create an instance of the class in which it is defined. In the lines trailing comment #3, you accomplish this task. You create a local instance of the class. A local instance of a class is one that you create within a method. Here are the lines that accomplish this work:

```
Functions functions = new CodeLab.Functions();
```

When you create an instance of the `Functions` class, you use the name of the class and then designate the name of the instance (`functions`). You then use the `new` keyword, which invokes the constructor for the class. The constructor for a class consists of a function that has the same name as the class. In this respect, `Functions()` is a default constructor. A default constructor is one that C# provides automatically for any class you create. A default constructor does not require any arguments. The result of invoking the default constructor using the `new` keyword is that you create an instance of the class that you assign to the `functions` identifier. You can now use the `functions` identifier to call methods you have defined in the `Functions` class. (How you define this class and its functions is explained momentarily.)

After creating an instance of the `Functions` class, at comment #4 you declare and define two local variables, `tonsOfC` and `tonsOfCO2`. The first variable allows you to track domain values, which in this case represent billions of tons of burned carbon (see Table 2.1). The second variable allows you to track range values. In this instance, the range values consist of the values you generate with the `calculateCO2Added()` method.

Using Repetition

At comment #5, you set up a `for` repetition statement so that you can repeatedly call the `calculateCO2Added()` method to generate a table of domain and range values. A `for` repetition statement allows you to create a block that repeatedly executes. Opening and closing curly braces mark the block. Statements you include within it repeat the number of times you designate in the control statement for the block. In this case, you use a variable name `ctr` to set up the control statement. To use this variable, you first declare it inside the parentheses following the `for` keyword. It is of the `int` type, and you define its initial value as 0. You allow the block to continue to repeat as long as the value of `ctr` is less than (<) 8. You use the increment operator (++) to increase the value of `ctr` from 0 by 1 each time the block repeats. Here is the shell of the `for` statement and its accompanying block:

```
for (int ctr = 0; ctr < 8; ctr++)
{
    //Statements to be executed . . .
}
```

Writing to a Table

As the lines following comment #6 show, each time the `for` statement repeats, you feed the domain value assigned to `tonsOfC` to the `calculateCO2Added()` method. The method then returns the range value, which you assign to the `tonsOfCO2` variable. Here is the line that performs these actions:

```
tonsOfCO2 = functions.calculateCO2Added(tonsOfC);
```

To display the domain and range values, you use the `displayArea` object to call `AppendText()` method. The `AppendText()` method is a member of the `RichTextArea` class, and `displayArea` is an instance of this class.

Note

If you position the cursor just after the "a" at the end of `displayArea`, remove the period, and then type a period, you see a complete list of all the member methods and attributes the `RichTextArea` class provides.

The `AppendText()` method takes an argument of the `string` type. In this instance, you create a string using double quotation marks and the concatenation (+) operator:

```
displayArea.AppendText("\n\t" + tonsOfC +
                       "\t\t" + tonsOfCO2);
```

The text placed within double quotes becomes a string. A *string* is a sequence of characters you can print to the client area using the `AppendText()` method. The backslash (\) and the character that follows it are known together as an *escape sequence*. You use escape sequences to format a string. When you use the "\n" escape sequence, you tell the compiler to start the string on a new line. When you use the "\t" escape sequence, you tell the compiler to insert a tab into the string.

To form one long string, you join together short strings. The concatenation operator ($\pm$) allows you to join together strings and identifiers. When you form strings in this way, you can include identifiers of the `double` type in your string (the `tonsOfC` and `tonsOfCO2` identifiers) because C# automatically converts identifiers (or variables) of the `double` type into strings when you use the concatenation operator.

Each time the `for` block repeats, the `AppendText()` method writes your results to the client area of the CodeLab form. After writing the results to the client area, you use the ++ operator to increase the value assigned to the `tonsOfC` variable by 1. Since the `for` control repeats 8 times, this value grows from 1 to 8. Here are these lines, repeated from the previous example:

```
//#6 Apply the function
   tonsOfCO2 = functions.calculateCO2Added(tonsOfC);
   //Write lines in the table
   displayArea.AppendText("\n\t" + tonsOfC +
                          "\t\t" + tonsOfCO2);
   //With each repeat of the block, increase
   //the carbon tons by 1
   tonsOfC++;
```

Programming a Function

Having viewed the code that generates the table in the Code Lab application, you can now turn your attention to the essential task of programming the function that allows you to generate a table of domain and range values that relate tons of

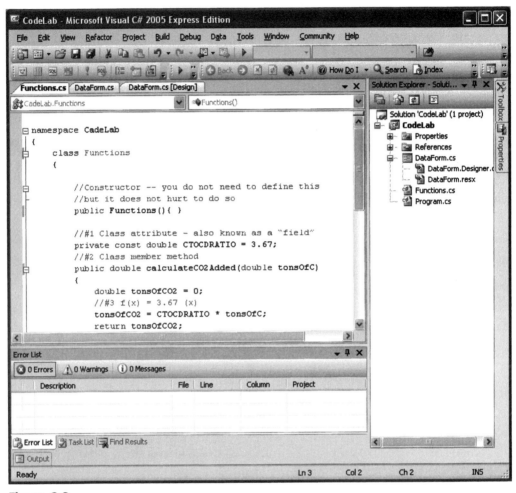

Figure 2.8
Click the Functions.cs listing in the Solution Explorer pane.

carbon to tons of atmospheric carbon dioxide. To accomplish this task, first double-click on the Functions.cs file in the Solution Explorer pane. If you do not see the Solution Explorer, select View > Solution Explorer. Figure 2.8 illustrates the Solution Explorer (on the right) and the top portion of the Functions.cs file.

To make it easier to review the code for the Functions.cs file, here is the code that constitutes the class. Subsequent sections discuss this code in detail:

```
namespace CodeLab
{
    class Functions
```

```
    {
        //#1 Class attribute - also known as a ''field"
        private const double CTOCDRATIO = 3.67;

        public Functions(){ }
        //#2 Class member method

        public double calculateCO2Added(double tonsOfC)
        {
            double tonsOfCO2 = 0;
            //#3 f(x) = 3.67 (x)
            tonsOfCO2 = CTOCDRATIO * tonsOfC;
            return tonsOfCO2;
        }//end of calculateCO2Added
    }//end of class Functions
}//end of namespace CodeLab
```

The first line of the Functions.cs file extends the CodeLab namespace. If you examine other files in the Code Lab project, you can see that the IDE automatically generates files wrapped in a namespace. A namespace is analogous to a large block that contains all the classes for a project. Given the use of a namespace, the compiler then identifies all elements of your program according to it. To designate a namespace, you employ the namespace keyword followed by the name of the namespace, which in this instance is CodeLab. After the namespace name, you create a block using opening and closing curly braces. Here is the shell of a namespace:

```
namespace CodeLab
{
    // The components (classes) of your program go here.
    // The same namespace can be used in a multitude of
    // different files. It applies wherever you create
    // a block like this one.
}
```

Namespaces are a necessary part of most programming routines, because they provide you with a way to avoid confusing situations in which you might assign the same names to two or more classes. In large programs, especially those in which you use pre-existing code, such redundancy easily occurs. Namespaces allow you to ensure that you can use the identifier names you find most meaningful in the context in which you are working without having to fret over whether some other programmer, in some other context, has used the same name.

Namespace Specifics

When you create a namespace for your project, the compiler identifies the elements of your project using the namespace identifier. As mentioned in another passage, the namespace identifier (or name) used for the Code Lab application is `CodeLab`.

One visible manifestation of the use of namespaces is that you can access the elements in your project using the namespace identifier. When you use this approach to identifying an item in your program, *qualify* it using the namespace identifier.

With the Code Lab application, you work with two classes (among others). One you know as `DataForm`. The other you know as `Functions`. Within each of these classes, you define methods.

To use the namespace path to qualify a class, you combine the identifier for the namespace with the identifier for the class using the dot (.) operator. To use the namespace path to qualify a method, you use the dot operator to combine the identifiers for the namespace, the class, and the method.

To draw upon a previous passage, consider the actions you took as you declared a local instance of the `Functions` class in the DataForm.cs file. Here is the line you employed:

```
Functions functions = new Functions();
```

To accomplish the same task, you might have included the namespace identifier as part of the name of the class identifier. The line then takes this form:

```
Functions functions = new CodeLab.Functions();
```

Because you have defined the `Functions` class within the `CodeLab` namespace, both forms of identification work. You do not need to include the namespace identifier to qualify a class identifier if you are working within the namespace in which you have defined the class.

Using a namespace path with a method involves the same actions you perform when qualifying classes. With method calls, however, you are not free to call the method using the name of the class in which you have defined the method unless you have defined the method in a special way. Such a special definition makes the method a *static method*. To call a static method, you employ the name of the class in which it is defined.

Here is a line that contains a call to the static `demo_Namespace()` method:

```
displayArea.AppendText("\n\t" + CodeLab.DataForm.demo_Namespace() );
```

In this call, you qualify the call to the method by appending the name of the method to the names of the namespace and the class in which the method is defined. You use the dot operator to join the names.

At comment #7 in the DataForm.cs file, you can find the definition of the static `demo_Namespace()` method. To create such a method, you use the keyword `static` in the signature line of the method. Here is the method definition, which returns a string that identifies the method:

```
public static string demo_Namespace()
{
   return "CodeLab.DataForm.demo_Namespace()";
}
```

To test the method for yourself, modify the `runButton_Click()` method so that it takes this form:

```
//Functions.cs
private void runButton_Click(object sender, EventArgs e)
{
   //#1 Call the display function
   performCCalculation();

   // A Call using a full namespace path
   displayArea.AppendText("\n\t"
               + CodeLab.DataForm.demo_NameSpace() );

   // B Call using only the class path
      displayArea.AppendText("\n\t"
               + DataForm.demo_Namespace());

   // C Call using only the method name
      displayArea.AppendText("\n\t"
               + demo_Namespace());
}
```

The three successive calls to the `demo_NameSpace()` method all accomplish the same task. The only difference is the way you qualify the call. The first qualification furnishes a *fully qualified* namespace path. The second provides the class path. The third identifies the method using only its name. You can perform this third type of call because you are calling the function from within the class in which it is defined. No namespace or class qualification is needed.

The Functions Class

The primary activity you perform when you work within the Functions.cs files involves defining the `Functions` class. When you define this class, you attend to three tasks:

- Declare and define a constant representing the ratio of carbon to carbon dioxide.

- Define a class constructor.

- Define a method, `calculateCO2Added()`, which implements the function defined by the equation $y = 3.67(x)$.

To define a class, you use the `class` keyword and the identifier (or name) you want to use for the class. When you define a class, the class opens and closes with curly braces, as does a namespace. Here is the shell of the `Functions` class:

```
class Functions
{
        //You define the attributes (fields) and methods
        //in the scope of the class (the area within the
        //curly braces.
}
```

Defining a Field

In the context of the class, you create an *attribute*. An attribute is a formal term for a variable that exists at the scope of a class. When a variable exists at the scope of a class, you can use it in any function you define within the class. When you define such a variable in C#, you can also refer to it as a field. A field is a variable defined at class scope. The one field you define for the `Functions` class is `CTOCDRATIO`. It is of the `double` type. As shown above, here is the line in which you define the field:

```
private const double CTOCDRATIO = 3.67;
```

To define this field, you use two keywords other than the keyword for the data type. The first of these is `private`. The keyword `private` makes it so that you cannot use the `CTOCDRATIO` field other than within the scope of the `Functions` class. In this way, you *encapsulate* it in the `Functions` class. (Encapsulation receives extended treatment in the next chapter.)

You also employ the `const` keyword. This keyword allows you to designate that the value you assign to a field cannot be changed in the methods in which you use it. Such a field is known as a constant. By convention, you capitalize constants to make clear to those who read your code (and possibly modify it) that the value of the field cannot be changed. Since it cannot be changed, you must assign a value to a constant when you declare it. To use the `CTOCDRATIO` field you assign the value of 3.67, which represents the ratio between carbon and carbon dioxide.

Defining a Constructor

Following the definition of the `CTOCDRATIO` field, you define a constructor for the `Functions` class. As mentioned previously, a constructor is a method that creates an instance of a class. Formally, you can describe a construction as a method that has the same name as the class and no return type. Recall from the discussion of the `DataForm` class that you employed the `Functions` constructor in this manner:

```
Functions functions = new Functions();
```

This statement tells the compiler to reserve memory and take a few other actions to formally define the `functions` identifier as a `Functions` object. In this context, you are using what is known as the explicit default definition of the constructor. Such a constructor is explicit because you define it. The lines in which you define it are as follows:

```
public Functions(){ }
```

This form of definition is known as an empty definition. It does nothing more in this setting than show the users of your program that you have not done anything special with the default constructor of your class.

Note

> In this context, you do not need to define a constructor at all. When you are working only with the default constructor and defining only specific instances of a class as you do in the `DataForm` class, C# proves an implicit default constructor for you. To test this notion, comment out the line in which the explicit default constructor is defined in the `Functions` class. Then press F5 to compile and run the program. It compiles and runs as before. While simple situations such as this one allow you to use the implicit default constructor, it remains that in more complex situations, you cannot proceed in this manner. Subsequent chapters discuss construction activities in greater detail.

Using a Method to Implement a Math Function

As your work with the methods in the `DataForm` class reveal, defining a method involves activities that resemble those involved in defining namespaces and functions. You provide a name and use opening and closing curly braces to designate the scope of the method.

A method definition begins with a signature line. The signature line designates the type of the value you return from the method and the arguments you supply to the method. It also identifies the accessibility and name of the method. Here is the signature line and the shell for the `calculateCO2Added()` method:

```
public double calculateCO2Added(double tonsOfC)
{
    //The content of the method goes here.
    return . . . ;
}
```

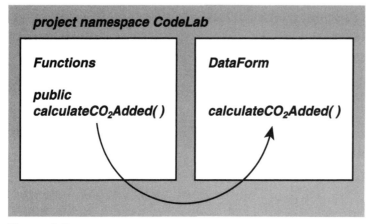

You define the method within the scope of the Functions class.

You use the public keyword.

You can then call the method in the scope of the DataForm class.

Figure 2.9
The public keyword gives you access to the method when you call it outside the class in which you define it.

In this example, you begin by using the public keyword. The public keyword performs an action that is the opposite of that of the private keyword. The private keyword made it so that users of your class *could not* access an item in your class outside the scope of the class, whereas the public keyword makes it so that users *can* access an item in your class outside the scope of the class. In this case, rather than a field, the item is the calculateCO2Added() method.

Access refers to scope, and scope refers to where you can use a given item in your program. Access to the scope of the Functions class allows you to call the calculateCO2Added() method in the DataForm class. The actions you perform in the DataForm class take place within the scope of the DataForm class, but they take place outside the scope of the FuntionSetA class. When you designate the calculateCO2Added() method as public, you make it so that your use of it is possible within the scope of the DataForm class. Figure 2.9 illustrates this phenomenon.

When you define the calculateCO2Added() method, the value you return is of the double type. The value returned is the number of tons of carbon dioxide a ton of burned carbon creates. To designate that the data the method returns is of the float type, following the *public* keyword, you use the double type identifier.

The method accepts a single argument, also of the double type. This is the amount of burned carbon. The formula you use for the calculation is as follows:

$$f(x) = 3.67(x)$$

To return the result of this calculation, you employ the return keyword. The return keyword complements the data type you identify for the return type in the signature of the method. Here's the code that implements the constant and the function:

```
private const double CTOCDRATIO = 3.67;
public double calculateCO2Added(double tonsOfC)
{
    double tonsOfCO2 = 0;
    //f(x) = 3.67 (x)
    tonsOfCO2 = CTOCDRATIO * tonsOfC;
    return tonsOfCO2;
}
```

The formula you use for the calculation reads $f(x) = 3.67(x)$. In this case, you can make the values explicit so that it is easier to understand the work the method performs. Accordingly, you declare a local identifier of the double type (tonsOfCO2) to designate the value you want the method to return. You initialize this identifier by assigning 0 to it. You then employ the multiplication operator (*) in conjunction with the CTOCDRATIO field to implement the function. You assign the result of the function to the tonsOfCO2 identifier. To make this value available to users of the function, you use the return keyword to return the value you have assigned to tonsOfCO2.

Implementing the method using a local variable and several lines of code makes the activity of implementing the function clearer, but it is generally preferable to reduce the amount of code as much as possible. Accordingly, you might reduce the code to one active line:

```
public double calculateCO2Added(double tonsOfC)
{
    //f(x) = 3.67 (x)
    return 3.67 * tonsOfC;
}
```

In this implementation, you supply the argument provided by the tonsOfC argument directly to the statement in which you implement the function. The flow of the program allows that the return keyword automatically returns the value that results. This implementation produces the same outcome as the previous implement. To demonstrate as much, alter the code in the Functions class so that is assumes the second form. When you call it in the `performCCalculation()` method, you then generate the same values you see in Figure 2.7.

Conclusion

In this chapter, you have explored how to merge the work of defining a function mathematically with that of implementing a method for the function in C#. This activity leads to recognition of how programming a method in many ways is analogous to developing an equation. In both instances, you can use the product of your effort to repeatedly achieve a given end in a consistent, predictable way. When you develop a mathematical function, you can gauge the results of the application of your function by creating a graph. In the case of the function that relates burning carbon with the amount of carbon dioxide added to the atmosphere, such a procedure results in a linear graph. The validity of the result can be confirmed in part by inspecting the plotted values to verify that the line that they create conforms to the horizontal line rule. Implementing a function in C# requires preliminary work to alter the Code Lab application so that the `Functions` class contains a method that embodies the function you use for relating carbon and carbon dioxide. Given the implementation of this method, you can then call it to generate a table of domain and range values.

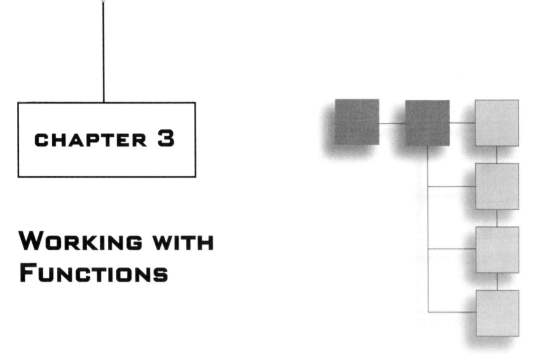

CHAPTER 3

WORKING WITH FUNCTIONS

In this chapter, you draw from the work you performed in Chapter 2 and program methods that implement mathematical functions that process limited ranges of values. When you program methods of this variety, you put to work the exception handling features of C#. The try, catch, and throw keywords form important elements in this group of features. To process data, you use a selection statement to determine the validity of the data. If the data proves invalid, then you generate an exception rather than returning an inconsistently calculated value. To understand how to implement methods that evaluate data and generate exceptions, you explore the following topics, among others:

- How domains and ranges can be considered both infinite and limited

- Factors that make it necessary to limit domain values

- Formal approaches to defining limited domains

- Implementing methods that can limit domains

- Using constructors to create customized error messages

- Processing exceptions and formatting numerical data

Domains and Functions

In Chapter 2, you investigated how you can create a method in a C# program to implement a mathematical function that generates values you can represent in a table. You also investigated how to use a linear graph to plot values from a table. Tables and graphs provide convenient media you can use to depict numerical relationships so that you can visually inspect them to discover patterns and trends.

It remains, however, that a notion that is fundamental to programming also applies to mathematical functions. This is the notion of "GIGO," which deciphers to "garbage in garbage out." You can write a perfectly reasonable program, but if you feed it invalid or corrupted data, then the output you receive itself is invalid or corrupted. When programmers design programs, then, they often exert efforts to ensure that they check the data for validity before they process it.

When you work with mathematical functions, you work in similar ways. You can discern when you read values displayed in a table whether they have been generated by a valid function.

In the example in Chapter 2 of a function that relates carbon to carbon dioxide, you saw that for each value of x (representing carbon), you were able to generate a corresponding value of y (carbon dioxide). A long way to express is to say that for each application of the function $f(x)$, a unique set of tabular value or coordinate pairs results.

That a valid function generates sets of unique values proves important to the definition, formulation, and testing of a function. If the function you create does not generate such values, then it is not valid.

In this light, consider the table that Figure 3.1 illustrates. Ostensibly, this table represents the domain and range values of a function. Although the specific

x	1	5	8	7	8
f(x)	4	11	25	30	5

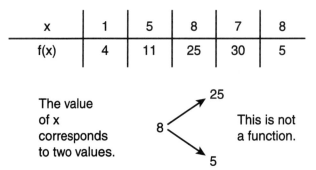

The value of x corresponds to two values.   8 →⟨ 25 / 5   This is not a function.

Figure 3.1
Functions express unique relationships.

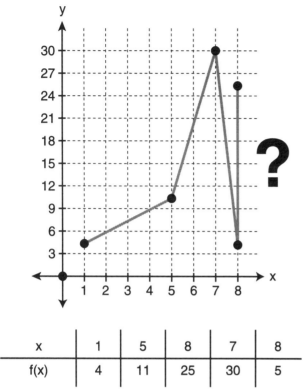

x	1	5	8	7	8
f(x)	4	11	25	30	5

Figure 3.2
A function requires that two values cannot correspond to one value of x.

equation the formula represents is not shown, if you inspect the domain (x) and range [f(x)] values, you can detect a flaw. In this table, you twice apply the function to 8. In one instance, the result is 25. In another instance the result is 5.

If in both instances the domain value remains the same and yet the function generates different range values, something is wrong. Each application of the function does not result in unique correspondences. Such a relationship does not characterize a legitimate function. As Figure 3.2 illustrates, another way to depict this inconsistency involves using a graphical representation. When you graph the values, you see that the graph extends vertically along the line that crosses the x axis at 8. When this happens, the graph violates the horizontal line rule, which establishes that when you plot a function, the function is legitimate only if you cannot connect any two of its coordinates using a vertical line.

Starting Values

A legitimate function relates domain and range values. It is the rule, procedure, or algorithm that allows you to see or understand how two values are related in a

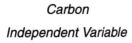

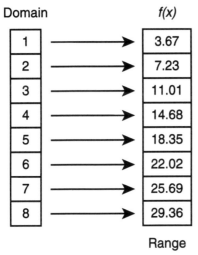

Range

Dependent Variable

Carbon Dioxide

Figure 3.3
Tons of carbon form independent values, while tons of carbon dioxide become dependent values.

unique way. As Figure 3.3 illustrates, expressed formally, you can view the value of *x* as an *independent variable.* You can view the function it generates as the *dependent variable.* In this instance, then, the values representing billions of tons of carbon burned each year become independent variables. The tons of carbon dioxide resulting become the dependent values. The function establishes the dependency. One set of values depends on the work of the function in relation to the other.

As mentioned previously, the dependency a function establishes is valid if the function and the data you use for your calculations is valid. Valid functions establish distinct, unique correspondences between domain and range values. The function Figure 3.2 illustrates proves invalid because it fails to establish unique correspondences.

In other situations, a given function might be perfectly sound but generates legitimate values only if you limit the numbers you include in the domain you use with the function. The next few sections discuss this situation in detail. Some functions produce consistent values for almost any number you choose to name. Other functions work only with restricted domains.

To accommodate this situation, you can specify the values of the independent variable (the domain) using the letter **D**. To make it so you can identify values for specific functions, you associate subscripts with the letter to identify the functions. Accordingly, here are a set of functions for which you specify limited domains:

$\mathbf{D_g}$ designates the domain of $g(x)$

$\mathbf{D_h}$ designates the domain of $h(x)$

$\mathbf{D_b}$ designates the domain of $b(x)$

In each instance, you make clear that the domain is specific to the function. Many functions possess a domain that is associated with the set of all real numbers. Others involve operations that require you to exclude certain values from consideration.

Real Numbers

The set of real numbers consists of the numbers you can write using decimal notation. Among these numbers are integers, which you can represent with a decimal point but that do not include a mantissa (or fractional part). Here are some integers represented in this way:

```
1.0
2.0
23.0
234.0
```

Also included in the real number set are fractions that include no integer part. Here are a few such numbers:

```
0.25
0.5
0.75
```

You might express these as 1/4, 1/2, and 3/4.

Fractions represented with decimal points are a form of rational number. Here are rational numbers that provide both integer and decimal parts:

```
1.25
1.50
1.75
```

Each of these rational numbers represent a definitive number. In addition to numbers that represent definitive values, the real number set includes those that do not. Those that do not are known as irrational numbers. Irrational numbers are characterized by sets of digits that repeat indefinitely. Such numbers usually result from divisions. Here are a couple of examples of such numbers:

```
1 / 13 = 0.076923076923076923
1 / 17 = 0.0588235294117647
```

For many other such numbers, visit this Internet site: http://thestarman.dan123.com/math/rec/RepeatDec.htm

In the first example, the division results in a set of numbers (076923) that repeats infinitely. In the second example, the division results in 16 repeating decimals.

There are divisions that result in numbers that provide no set of repeat digits. Such numbers are known as non-repeating irrational numbers. One such number is pi. Pi has been calculated to a billion or more decimal places, and a set of its decimal values that repeat has yet to be found. Here is pi calculated to 50 digits.

3.14159265358979323846264338327950288419716939375

For other calculations, visit this Internet site: www.angio.net/pi/piquery

All Real Numbers

A multitude of functions use domains that include the set of all real numbers. If you represent the set of all real numbers with **R**, then, you can designate the domain of such a function as D_R. Here is a function that allows you to employ the set of all real numbers:

$$f(x) = 3x + 2 \qquad \{x \mid x \in R\}$$

This function provides a rule that allows you to substitute for x any value you care to name from the set of real numbers. The expression to the right of the equation $(x \mid x \in R)$ explicitly qualifies the value of x, stipulating that x must be a member of the set of real numbers.

When the work of a function is bound by the set of real numbers, in addition to the domain values, the range values are also real numbers. With the function currently under consideration, the rule states that you multiply x by 3 and then add 2 to the product. This operation and all variants of it result in range values that are real numbers. Here are a couple of substitutions that involve single values:

$$f(3) = 3(3) + 2 = 9 + 2 = 11$$
$$f(3.5) = 3(3.5) + 2 = 10.5 + 2 = 12.5$$

The function works with all real numbers, and integers and rational numbers are part of the set of real numbers. In the first equation, you substitute an integer, 3, as the independent variable. In the second equation, you substitute a rational number, 3.5, as the independent variable.

It is also the case that you can substitute an expression or even another function for an independent variable. Use of a function in this capacity receives attention later on in this book. With respect to the use of an expression, you can substitute expressions for the independent variable. For example, you can equate x with an expression that reads $x + 2$. You then end up with this equation:

$$b + 2 = x \qquad\qquad \{b \mid b \in R\}$$

$$f(x) = 3x + 2$$

$$f(b + 2) = 3(b + 2) + 2 = 3b + 6 + 2 = 3b + 8$$

In each instance, $\mathbf{D_f}$ consists of the set of all real numbers. When $\mathbf{D_f}$ consists of the set of all real numbers, a condition for a valid solution is that the values that result all prove meaningful and consistent with relation to real numbers. That the domain consists of the set of all real numbers implies in certain instances, however, that you limit values you include. The next few sections explore a few scenarios that characterize such explorations.

Restricting the Domain

Some functions restrict you to a domain that excludes a range of values. If you work with the set of real numbers, you cannot find the square root of a negative number. For this reason, if you develop a function that involves taking the square root of a given independent variable, then you must stipulate limitations for the values you employ. Here is an example one such function:

$$g(x) = \sqrt{x + 25}$$

With this function, a value that is less than -25 results in a negative value, and if you are seeking a solution in the set of real numbers, the square root of a negative number does not prove meaningful. Other values do, however.

$$g(x) = \sqrt{x + 25}$$

$$\sqrt{0 + 25} = \sqrt{25} = 5$$

$$\sqrt{-9 + 25} = \sqrt{16} = 4 \qquad\qquad \text{Values greater than } -25 \text{ are meaningful.}$$

$$\sqrt{11 + 25} = \sqrt{36} = 6$$

$$g(x) = \sqrt{-26 + 25} = \sqrt{-1} \quad \text{Values less than } -25 \text{ are not meaningful.}$$

$$g(x) = \sqrt{-61 + 25} = \sqrt{-36}$$

To restrict the values you employ with such a function, you qualify the domain using a limiting expression along the lines explored in the previous section. Here is an example:

$$g(x) = \sqrt{x + 25} \qquad \{x \mid x \in R\} \text{ and } \{x \mid x \geq -25\}$$

Specific Values

Functions involving quotients require restrictions for the values you provide to variables or expressions in numerators. Division by zero is not defined, so if the values you include result in zero, then your function is no longer valid. This equation illustrates a common scenario:

$$g(x) = \frac{1}{x - 4}$$

With this function, if you assign 4 to the independent variable, the value of the numerator is 0. Even though any other operation involving a rational number renders a consistent result, since division by 0 is not defined, allowing 4 to be part of your domain renders this function invalid:

$$\frac{1}{(5) - 4} = \frac{1}{1} = 1$$

An infinite number of substitutions prove valid.

$$\frac{1}{(-4) - 4} = \frac{1}{-8}$$

$$\frac{1}{4 - 4} = \frac{1}{0} \Rightarrow ? \quad \text{Use of 4 results in an invalid function.}$$

To remedy the situation, you define the domain of the function so that you exclude 4 from the domain. You can accomplish this with a domain definition that takes this form:

$$g(x) = \frac{1}{x - 4} \qquad \{x \mid x \in R\} \text{ and } \{x \mid x \neq 4\}$$

In this way, you prevent the use of the one value that causes problems.

Methods That Use Restricted Domain Values

To explore how you can program functions that incorporate restricted domains, open the Chapter 3 project. In Functions.cs you find the Functions class, and in this class you see the showResDA() method. This method implements a function that requires you to restrict the values you provide to it to those that are equal to or greater than -25. The function you implement to create the method is familiar from the previous section. It reads this way:

$$g(x) = \sqrt{x + 25} \qquad\qquad \{x \mid x \in R\} \text{ and } \{x \mid x \geq -25\}$$

Because you are extracting the square root of the value that you create when you add x to 25, the value of x cannot be such that you end up with a negative number. The numbers you generate must be real numbers. You can use two approaches to defining the domain for this function. One is to allow values *greater than or equal to* -25. The other is to exclude values *less than* -25. Here are the expressions that communicate these notions:

$$\{x \mid x \in R\} \text{ and } \{x \mid x \geq -25\}$$
$$\{x \mid x \in R\} \text{ and } \{x \mid !x < -25\}$$

The second approach proves convoluted because it defines the value of x such that x is *not* a value less than -25. While a mathematician might frown on this approach to defining a domain, it proves useful to a programmer because it allows you to use a selection statement in a way that simplifies your processing tasks. The next section reviews how this happens.

Single Selection and Throwing Exceptions

When you exclude a range of values from processing, you do so using a *selection statement.* A selection statement consists of three parts. One part is a keyword, such as if, which determines the specific type of selection you want to use. The second is a *control expression.* The third is the block of statements the control expression governs. Curly braces open and close this block. Here's the shell of a simple selection statement:

```
if(control expression)
{
    //Statements that enter the flow of the program
    // if the control expression evaluates to true
}
```

The control expression logically evaluates the information you provide to it. If the condition evaluates to true, then the control statement allows the block of statements it governs to be included in the flow of the program. If the condition evaluates to false, then the statement excludes the block of statements it governs from the flow of the program.

The showResDA() method in the Functions class includes a single selection statement that evaluates whether the value (val) you supply to the method is less than −25. The purpose of the selection statement involves preventing the method from generating values that are not in the appropriate range. To use the selection statement in this way, you employ a programming technique that involves throwing an exception. Here is the code you used to throw an exception in the showResDA() method. Discussion of details follows.

```
public double showResDA(double val)
{
    if (val < -25)
    {
            throw new System.
ArgumentException("Value is" + val
                                    +"but must be >= -25" );
    }
    //If not reached, returns 0
    return System.Math.Sqrt(val + 25);
}
```

If the value you provide to the function is less than −25, then the if selection statement evaluates to true and the flow of the program enters the selection block. The flow of the program then encounters the throw keyword. The throw keyword causes the method in which you place it to terminate. When it terminates, it exits the method, and the method does not return a value.

At the same time that it terminates your method, the throw keyword also releases a message. The message consists of an object of the ArgumentException type. You define the object in much the same way that you define any other object in C#. You use the new keyword and the constructor of the object.

In this case, the constructor is for a special category or data known as an *exception type*. Many exception types are available to you in C#. Exception types constitute special classes that accommodate commonly encountered program malfunctions. In this case, the malfunction is that of a general argument to a function. The exception data type that best addresses such a malfunction is ArgumentException. Since this data type is included in the System namespace, you prefix it with System identifier when you use it.

The constructor for the ArgumentException class takes one argument. This argument is of the string type. In this instance, you compose a message that identifies the value that causes the exception. Your message also includes a brief explanation of the problem. If you were to assign a value of -26 to the method, then the constructor would create the following message:

```
Value is -26 but must be >= -25
```

When you provide this message to the constructor, the constructor assigns it to a data property of the ArgumentException class called Message. As discussion later in the chapter reveals, you can then access this message using the ToString() method, which is also part of the ArgumentException class.

When the flow of the program encounters the throw keyword, it constructs an object of the named exception type and inserts this object into a protected memory location that allows your program to pick it up and process it through an exception handler. A catch block (discussed momentarily) is such a handler. You provide code in the catch block to handle the exception in a way that does not disrupt the flow of your program.

If you supply a value to the showResDA() method that is within the defined domain, then the if selection statement evaluates to false, and flow of the program skips the statements within the selection block. The flow of the program progresses in a normal way and encounters the statement that processes $\sqrt{x + 25}$. To implement this statement, you call the Math.Sqrt() method:

```
return System.Math.Sqrt(val + 25);
```

The Math class resides in the System namespace. For this reason, you prefix the call to Math.Sqrt() with the namespace identifier, System. The Math.Sqrt() method requires an argument of the double type and also returns a value of the double type. To supply this value, you retrieve the val argument from the function parameter list and add it to 25.

The val argument is of the double type. The double type accommodates large real numbers (numbers with a mantissa). When you add the val argument to an integer, 25, the + operator causes the result to be changed (or *promoted*) to the double type. For this reason, the Math.Sqrt() method accepts the argument without problems.

Generating Values and Catching Exceptions

The throw keyword, combined with a constructor of an exception type, allows you to issue (or throw) an exception when the method you program encounters a number that lies outside a defined domain. To process exceptions, you implement an exception handler. An exception handler consists of two parts. The first part is a try block. The second part is a catch block. Here is the shell of a try ... catch exception handler:

```
try
{
    //A call to a method that throws an exception (E, for instance)
}
catch(type for exception E)
{
    //Statements that process the exception E
}
```

The first part of the handler consists of the try keyword and opening and closing curly braces that define the try block. The flow of your program always enters the try block and attempts to process the statements the try block contains. The most important such statement consists of a call to a method that can throw an exception. As the previous section discussed, such a method contains the throw keyword.

If the method call within the try block generates an exception, then the catch block processes it. The catch block consists of the catch keyword, an argument list defined between parentheses for the catch keyword, and opening an closing curly braces that enclose the statements you include in the catch block. The catch block processes the exception as an argument. You process the exception argument the same way that you process arguments passed to a method. The exceptions the catch block can process are of the exception type you define for the catch argument list. Exceptions of other types are not processed.

The performCalcB() method in the DataForm class calls the showResDA() method and processes its exceptions using a try ... catch handler. Here is the code. Subsequent sections provide discussion of specific details:

```
private void performCalcB()
{
    //#1 Create an instance of the Functions class
    Functions functions = new CodeLab.Functions();

    //#2 Set up domain and range variables
    double localA = -27;
    double localB = 0;

    //Write the output to the table
    displayArea.AppendText("\n\t Domain \t\t Range");
    List<string> errors = new List<string>();
```

```
    //#3 Repeat the calculation 8 times.
    for (int ctr = 0; ctr < 8; ctr++)
    {
      //#4 Apply the function
      // Use a try catch block to process
      //values that are not within the range
      try
      {
      //#5 Call the method and possibly generate exceptions
      localB = functions.showResDA(localA);
      }
      catch (ArgumentException ex)
      {
    //#6 Catch exceptions and call methods to process them
    //In this case, you add them to a List
    errors.Add(ex.Message.ToString());
      }
      //Write lines in the table during normal processing
      ////#7 Use the double ToString method to format the numbers
      displayArea.AppendText("\n\t" + localA +
                            "\t\t" + localB.ToString("0.00") );
      localA++;
      localB = 0;              //reset the value to 0
    }
    //#8 Pass the array to the display method to show the
    //values that were outside the acceptable range
    showErrors(errors);
}//end method
```

At comment #1 in the performCalcB() method, you create an instance of the Functions class and assign it to the functions identifier. Later in the method, this instance of the Functions class allows you to call the showResDA() method.

At comment #2, you define two local variables of the double type. These variables allow you to work with the domain and range values you display in the table Figure 3.5 illustrates.

In the lines associated with comment #3, you create a for repetition statement. This statement received detailed discussion earlier, but reviewing a few features does not hurt. The three primary ways you control the flow of a program involve repetition, sequence, and selection. The for repetition statement allows you to use a counter to control the number of times a block of statements repeats. In this instance, the name of the counter is ctr.

The first of the three expressions in the for statement defines ctr and sets its initial value (0). The second sets the limit. In this instance, you allow the value of the counter to start at 0 and increase as long as it remains less than the limit of 8. In this way, the block repeats 8 times. The third expression establishes how you increase the value of ctr. To increase the value of ctr, you employ the increment operator (+ +), which increments it by 1 with each iteration of the block.

Within the for block you include a try . . . catch handler that processes a call to the showResDA() method. In the lines trailing comment #4 you implement the try block. Within the try block, the method call involves this statement:

```
localB = functions.showResDA(localA);
```

You call the method using the functions identifier, which is of the Functions type. The localA variable represents the domain value. As mentioned several times in previous sections, this value cannot be less than −25. You assign the result of the showResDA() method to the localB variable. As the earlier discussion of the showResDA() method emphasized, if you submit a legitimate value to the method, a range value consistent with the defined domain results.

The method does not return a value if you supply an inappropriate domain value. Instead, it generates an exception of the ArgumentException type. To process this exception, in the catch block that follows, you use the ArgumentException type to define the argument. The argument's name is ex, designating "exception."

Within the catch block, in the lines associated with comment #6, you supply statements that process the ex argument. Processing the argument in this case features a few fairly involved activities. First, you make a call to the ToString() method. This method allows you to return the value of an ArgumentException *property* called Member. To make the call, you cascade the object name, the property name, and then the method name:

```
ex.Member.ToString()
```

The effect of this call is to retrieve only the message that you defined in the constructor of the ArgumentException class when you implemented the showResDA() method. Recall from the previous discussion that this activity assumes the following form:

```
throw new System.ArgumentException("Value is" + val
                          + " but must be => -25" );
```

The message you provide to the ArgumentException constructor consists of a sentence that identifies the value fed to the method, and then tells you what is wrong. When you employ the ToString() method to access the Member property of the ArgumentException object, you retrieve this sentence. As Figure 3.5 shows, you retrieve such a sentence for every exception the method throws.

Fields and Properties

The data members of a class are called *fields*. The generic software engineering term for a field or data member is *attribute*. An attribute of a class is an item of data as opposed to a method.

A *property* is a special type of field in C#. For practical purposes, it is a field, but on the other hand, it is also a substitute for a field. It provides you with an indirect way to access the value of a field.

To employ the ArgumentException object (ex) to access the Member property of the ArgumentException class, you use this approach:

ex.Member;

The ex object calls the value you have assigned to Member. Member, again, is a property, not a field, in the ArgumentException class.

Properties are important because they make it so that you do not directly access fields. Not directly accessing fields proves significant to practitioners of object-oriented programming. Good practices in object-oriented programming stipulate that you are not supposed to directly access the data in a class. Data is supposed to be private.

To access data in a way that is consistent with good object-oriented practices, one approach you can use involves creating a special method known as an *accesor* or *get* method. Such a method usually contains a single line of code that returns the value of the field.

To see how this happens, consider some of the work discussed in Chapter 2. Assume that you want to allow users to access the constant in the Functions class. Here is the line that defines the constant:

private const double CTOCDRATIO = 3.67;

Following good object-oriented practices, you qualify the definition of the constant (or field) with the private keyword. Because the field is private, you cannot use the functions identifier in the DataForm class to call it. Such a call assumes this form:

functions.CTOCDRATIO;   //Direct access denied, so this fails

The compiler issues an error because a private data member cannot be accessed directly in this way. If you changed the private keyword to public, then the compiler would no longer generate an error, but then you would also be in violation of good object-oriented programming practices.

To remedy this situation, a common solution involving leaving the private keyword in place and implementing an accessor method in the Functions class can be used. Here's how you implement such a method:

```
//Accessor or get method for the constant
public double getCToCO2Ratio()
{
    return CTOCDRATIO;
}
```

The method returns the value of the constant. The constant remains private. The method, on the other hand, is public. The user can in this way call the public method to access the private field. Good object-oriented practices are preserved. Now the user of your class can create an instance of the Functions class (such as functions) to access the value assigned to the CTOCDRATIO constant. Here is an example of such a call made in the DataForm class:

```
displayArea.AppendText("\n\tConstant: " + functions.getCToCO2Ratio() );
```

As convenient and sound as this practice might seem, it remains that calling accessor or get methods have certain drawbacks, one of which is that they can add processing overhead to your program. For this reason, to make it possible to observe object-oriented programming practices and yet be able to access the values in fields in a fairly direct way, the developers of C# allow you to create properties.

A property basically replaces an accessor method. The procedure to create a property involves writing a few lines of code that resemble a method. What distinguishes these lines from a method is that they do not include opening and closing parentheses. You use only opening and closing curly braces. Here is the code:

```
public double CToCO2Ratio
{
    get { return CTOCDRATIO; }
}
```

The developers of C# provide a get keyword that allows you to stipulate the field from which you want to return a value (in this case CTOCDRATIO). You follow the get keyword with its own set of opening and closing curly braces. Within the curly braces you employ the return keyword followed by the name of the field. You can now use the name of the property rather than the name of the field to access the constant value. Here is how you perform this action in the DataForm class:

```
displayArea.AppendText("\n\tConstant: " + functions.CToCO2Ratio );
```

Once again, since the property is public and allows you to access a private field, you still follow sound object-oriented programming practice. No field is accessed directly. You use the instance of the Functions class to access the property rather than the field. You use the name of the property rather than the name of field.

The List Collection

When you process single values, as with the localA and localB identifiers, you deal with what programmers refer to as *scalar values*. A scalar value is a single value you associate with a single identifier. In contrast to scalar values

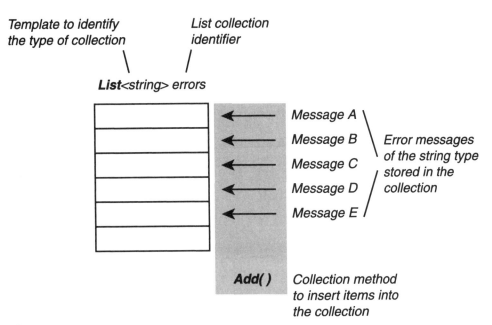

Template to identify
the type of collection

List collection
identifier

List<string> errors

Message A
Message B
Message C
Message D
Message E

Error messages
of the string type
stored in the
collection

Add( )   Collection method
to insert items into
the collection

Figure 3.4
The List collection object allows you to store all the error messages.

are those characterized by collections. The List object is an example of a collection.

As Figure 3.4 illustrates, a List collection allows you to associate a large number of separate values with one identifier (in this case errors). The List identifier designates a single object. The object provides an expandable number of slots. In each of the slots you can store a distinct value. For the errors collection, each value is a message you retrieve when you call the ex.Member.ToString() method.

To insert the error message into the List collection, you call the Add() method of the List class. The type of argument this method requires depends on how you have defined your collection. You define a collection using a template constructor. As is shown in the lines trailing comment #2 in the performCalcB() method, a template constructor consists of the name of the collection you want to use followed by less than and greater than signs (<>). Between these signs you place the name of the class or data type you want to associate with the collection. After that, you then use open and close parentheses to complete the constructor. Here is the line featuring the List constructor:

```
List<string> errors = new List<string>();
```

You assign the instance of the List class to the errors identifier. When you define the identifier, you follow the data type with less than and greater than signs in which, again, you identify the class or data type you want to associate with the collection.

Generally, then, with both the declaration of the identifier (errors) and the use of the constructor, you identify the type of data you want your collection to accommodate by making use of the template (<>) operators and the name of the associated data type (in this case string). Given this start, when you call the Add() method of the List class, you can then insert objects of the string type into your collection.

Iterations and Retrieval of Error Messages

The messages you retrieve from the exception object (ex) in the catch block are of the string type. In the lines associated with comment #6 in the performCalcB() method, you use the errors collection to call the Add() method to insert the error messages into the errors collection. Here is the line that accomplishes this task:

```
errors.Add(ex.Message.ToString());
```

Each time a call using showResDA(localA) encounters a value assigned to the localA variable that is less than −25, it throws an exception. The exception carries a message. When you retrieve the message and assign it to the List collection, it is available for retrieval at a later time.

You retrieve the exception message after the flow of the program exits the for block. In the lines associated with comment #7, you then call the showErrors() method and pass the errors collection to it as an argument. At this point the errors collection contains all the error messages you have collected while processing data. The purpose of the showErrors() method is to display the messages you have collected.

In the comments accompanying comment #8, you define the showErrors() method. To define the method so that you can pass the errorsList collection to it, you employ the template List<string> to declare the data type of the method's argument (col). As with the declaration of the errors collection, you use the string keyword to identify the data type. Here is the code that implements the argument type and the rest of the method:

```
private void showErrors(List<string> col)
{
    displayArea.AppendText("\n\n\tDomain value errors:\n");
```

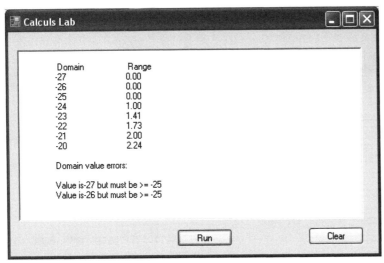

Figure 3.5
Exceptions identify values that lie outside the legitimate domain for the function.

```
foreach (string message in col)
{
    displayArea.AppendText("\n\t" + message);
}
}
```

Within the showErrors() method, you make use of the displayArea object. This is of the RichTextBox class. This class offers the AppendText() method, and your first statement in the showErrors() method calls this method to display messages stored in the col collection. At this point, the col collection holds the values you passed to the method with the errors collection.

To retrieve messages from the col collection, you use a foreach block. The foreach keyword works in conjunction with the in keyword. It fetches successive items from the col collection and transfers them to a local variable, message, which you define in the parentheses that accompany the foreach keyword.

You then use the message identifier as an argument to the AppendText method. The AppendText() method writes the error messages you retrieve from the col collection at the bottom of the text area you see displayed in Figure 3.5.

Events and Displays

In the DataForm class, you employ the runButton_Click() method to invoke the methods that create the table of values you see in Figure 3.5. This method assumes the same form it assumed in Chapter 2, with the difference that you are now calling the `performCalcB()` method.

```
private void runButton_Click(object sender, EventArgs e)
{
   //#1 Call the display function
   performCalcB();
}
```

When you click the Run button, you generate the values and error messages Figure 3.5 illustrates.

Formatting

The formatting of numbers proves to be an important aspect of your work with numbers. Figure 3.6 illustrates a few of the ways you might format the double values that you assign to the `localB` variable in the `performCalcB()` method.

For review, here is the line in the `performCalcB()` method that allows you to assign values to the `localB` variable:

`localB = functions.showResDA(localA);`

Given this assignment, you can the employ the `localB` variable to create a line of text that you use as part of the table of values the function generates. To create the line of text, you call the `AppendText()` method of the `RichTextBox` class. This method takes a data of the `string` type as its argument. The values you combine using the concatenation (+) operator are automatically converted into data of the `string` type.

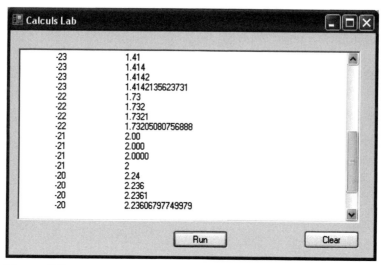

Figure 3.6
Use the `ToString()` method to format numbers in different ways.

At the same time, the double data type contains a ToString() method that allows you to format how the value it stores appears when you pass it to the AppendText() method. Here are the calls to the ToString() method that generate the lines displayed in Figure 3.6:

```
// 2 decimal places    1.41
displayArea.AppendText("\n\t" + localA +
                    "\t\t" + localB.ToString("0.00"));
// 3 decimal places    1.414
displayArea.AppendText("\n\t" + localA +
    "\t\t" + localB.ToString("0.000"));
// 4 decimal places    1.4142
displayArea.AppendText("\n\t" + localA +
    "\t\t" + localB.ToString("0.0000"));
// default decimal places  1.4142135623731
displayArea.AppendText("\n\t" + localA +
                    "\t\t" + localB);
```

To implement the formatting, you use the double variable (localB) to call the ToString() method. Then, as an argument to the ToString() method, you provide a *mask*. The mask designates the formatting you want to use for your numerical output. The mask in this instance involves double quotes containing zeros and a decimal point to show how many digits after the decimal point you want to allow. Here are summary descriptions of a few of the items:

ToString("0.00")	Allow 2 decimal places.
ToString("0.000")	Allow 3 decimal places.
ToString("0.0000")	Allow 4 decimal places.
ToString()	Allow the default number of decimal places.

Division by Zero

Many of the previous sections have dealt with how to program a function that requires that you exclude from your domain all the values that are less than -25. This set of values proves infinite. Other functions require that you exclude only a single value or a small set of domain values. Among such functions are those in which you seek to eliminate values that make the denominator 0.

Here is the function discussed earlier in the chapter.

$$g(x) = \frac{1}{x - 4} \quad \{x \mid x \in R\} \quad \text{and} \quad \{x \mid x \neq 4\}$$

Programming this function requires only that you check for a specific value that can make the denominator 0. The specVal() method in the FuntionSetA class implements this function. Here is the code for the method.

```
public double specVal(double val)
{
    if (val == 4)
    {
        throw new System.ArithmeticException(
                        val + " invalid; division by 0");
    }
    return 1 / (val - 4);
}
```

In this instance, when you implement the method, you use an if selection statement to determine whether the argument (val) for the method equals 4. If it equals 4, then the flow of your program enters the selection block, where you use the throw keyword to throw an error of the type ArithmeticException. This is an error type that you can use to process errors involving division by zero or other such basic problems.

To use the constructor for this exception type, you follow the same procedure you followed with the ArgumentException constructor. You create a message in which you identify the offending value and then explain why the exception occurs.

To call the specVal() method, you can reuse much of the code you have implemented previously. In this case, you create the performCalcC() method.

```
public void performCalcC()
{
    Functions functions = new CodeLab.Functions();
    double localA = 0;
    double localB = 0;
    displayArea.AppendText("\n\t Domain \t\t Range");
    List<string> errors = new List<string>();
    for (int ctr = 0; ctr < 8; ctr++)
    {
        try
        {
            //#1 Call the method and possibly generate exceptions
            localB = functions.specVal(localA);
        }
        //#2 Use the new type for the exception
        catch(ArithmeticException ex)
        {
            errors.Add(ex.Message.ToString());
        }
```

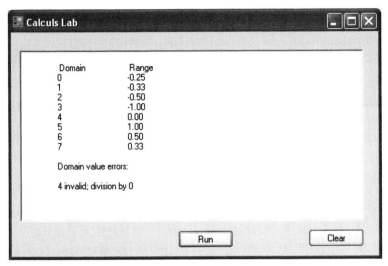

Figure 3.7
Processing an exception allows you to confirm when you have attempted to process a domain value that results in division by 0.

```
    displayArea.AppendText("\n\t" + localA +
                           "\t\t" + localB.ToString("0.00"));
    localA++;
    localB = 0;            //reset the value to 0
  }
  showErrors(errors);
}
```

At comment #1 of the performCalcC() method, you call the specVal() function and pass it the value you have assigned to the localA variable. As Figure 3.7 illustrates, the for repetition statement allows you to generate values for this variable that range from 0 to 7. One of the numbers in this range is 4. This number generates an exception.

As comment #2, you implement a catch block that processes exceptions of the exception, which in this case is of the ArithmeticException type. You access the Message property of the exception object and call the ToString() method to extract the text of the customized message.

At the bottom of Figure 3.7, you see that the only exception message generated relates to the number 4. This value is not allowed, so the specVal() function itself does not return a value for it. In the table of values above, you see 0 as the range value that corresponds to the domain value of 4. The range value rests at

0 because with each iteration of the `for` block you reset the `localB` variable to 0, and when the `specVal()` returns no value to assign to it, it remains 0.

Conclusion

In this chapter, you have carried forward the work of the previous chapter to extend to creating methods for mathematical functions that require you to handle domain values that are not valid. Such values include sets of numbers that extend indefinitely and those that you can identify individually or as members of a small set. A common domain problem involves functions that contain variables that, set to a given value, result in division by 0. To handle such situations, you can make use of `try` ... `catch` blocks and the classes of C# that allow you to process exceptions. You also make use of the `throw` keyword, which allows you to generate an instance of an exception class when your method encounters invalid or inconsistent values.

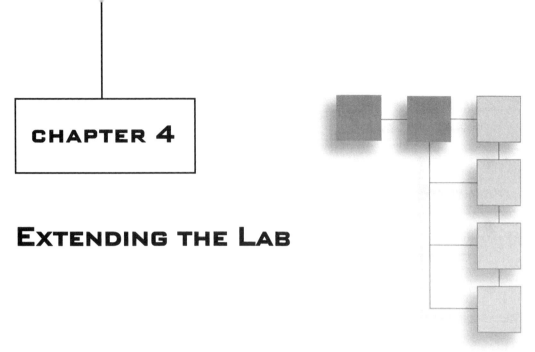

CHAPTER 4

EXTENDING THE LAB

This chapter begins a two-part adventure into extending the Code Lab application so that it incorporates a Cartesian plane. To extend the application, you explore several language features of C#. These features include developing a data type using a struct, incorporating this data type into the definition of a collection object, and adding static fields to your application. You also investigate how to set up forms so that you can process events that refresh the graphical images you include in your application. The central data type in this respect is PaintEventArgs. Using this data type involves painting designated objects you include in your application. One such object is a PictureBox. This is just one of many objects you can use as a background or container for graphical objects. You can pass along the Graphics object (or reference) to the methods in which you want to include graphical operations. This chapter covers the following:

- Using the struct keyword to create a data type

- Employing a collection object as a class field

- Adding a new form to your application

- Graphics and how to use paint events

- Approaches to implementation and testing

- Approaches to testing what you have developed

Graphing Functions

Access the CodeLab.sln project file for Chapter 4 and open it in Visual Studio. When you compile and run the project, you see the form that Figure 4.1 illustrates. This form represents a revised version of the DataForm class you have worked with in previous chapters. In addition to revisions of the DataForm class, you add another form to the Code Lab application. If you click the Run and Show Graph buttons, you see a graph. The graph allows you to use the domain and range values you generate with functions to create graphical representations within a Cartesian coordinate system. Adding such features involves building a class called CoordSystem and building on the skills you have already acquired working with C#. Among other things, you explore a number of methods provided by the C# Graphics class.

In this chapter, you implement only the Graph form (see Figure 4.7). In Chapter 5, you add the graph. Once you perform the work in Chapter 5, Figure 4.2 illustrates the Graph form that you see after you click the Show Graph button. The Cartesian coordinate system allows you to plot points, lines, and curves for limited sets of domain and range values. The values the plane can accommodate range from -20 through 20. However, you can work with larger values if you scale them to accord with the plane. For example, you might divide 200 by 10.

For purposes of exploration, the code for the plane is intentionally left simple. One goal of this chapter and the next is to work through a basic programming

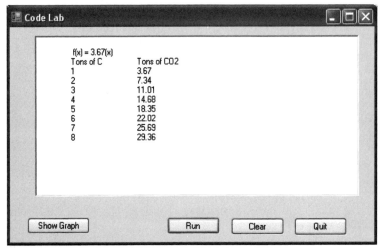

Figure 4.1
You add buttons and new features to your primary form.

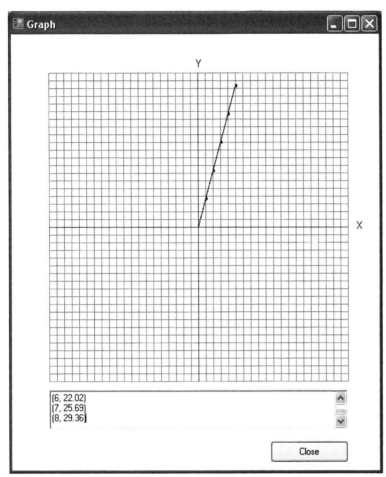

Figure 4.2
A second form allows you to plot values.

project to investigate how it is possible to create a Cartesian coordinate system and methods to plot points, lines, and curves. From this framework, it is hoped you can then work on your own to develop an application with more advanced capabilities. For example, you might proceed to use your knowledge of C# to implement functionality that scales the grid to match the values generated.

Aggregation and Composition

To work with the Code Lab application, it is helpful to view its primary component classes schematically. Accordingly, Figure 4.3 shows you a class diagram

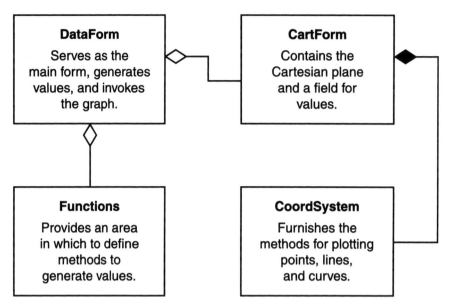

Figure 4.3
The classes are related to each other through composition and aggregation.

of four of the classes you find in the Code Lab project. These are the classes that you work with to implement the functionality that allows you to store and retrieve generated values and to plot graphs.

Diamonds cap all of the lines in Figure 4.3. Software engineers use such lines to illustrate that one class *contains* an instance of another class. When one class contains an instance of another, the general name for the containment is *association*. Two general types of association characterize the relations between the four classes. One type, indicated by the open diamond, is called *aggregation*. The other type, indicated by the filled diamond, is called *composition*.

Note

> The terms and the devices shown in Figure 4.3 illustrating associations between the classes originate in practices of software engineers. A fairly extensive set of practice included in the Unified Modeling Language (UML) provide language and schematics that you can use to communicate about how classes and other software components relate to each other. You can find out more about the UML at www.uml.org/.

The CartForm class is composed of an instance of the CoordSystem class because you always create an instance of the CoordSystem class when you create an instance of the CartForm class. Composition characterizes an association in which one class always contains an instance of another.

In contrast to composition, when you click the Show Graph button in the form you create with the DataForm class, you invoke an instance of the CartForm class, which shows you the graphical representation of data you see in Figure 4.2. You do not always have to click the Show Graph button. In some instances, you might be content to just view the table of values you see after you click the Run button. Because it is discretionary whether you create an instance of the CartForm class, the relation between the DataForm and CartForm classes is characterized by aggregation. Aggregation constitutes an association in which one class can but need not contain an instance of another.

When you click the Run button, you create an instance of the Functions class in the DataForm class. As with the relation between the CartForm and the DataForm classes, a relation of aggregation also characterizes the relation between the DataForm and the Functions classes. You do not have to click the Run button. Rather than generating a table of values, you might be content to view the general features of the application and then click the Quit button. In this case, you would not create an instance of the Functions class.

Dependencies

Aggregation and composition prove to be helpful concepts because they reveal *dependencies*. When you add features to an application that consists of several classes, you can proceed without problems if you know the classes you must develop first. As you go, you might have to comment certain lines or delay implementation of certain features until you have taken care of dependencies. A smooth development effort involves anticipating dependencies. Here are dependencies that affect how you might proceed:

- **Values.** You create a struct (or data type) named Values that has two fields, X and Y, both of the float data type. You use the Values data type extensively in the DataForm class.

- **DataForm.** You extend the DataForm class. Among other things, you add buttons to open a new window (Show Graph) and to quit the application (Quit). The method that opens the new window depends on the creation of a second class, CartForm. The button to quit the application makes use of a class in the C# class hierarchy, Application. You need only to call a method from this class. In addition to buttons, you make it so that you can store and retrieve data that you generate when you implement functions. To accomplish this, you add a collections field of the List type to the class. To add this field, you make use of the Values data type. Also, you create a new method for the DataForm class that allows you to create tables. This method makes use of the List field.

- **CartForm.** To display a Cartesian coordinate system, you add a form to the Code Lab application. This form is made possible by the CartForm class. In this class, you create instances of the PictureBox and RichTextBox classes. You also create a Close button and implement a paint method that allows you to work with an EventArgs event to manipulate various methods from the Graphics class. These components and methods provide a framework in which you can implement the features of a Cartesian coordinate system. To fully implement the class, you must introduce an instance of the DataForm class to access its List field and an instance of the CoordSystem class so that you can implement the Cartesian grid. You implement the CartForm class first, without the grid, so that you have a form in which to test the grid.

- **CoordSystem.** To provide all the functionality needed to create a Cartesian coordinate system and to plot points, lines, and curves in it, you create the CoordSystem class. You can program the methods of this class independently of other classes, but to test it, you require the CartForm class.

- **Functions.** You carry forward most of the features of the Functions class unchanged from Chapter 2. You require this class from the first. To make it easier to work with, you can reduce its methods to one, calculateCO2Added().

Note

When one class has a dependency on another, the class that has the dependency is known as the *client* class. The other class is known as the *service* class. The DataForm class is the client class of the CartForm and Functions classes. The CartForm class is a service class for the DataForm class.

Adding a Struct

In the DataForm.cs file, you begin your work by creating a *struct*. You create a struct in the same way that you create a class, with the difference that you do not, as a matter of practice, include methods in it. A struct is a data type. When you define the Values struct, then, you create a data type named Values that you can use throughout your project.

A struct provides a way to combine two or more fields into a single manageable unit. In the code associated with comment #1 in the DataForm.cs file, you create the Values struct just prior to creating the DataForm class. This struct provides you with a set of two fields, X and Y, which you can use together to store the domain and range pairs that functions generate. You work repeatedly with such pairs in the DataForm class, so the Values data type appears several times. Here is the code that defines the Values struct:

```
//#1
   public struct Values
   {
      public float X;
      public float Y;
      // Constructor
      public Values(float xVal, float yVal)
      {
         X = xVal;
         Y = yVal;
      }
   }// end of struct definition
```

To create a struct, you identify the scope of the struct with the appropriate access keyword. In this instance, you use the public keyword. This makes the struct public so that you can use it without restrictions in any class in your project.

You also use the public keyword to define the two fields you create in the Values struct, X and Y. Making fields public constitutes an important distinction between a struct and a class. You make the fields of a struct public because you access them by name, not via methods. You access them by name using the name of the instance of the struct and a dot operator.

You also create a constructor for the Values struct. The constructor provides a convenient way to initialize the fields of the struct. The constructor has the same name as the struct, Values. The scope of the constructor is public, and it accepts two arguments of the float type. This allows you to set the X and Y fields when you invoke the constructor.

Note

When you define a struct data type, you can include private fields and then access the fields using properties, just as you do when you develop classes. Here is an example of how this might be done.

```
public struct Values_With_Property
{
    private float Xval;
    public float X
    {
        get { return Xval; }
        set { Xval = X; }
    }
}
```

This approach proves excessive in the current context, where a one-to-one relationship exists between the fields and the properties. In other situations, such an approach might prove extremely helpful. One such situation might be characterized by a large array of color values that you use properties to access.

Adding a Static List to the DataForm Class

The first use you make of the Values data type occurs when you employ it to define the type of a List field of the DataForm class. The line that defines this field follows comment #2. Here is the line:

```
static List<Values> coordSets = new List<Values>();
```

The definition of the coordSets object in this case follows the same pattern you followed in Chapter 3 when creating a collection (List) object there. You use template forms of declaration and construction. Between the greater and less than signs, you state the name of the data type you want to assign to the List collection object. In this instance, you use the Values data type. As with your previous work with List object construction, you first declare the identifier for the List object (coordSets), and then you call the constructor for the List class to create an instance of the class to assign to the identifier.

When you define the coordSets identifier, you make use of the static keyword. The static keyword allows you to create a *class field*. The fields you define without the static keyword are *instance fields*. The values of an instance field are restricted to a single instance of a class. In other words, every instance or object of the class has its own set of fields. A class field differs from an instance field because all instances or objects of a given class share the class field.

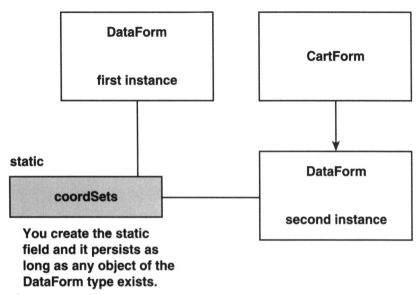

Figure 4.4
The class (or static) field persists as long as your application maintains an instance of the class that contains the static field.

Given this situation, the coordSets field comes into existence when you create the first instance of the DataForm class and continues to exist, shared by all instances of the DataForm class that you create after that. The field is deleted only when you have deleted all instances of the DataForm class. Figure 4.4 illustrates what happens.

As Figure 4.4 shows, you create the first instance of the DataForm class when you start the Code Lab application. When you create the first instance of the DataForm class, the coordSets field is also created. This field is a List object of the Values type, so you can store pairs of domain and range values in it. As you will see in the sections to come, the actions you invoke when you click the Run button assign data to the coordSets field.

Next, when you click the Show Graph button (see Figure 4.1), you create an instance of the CartForm class (shown in Figure 4.2). Within the CartForm class, you create a second instance of the DataForm class. This second instance of the DataForm class provides you with access the coordSets field in the plotCToCO2 function. Because the coordSets field is a static field, the data you stored in it when you clicked the Run button still exits. You are working now with two instances of the DataForm class. Both instances share the same coordSets field. That this is so becomes evident if you inspect the text field in the lower part of the

Graph window (see Figure 4.2). The values the text area display are from the coordSets you call using the second instance of the DataForm class. (A later section provides detailed discussion of this activity.)

Using the List Object

You defined the performCCalculation() method in Chapter 3. This method attends to calculating the amount of carbon dioxide that results when you burn fossil fuels and other carbon substances. In your previous work, you called this method in the DataForm class and wrote its results to the text area of the DataForm class. Now this procedure changes. Now you store the results of the method in the coordSetsList object, which is a field of the DataForm class. Here is the revised version of the performCCalculation() method, which you can find in the lines following comment #6 in the DataForm class:

```
private void performCCalculation()
{
  // Create an instance of the Functions class
    Functions functions = new CodeLab.Functions();
    double tonsOfC = 1;
    double tonsOfCO2 = 0;
    // Repeat the calculation 8 times.
    for(int ctr = 0; ctr < 8; ctr++)
    {
      // Apply the function
      tonsOfCO2 = functions.calculateCO2Added(tonsOfC);
      coordSets.Add( new Values( (float) tonsOfC,
                                 (float) tonsOfCO2 ));

      tonsOfC++;
    }// end for
  }// end method
```

In this version of the method, as in the previous version, you start off by creating an instance of the Functions class and assigning it to the functions identifier. You then use the functions identifier to call the calculateCO2Added() method.

The revised method differs from the older form because you now preserve the data that the calculateCO2Added() method returns by storing it in the coordSets collection. To store it in the collection, you call the Add() method. The Add() method is a member of the List class. It allows you to add an object to a List collection. In this case, the item you add is of the Values struct type.

When you add the object of the `Values` type to the `coordSets` collection, you make use of the `Values` constructor. Here is an isolated view of this activity:

```
coordSets.Add( new Values( (float) tonsOfC, (float) tonsOfCO2 ));
```

Several actions occur within this statement. As an argument to the `Add()` method, you call the `Values` constructor. As arguments to the `Values` constructor, you provide the values you have assigned to the `tonsOfC` and `tonsOfCO2` variables. These values allow you to set the `X` and `Y` fields of the `Values` struct. With each repetition of the block, you create a new instance of the `Values` struct and assign this instance to a slot within the `coordSetsList` object.

To the first (`X`) field, you assign the value assigned to `tonsOfC`. This is a `double` value that grows as the `for` block repeats. It begins at 0 and grows to 8. To make it suitable as an argument for the `Values` constructor, you cast it using the `float` data type. To cast one type to another, you place the name of the data type to which you want to cast a given value in parentheses preceding the name of the variable to which the cast applies.

For the second `Values` constructor argument, you use the `tonsOfCO2` variable, which holds the value returned by the `calculateCO2Added()` method. The returned value is of the `double` type.

Note

Certain risks accompany casting a `double` as a `float` value because the `double` data type accommodates larger values than the `float` data type. However, in this instance, the values you are dealing with are small enough that the effects are not harmful.

Each `Values` object you create in this way you assign anonymously to the `coordSetsList` object. You can then use the appropriate `List` methods to retrieve the data for later use. Since the `Values` objects you store in the `List` collection are anonymous, you can identify them only according to their positions within the `List` collection. As you see later on, if you first assign the `coordSets` objects to an array (or a collection with an explicit index), then you can conveniently retrieve the `Values` objects individually.

Using the List Object for Display Purposes

As mentioned previously, you change the `performCCalculation()` method so that it stores the values that result from its operations in the `coordSets` field. You no longer immediately display these values. Instead, you now retrieve them in another method to display them. This is the `displayTable()` method. The definition of the `displayTable()` method follows comment #7 in the `DataForm` class.

The `displayTable()` method generates a two-column table of domain and range. To define the method, you assign it an argument list that consists of two items. The first argument is of the `String` type and allows you to furnish a line of text to identify the mathematical formula you are working with. The second argument is also of the `String` type. This allows you to supply text for the column headings of your table of data. Here is the code for the method:

```
void displayTable(String formula,
          String heading)
{
    // Write the output to the table
    displayArea.AppendText(formula);
    displayArea.AppendText(heading);
    foreach(Values valSet in coordSets)
    {
        // Write lines in the table
        displayArea.AppendText("\n\t" + valSet.X.ToString() +
                            "\t\t" + valSet.Y.ToString());
    }// end foreach
}// end of method
```

You have seen the work of the `AppendText()` method several times in previous chapters. In this context it performs the same activity as before. It prints text in the `DataForm` text area.

Within the `foreach` block, you implement code that takes care of the primary responsibilities of the method. This activity involves printing the two columns of the table. To accomplish this, you use the `foreach` action to retrieve pairs of values (stored in `Values` objects) from the `coordSets` collection and assign them to the `valSet` variable.

Since `coordSets` is a class field, all methods in the class can access it. The `performCCalculation()` method accesses it to store data in it. Now the `displayTable()` method accesses it to retrieve data. You use the `foreach` statement to retrieve copies of all the objects stored in it, which you assign individually to the `valSet` variable.

The `valSet` variable is of the `Values` type, so you can use the dot operator to access the X and Y fields to retrieve values from it. These two fields are of the float type, so to make them suitable for display in a text field, you call the `ToString()`

method to convert them to the String type. They can then be made a part of a line of text you print using a call to the AppendText() method.

Setting and Using a Flag

When you call the performCCalculation() method to assign values to the coordSets collection, you make it possible to retrieve the values in a number of places for use in a number of ways. In the context provided by the DataForm window, you make two basic uses of the data. The first is to display it locally, in the text area of the DataForm window. To accomplish this task, you click the Run button. The second is more involved. You pass the data to another class, which uses it to generate a graph.

Using data in this way can create problems unless you devise a way to track your use. For example, if you implement methods that cannot function properly unless you have data at hand for them to use, then you can end up with invalid results. You can also create a situation in which you cause your application to crash.

To deal with such dangers, you can create control mechanisms. One such control mechanism is a *flag*. A flag is often of the bool type, so it can take one of two values: true or false. One use of a flag is to set it to true if a given preliminary event has been completed and false if it has not.

Such an event characterizes generating a body of data to assign to the coordSets collection. When you have generated the data and are ready for further actions, you can set the flag to true. You accomplish this task in the definition of the runButton_Click() method. The definition of this method accompanies comment #4 in the DataForm class. Here are the lines for the method:

```
private void runButton_Click(object sender, EventArgs e)
{
   if (run == false)
   {
     // Generate initial values
     performCCalculation();
     displayTable("\n\t f(x) = 3.67(x)",
                  "\n\tTons of C \tTons of CO2");
     run = true;
   }// end if
}// end of method
```

As the previous discussion emphasizes, you call the performCCalculation () method to generate initial domain and range values and store them in the coordSets object. You then call the displayTable() method to display the values in the text area of DataForm. To call the displayTable() method, you supply it with arguments that identify the equation you have used to generate the domain and range values. You also provide text for the column headings of the table.

To determine whether to perform the two methods, you implement an if selection statement. This statement serves as a toggle to change the value of your flag to indicate that you have generated the domain and range values. In this case, the flag is the run field, which you define in the line associated with comment #3.

The run field is a static field of the bool type. It is static because it provides information about a static field, coordSets. You make the run field static so that it can be a fellow traveler with the coordSets field. You must be able to use it in different instances of the DataForm class.

You can assign only two values to the run field, true and false. In light of this, after you have generated the data for the coordSets collection and displayed it in the DataForm text area, you set the run flag to true. This action has several results, one of which is that you are now prevented from repeatedly generating new data by clicking the Run button. The second is that that you can now perform other actions, such as clicking the Show Graph button to generate a graph of the data.

Initializing the Flag

The initial value of the run field is false. It is not necessary to explicitly set the run flag to false because, if you do not initialize it, its value is set to 0, or false. However, to ensure that the value is initialized as false, find this statement in the DataForm constructor:

```
run = false;
```

When your application starts, then run is set to false. It remains false until you click the Run button, which invokes the runButton_Click() method. The if statement in the runButton_Click() method evaluates the run field, and finds its value to be false. It allows the flow of the program to invoke the performCCalculation() and displayTable() methods. It then changes the value of run to true.

Clear and Reset

You visit the run field in places other than the constructor and the runButton_Click() method. One such place is the clearButton_Click() method, which you define in the lines associated with comment #5. The definition takes this form:

```
private void clearButton_Click(object sender, EventArgs e)
{
    displayArea.Clear();
    coordSets.Clear();
    run = false;
}
```

The actions the method invokes consist of using the Clear() method of the RichTextBox class to delete the contents of the text area in DataForm. You then call another Clear() method, this one for the List class, which deletes the contents of the coordSets collection. Given these two actions, you have now deleted the displayed data and the data you have stored in the coordSets collection. Having cleared the data in this way, you reset the run field to false, indicating that no data any longer resides in the coordSets collection.

Defining the Run Property

To make it so that you can access the run field in a formal way, you create the Run property. The name of this property differs from the name of the field only with the capitalization of the first letter. Here is the code that implements the Run property:

```
public bool Run
    {
        get { return run; }
        set { run = Run; }
    }
}
```

The implementation of this property differs slightly from the work you performed previously. Here, you use both the get and set keywords to define the property. Given the use of these keywods, you can both assign a value to and retrieve a value from the Run property.

The effect of this activity is that you can now access the value of the run field using the Run property. On the other hand, you cannot access the run field directly. That it is a static field makes no difference in this respect.

Defining the Vals Property

In the lines associated with comment #9 of the DataForm class, in addition to defining the Run property, you also define the Vals property. When you set up the Vals property, you use only the get keword. Using only the get keyword allows you to make it so that users of the DataForm class have a relatively safe way to access the values you have stored in coordSets collection.

As with the run field, after you define a property for the coordSets field, your sole means of accessing the values in the coordSets field is through the Vals property. Here are the lines you employ to define the Vals property:

```
public List<Values> Vals
{
   get { return coordSets; }
}
```

The Vals property returns copies of all the items in the coordSets List object. This proves to be a convenient way of accessing the items without at the same time exposing them to the danger of being deleted. You are able to use this capability in an effective way in the CartForm class when you create an instance of the DataForm class to retrieve values that you use to generate graphs.

Opening the Graphics Window

In the code associated with comment #8 in DataForm, you implement the showButton_Click() method. Here is the code for this method:

```
private void showButton_Click(object sender, EventArgs e)
{
   if (run == true)
   {
     CartForm cartForm = new CartForm();
     CartForm.Activate();
```

```
    CartForm.Show();
  }
  else
  {
    MessageBox.Show(this, "Click Run to "
                     + "generate a table first.");
  }// end if-else
}// end of method
```

This method creates an instance of the CartForm class. Creation of this class exposes a dependency that you must account for prior to implementing the method. The next several sections deal with the development of the CartForm class. To work with this method prior to full implementation of the CartForm class, you can comment out the three lines beginning with CartForm.

For now, the primary action involves an if. . .else selection structure. This structure evaluates the value currently stored in the run field to determine if it has been set to true. If the run field is set to true, then the flow of the program enters the if block and you create an instance of the CartForm class.

You check the flag in this way to ensure that when you commence with the generation of a graph, you have data to work with. If you tried to generate a graph without any data (if the coordSets collection were not yet populated), then your results would prove dissatisfying. You might find a Cartesian plane devoid of plotting, or you might crash your application.

If the run flag is set to false, then the flow of the program enters the else block. In the else block, you create a MessageBox object. A MessageBox object is a dialog. Technically, a MessageBox is a *modal* dialog. A modal dialog halts your interaction with an application until you respond to it. Responses are usually made possible through a routine that is familiar to most Windows users. You click OK, Cancel, No, and Yes buttons, among others. The dialog then vanishes, and you can proceed.

Among other things, a modal dialog serves to explicitly advise you of a hazard. It is something like a warning label. On the other hand, it serves as a way to tell you that you must perform a necessary action. In this case, the dialog tells you that before you can generate a graph, you must generate some data. Figure 4.5 illustrates the MessageBox dialog as implemented to inform you that you must generate data for the coordSets collection.

Figure 4.5
A `MessageBox` object allows you to create modal dialogs.

Note

The dialog provides a proactive advisory. Rather than providing a message about an error, it simply tells you what to do to avoid the error. Imagine the contrary. Suppose you were using the application for the first time and encountered a message that read, "Error: no data in data field." Such an error leaves you hanging.

To implement a message box, you use the `MessageBox` class name to call the `Show()` method. Several versions of the `Show()` method allow you to create message boxes with varying appearances. They also provide you with the ability to return different values. For example, you can implement a `MessageBox` dialog to confirm whether the reader wants to perform a given action, such as exiting an application. In this instance, you provide only an advisory. To provide an advisory, you supply the `Show()` method with one argument, the advisory that the dialog displays.

Redevelopment and Exploration

Chapters 4 and 5 provide a fully implemented system of classes, but you can redevelop the system if you want to explore programming activities on your own. In fact, this is the suggested approach to learning programming. See if you can redevelop a given body of code on your own by following an example line by line, understanding things as you go.

One approach to this type of learning is to make copies of the files and then delete selected features. For example, you reduce a class to the signature lines of its methods and rebuild them from there.

Along with the signature lines, you include the shells of the methods. The shell of a method includes opening and closing braces and a `return` statement. In some cases, you must fabricate a temporary `return` statement. If the `return` statement involves a number, such as a `float`, an `int`, or a `double`, then you can use a literal value. You might use statements along these lines:

```
return 0.0;   //Double
return 0.0F   //Float
return " ";   //Empty string
return 0;     //integer
```

The CartForm class offers only methods that have void return types. If a method possesses a void return type, the shell of the method does not include a return statement. In this respect, then, to implement this set of methods, you do not employ the return keyword as you complete the methods. This situation changes with the CoordSystem class, where almost all of the methods use return types. This becomes a topic of Chapter 5. Here is the CartForm class with the shells of its methods.

```
public partial class CartForm : Form
{
   // #1 Define the fields for the class

   public CartForm()
   {
   }
   // #2
   private void CartForm_Load(object sender, EventArgs e)
   {
   }

   private void pictureBox1_Paint(object sender,
                                  PaintEventArgs e)
   {
      // #3 Create a local version of the graphics
   }
   // #4 Show data and draw graph
   public void plotCT0CO2(Graphics e)
   {
   }
   // #5 Close the form
   private void closeButton_Click(object sender, EventArgs e)
   {
   }
}//end of class
```

To implement this class, you can use a number of approaches. One is to copy the file to a backup name, and then go through the original and delete lines until you have only the shell. You can then follow the explanations this book provides and retype the code.

In this book and many other contexts, it is your prerogative to change and improve the code you start with. Seeing changes constitutes a key activity in any learning exercise. You add a feature to a program and then test your addition by seeing what it does. In this way you both test the feature you have implemented and confirm your knowledge of programming.

The CartForm Class

The CartForm class serves as a kind of drawing board for your coordinate system. It contains few lines of code, and it does very little beyond displaying information or graphical images that other classes generate. The implementation of the CartForm class includes code that you might not see in a form you generate using the wizard. Still, it conforms generally to the classes you generate using the wizard. Here is the code for the CartForm class:

```
public partial class CartForm : Form
{
    // #1 Field declarations and definitions
    CoordSystem cSys = new CoordSystem();        //dependency
    private int FW, FH;
    private PictureBox pictureBox1 = new PictureBox();

    public CartForm()
    {
        InitializeComponent();
    }
    // #2
    private void CartForm_Load(object sender, EventArgs e)
    {
        FW = 500;
        FH = 600;
        this.Width = FW;
        this.Height = FH;
        pictureBox1.Dock = DockStyle.Fill;
        pictureBox1.BackColor = Color.White;
        //Connect the Paint event of the PictureBox
        //to the event handler method.
        this.pictureBox1.Paint + =
                new System.Windows.Forms.PaintEventHandler(
                                this.pictureBox1_Paint);
        // Add the PictureBox control to the Form.
        this.Controls.Add(pictureBox1);
    }

    private void pictureBox1_Paint(object sender,
                            PaintEventArgs e)
    {
        // #3 Create a local version of the graphics
        cSys.drawGrid(e);                // dependency
```

```
      cSys.drawAxes(e);                    // dependency
      plotCTOCO2(e);
   }
   // #4 Show data and draw graph
   public void plotCTOCO2(Graphics e)
   {
      DataForm item = new DataForm();
      Values[] locVals = sets.Vals.ToArray();
      richTextBox1.AppendText("\n(CO, CO2)");
      foreach (Values val in locVals)
      {
        if (val.Y < 20)
         {
            richTextBox1.AppendText("\n(" + val.X
                              + ", " + val.Y + ")");
            cSys.plotPoint(e, val.X, val.Y);        // dependency
            cSys.plotLinear(e, 0, 0, val.X, val.Y);  // dependency
         }
       }
   }
   // #5 Close the form
   private void closeButton_Click(object sender, EventArgs e)
   {
      this.Close();
    }
}//end class
```

The sections that follow discuss a few basics of creating your form and working with the code that comes with this book. To review approaches to development, see the previous sidebar, "Redevelopment and Exploration." To review how to work with dependencies, see "Commenting Out Dependencies" later in this chapter. Also, for connecting different forms, see the following sidebar, "Creating a Form and Connecting."

Creating a Form and Connecting

To create a fresh form for the CartForm class, use this procedure:

1. From the main menu of the Microsoft Visual Studio, select Project > Add New Item. You see the Add New Item dialog.

2. In the pane for the Visual Studio installed templates, click Windows Form. Press the Tab key to move the focus to the Name field. To identify your own version of the CartForm class, type MyCartForm. This class can then reside in the CodeLab class with the CartForm class, and you can switch back and forth as needed.

3. Click Add.

4. You then see the MyCartForm.cs[Design] view.

5. Double click the form to open the code, and proceed from there. You can type or copy the code from the file that comes with the book.

To make it so that you can invoke the form using the Run button in the DataForm window, change the code in the showButton_Click() method so that you comment out the original code and add code for your own form. Keep both sets of code so that you can alternate between the two versions of the form as you test and review your work. In this example, the MyCartForm class replaces the CartForm class.

```
// Test array of coordinate values
// #8 Verify values and open an instance of CartForm - the graph
private void showButton_Click(object sender, EventArgs e)
{
    if (run == true)
    {
        // CartForm cartForm = new CartForm();
        // cartForm.Activate();
        // cartForm.Show();
        MyCartForm cartForm = new CartForm();
        cartForm.Activate();
        cartForm.Show();
```

Figure 4.6
Click the starter form to begin implementing the code on your own.

```
    }
    else
    {
        MessageBox.Show(this, "Click Run to "
                               + "generate a table first.");
    }//end if-else
}//end method
```

Given these changes, click the Run and Show Graph buttons in the main window. Your application invokes a basic form, as Figure 4.6 illustrates.

The CartForm Code

In the lines associated with comment #1 in the CartForm class definition, you declare four fields for the class. These fields consist of an instance of the CoordSystem class, two variables of the int type for the width and height of the form, and a PictureBox object. The CoordSystem class provides the code that draws the grid for the Cartesian plane and allows you to plot the data you obtain from the DataForm class. The PictureBox object (pictureBox1) provides a pane that fills your form and allows you to paint on it. Here are the lines you use to create these fields:

```
CoordSystem cSys = new CoordSystem();        //dependency
private int FW, FH;
private PictureBox pictureBox1 = new PictureBox();
```

In addition to declaring fields for your class, you also implement a constructor. Visual Studio automatically generates the code for the constructor if you use the wizard. (See the sidebar, "Creating a Form and Connecting.") The call to the InitializeComponent() method constitutes a standard feature of the code the wizard generates. The code that you add to the constructor sets the FW and FH attributes. Here are the lines that implement the constructor:

```
public CartForm()
{
    InitializeComponent();
    //set width and height
    FW = 500;
    FH = 600;
}
```

Trailing comment #2, you define the CartForm_Load() method. This method attends to setting the size of your form and associating a Paint event handler with the pictureBox1 object. Here is the code for the method:

```
private void CartForm_Load(object sender, EventArgs e)
{
    this.Width = FW;
    this.Height = FH;
    pictureBox1.Dock = DockStyle.Fill;
    pictureBox1.BackColor = Color.White;
    // Connect the Paint event of the PictureBox
    // to the event handler method.
    pictureBox1.Paint +=
    new PaintEventHandler(pictureBox1_Paint);
    // Add the PictureBox control to the Form.
    this.Controls.Add(pictureBox1);
}
```

The this keyword refers to the CartForm class. It is used here for purposes of demonstration. You could just as well use the Width and Height properties alone, without qualifying them with the this keyword. The keyword allows you to recognize that the items it qualifies belong to the current class or the class from which the current class is derived. The Width and Height attributes are features of the Form class. The CartForm class is derived from the Form class and has its own copies of these properties.

Next you attend to the PictureBox object. First you access the DockStyle.Fill property to make it so that the PictureBox object entirely fills the CartForm area. You use the Color.White property to set white as the color of the PictureBox object. This becomes the color of the form as you see it in Figure 4.2.

After setting the appearance of the PictureBox object, you then make it so that the PictureBox object is repeatedly repainted. Repainting might be viewed as an action that occurs whenever the form is changed. To repaint the form, you construct a new instance of the PaintEventHandler class. As an argument to the constructor for the PaintEventHandler object, you provide the name of a method. This method contains the code that creates the items you want to repaint. You use the pictureBox1_Paint() method. This method you define momentarily.

You assign the instance of the PaintEventHandler to the Paint property of the pictureBox1 field. Painting constitutes an activity that repeatedly occurs while your application runs. If you collapse an application or move it so that the edge of your monitor obscures part of it, you generate an event that you can process to tell your application to repaint itself.

As a final action, you call the Add() method to add the pictureBox1 object as a visible feature of your form. If you add controls using the IDE ToolBox, such activities are often taken care of for you. In this instance, however, you can see first hand how to implement the repainting features of your form.

Painting

As mentioned previously, you create a method that contains the code that implements the graphical features you want to have repainted. The function you use for this purpose is the pictureBox1_Click() method. This method contains only three lines. It might contain many more, but as it is these three lines serve to create the graphical features of your Cartesian plane, including the plotting of your data. Here are the lines for this method:

```
private void pictureBox1_Paint(object sender,
                               PaintEventArgs e)
{
   // #3 Create a local version of the graphics
   cSys.drawGrid(e.Graphics);          // dependency
   cSys.drawAxes(e.Graphics);          // dependency
   plotCTOCO2(e.Graphics);
}
```

Methods of the pictureBox1_Paint() type are known as *event handlers*. This event handler handles events of the PaintEventArgs type. Such events trigger painting activities. When you process a PaintEventArgs event (e), you receive an object that carries information that you can use when you want to perform actions related to drawing graphical images. This object is associated with the Graphics class. The Graphics class contains methods that allow you to draw lines and many other geometric objects.

You can paint and repaint objects on your form by passing along the Graphics object (e) from function to function. This is the approach used here. Accordingly, each method that draws something has as its standard argument an argument of the Graphics type.

Commenting Out Dependencies

In the lines associated with comment #1 in the CartForm class, you create an instance of the CoordSystem class. As was discussed previously, your work takes place in the context of a set of dependencies, and one dependency is that you have yet to implement the CoordSystem class. Even if you have not yet implemented the CoordSystem class, you can still develop and test the CartForm class. Toward this end, toward the right margin of selective lines you find this comment:

//dependency

To work with the code so that you can compile the CartForm class, type the statement that creates an instance of the CoordSystem class and then comment it out. Follow the same procedure for each line on which you see the dependency comment. Five such comments appear in the code. When you compile your project without these lines, you see a blank form with a white background, as illustrated by Figure 4.7.

Figure 4.7
When you remove statements from the CoordSystem class, the coordinate system no longer appears, but you can still test data.

Plotting

The plotCTOCO2() method performs many of the same activities in this version of the Code Lab application that it performed in the last version. Some significant changes characterize how it performs its work, however. Central in this respect is the use of an instance of the CartForm class. You find the implementation of the method in the lines trailing comment #4. Here is the code:

```
// #4 Show data and draw graph
public void plotCTOCO2(Graphics e)
{
   DataForm sets = new DataForm();
   Values[] locVals = sets.Vals.ToArray();
   richTextBox1.AppendText("\n(CO, CO2)");
   foreach (Values val in locVals)
   {
     if (val.Y < 20)
     {
        richTextBox1.AppendText("\n(" + val.X
                               + ", " + val.Y + ")");
        cSys.plotPoint(e, val.X, val.Y);          //dependency
        cSys.plotLinear(e, 0, 0, val.X, val.Y);   //dependency
     }//end if
   }//end foreach
}//end method
```

In the first line of the body of the plotCTOCO2() method, you create an instance of the DataForm class using the default constructor. You assign the instance of the DataForm class to the sets identifier. You then use the sets identifier to access the Vals property of the DataForm class. The Vals property allows you to access the domain and range values you have stored in the coordSets.

Note

Recall that the Vals property allows you to access the coordSets collection. In practical terms, Vals and coordSets name the same entity, a collection of objects of the Values type. For a review of these two items, see the discussion of the DataForm class.

As the discussion of the DataForm class emphasized, the coordSets field is a static (or class) field, so the values you store in it can be accessed by any object of the DataForm class that you create during the lifetime of your application. Given this situation, you can now use the ToArray() method. This method is a member of the List class. The coordSets collection is of the List type. The ToArray() method allows you to retrieve copies of all the objects stored in the coordSets collection and assign them to an array.

To assign the objects to an array, you define an array of the Values type (locVals). You can then easily access the items in the array individually by employing index numbers or sequentially using a foreach structure. Since you have no need in this instance to access values by using indexes, the foreach structure proves the best choice. Using it, you access the coordinate pairs one after the other and print them to the RichTextBox.

In this way, the RichTextBox field displays the values you printed previously in a tabular form in the text area of the DataForm window. Given that you comment out the lines showing the dependency comment, you have a way to readily test the values you have generated and the connectivity of the different forms through the static List object. Figure 4.7 illustrates the values as they appear when generated in this way. You can use the scroll bars to view all the sets.

The foreach statement copies each Values object in sequence from the locVals array to the val variable. You can then use the X and Y fields of the Values struct to retrieve the domain and range values of each pair. These values are automatically converted to strings when you use them as arguments in the AppendText() method.

One limitation pertains to the values you generate. You employ an if selection statement to test the Y attribute of the Value objects you retrieve from the locVals array to determine if it is less than 20. Larger values are not displayed. This measure is taken to limit values to those that you can plot in the plane the form provides. If you want to see all values, you can move the call to the AppendText() method outside the if statement block. The code in this instance takes this form:

```
foreach (Values val in locVals)'
{
    // Moved to allow you to see all values in the List object
    richTextBox1.AppendText("\n(" + val.X
                        + ", " + val.Y + ")");
    if (val.Y < 20)
    {
        cSys.plotPoint(e, val.X, val.Y);          // dependency
        cSys.plotLinear(e, 0, 0, val.X, val.Y);   // dependency
    }
}
```

Calling the CoordSystem Methods

In the lines trailing comment #3 in the CartForm class, you call the picture-Box1_Paint() method. This method directly and indirectly calls methods from the CoordSystem class. The methods called directly are drawGrid() and draw-Axes(). The method that contains an indirect call to the CoordSystem class is the plotCTOCO2() method.

The drawGrid() method creates a Cartesian plane. The drawAxes() method draws *x* and *y* axes on this plane. As you develop the CoordSystem class, you can work in steps to implement the methods, including first the drawGrid() and next the drawAxes() method to construct your coordinate system. Then you can call other functions to plot values in the system.

As mentioned previously, you can call the plotCTOCO2() method without first implementing the CoordSystem class, but to do so, you must first comment out the two lines in which you make calls to methods of the CoordSystem class. Here is the code for the pictureBox1_Paint() method. You can remove the comments from the indicated lines as you proceed with development and testing efforts.

```
private void pictureBox1_Paint(object sender,
                               PaintEventArgs e)
{
    // #3 Create a local version of the graphics
    cSys.drawGrid(e);  // dependency - implement CoordSystem
    cSys.drawAxes(e);  // dependency - implement CoordSystem
    plotCTOCO2(e);     // Comment out 2 lines within this method
}
```

Closing

The CartForm class includes a method that allows you to process events generated by the Close button. In the lines associated with comment #5, you define this method. Here are the lines:

```
private void closeButton_Click(object sender, EventArgs e)
{
    this.Close();
}
```

The this keyword identifies the currently active object of the CartForm class. When you click the Close button, the result is that the CartForm window is disposed of. The object is deleted. Another method, Dispose() is usually associated with this action, but you do not need to call it in this context. You need only the Close() method. To close a window is not the same as to close an application. The action pertains only to the form in which you invoke it.

Conclusion

In this chapter, you have implemented the first of two classes that allow you to display a Cartesian coordinate system. The discussion in this chapter primarily focuses on preliminary activities involved in setting up a window (or form) so that you can paint features to it. Along the way, you developed a data type using a struct, implemented class fields, and explored how paint messages can be processed. When you introduced a second form, you examined how a class field can be used to temporarily transfer data from one form to another. In this respect, the `Values` data type combined with a list collection object proved central. This chapter also included discussion of simple approaches using development as a way to learn programming. One approach involves using the shells of methods as a way to outline your development work.

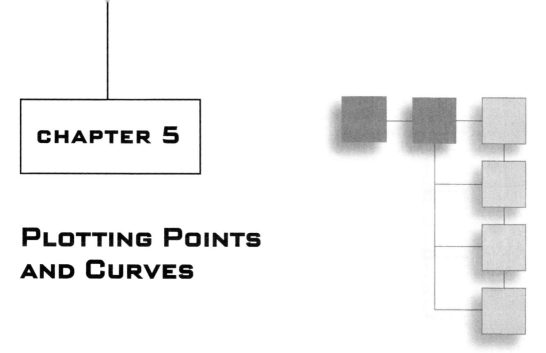

CHAPTER 5

PLOTTING POINTS AND CURVES

In this chapter, you implement the class that allows you to generate points, lines, and curves in the form you created in Chapter 4. To perform this work, you begin with an exploration of how to translate one coordinate system into another. This type of translation allows you to review how the coordinate system for a window differs from that of a standard Cartesian coordinate system. After exploring how to translate coordinate systems, you then proceed with the details of implementation. This activity involves exploring the use of four of the methods you can access from the C# Graphics class. These are the FillEllipse(), DrawLine(), DrawCurve(), and DrawString() methods. You also explore Brush and Pen objects and uses of such classes as Point. The result is that in the end you arrive at a version of the CoordSystem class that allows you to create several types of figures in your co-ordinate system. Toward this end, you explore these topics, among others:

- Planning the layout of a graphical image

- The differences between systems of plotting

- Creating a grid and axes for it

- Plotting an ellipse and a line

- Turning a rational value into a decimal value

- Drawing a curve using the DrawCurve() method

Creating a Cartesian Plane

Your work in Chapter 4 allowed you to create the framework of a form in which you can display graphs. Now you can proceed to implement the `CoordSystem` class, which provides the functionality that generates the graph.

To create a class that allows you to plot points, lines, and curves, you proceed in two steps. In the first step, you draw a grid. In the second step, you establish procedures that allow you to translate points from the Windows coordinate system to the Cartesian coordinate system. Both of these steps involve understanding from the start that a form (or window) is organized according to a coordinate system that corresponds to a Cartesian system but at the same time differs from the usually quadrant system you see in math books. The difference lies in the position of the origin of the coordinate system. You measure the dimensions of a window in pixels.

Note

The term *pixel* originates from the expression "picture element." A picture element is a point of color on your monitor and is familiar to most users of Windows. You set the resolution of your monitor using pixel measurements.

If you define a form to be 500 pixels high and 600 wide, its size changes as you see it on your monitor, according to the resolution of your monitor. For this reason, it makes little sense to think of a window as so many centimeters or inches across or high. Still, size remains important. Most people elect to use a setting of approximately 1024 × 768 for desktop computing, and many developers design applications so that they are most easily viewed in this range of resolution.

Redevelopment and Exploration

In this chapter, as in the last, you can learn most effectively if you redevelop the code on your own, exploring features as you go. Exploration often includes extending and improving the features that you work with. Such activity constitutes a central feature of much software development. Such development activity falls under the heading of *iteration* and *incrementation*. In other words, you repeatedly revisit a given feature or passage of your program, refining it and improving it. There is much room for such activity in the Code Lab.

When you refine a given passage in a program, the term that applies to your work is *refactoring*. When you refactor software, you change it so that you eliminate redundancies, provide meaningful names, and in other ways make your software easier to understand and maintain.

As in the last chapter, you can benefit if you develop classes from the signatures of shells of methods. Using shells of methods as a starting point constitutes a common practice in software development. Developers know that a given method must be implemented because the design of the software calls for a given type of functionality. Signatures and method shells serve as an outline for a program or a class.

As mentioned in Chapter 4, the shell of a method includes opening and closing braces and a `return` statement. If the `return` statement involves a number, such as a `float`, an `int`, or a `double`, then you can use a literal value. Here are some examples:

```
return 0.0;
return 0;
```

If the `return` statement involves a `String`, you can use a similar approach, one with a word, the other with empty quotations:

```
return "Okay";
return " ";
```

For the `CoordSystem` class, most of the methods return copies of `String` objects bearing the domain and range values you have used to plot points, lines, or curves. To the approaches just shown for dealing with `String` objects, you can add a third, one that involves declaring a `String` object. Consider this approach to the `drawCurve()` method:

```
public String drawCurve(Graphics e , float[] coords)
{
    String cmsg = "";   // Temporary lines for the return value
    return cmsg;
}
```

As mentioned in Chapter 4, to implement properties, you must include at least one accessor statement. The compiler issues an error if you leave out both of the accessors. If you want to redevelop the `CoordSystem` class on your own, here are the signature lines of the `CoordSystem` class. Always remember to make backup copies of your programs so that you can revert to them if you run into problems.

```
class CoordSystem
{
    const int BOTTOM = 450, RIGHT = 450;
    const int TOP    = 50,  LEFT  = 50;
    const int GRID   = 10;
    const int CENTER = 250;
public void drawGrid(Graphics e)
{
    // To do: implement code
}
```

```
public void drawAxes(Graphics e)
{
  // To do: implement code
}
public String plotPoint(Graphics e,
                         float x, float y)
{
  //To do: implement code
  return "(" + x + "," + y + ")";
}


public String plotLinear(Graphics e,
                  float xfrst, float yfrst,
                  float xsec, float ysec)
{
  // To do: implement code
   return "(" + xfrst + ","
          + yfrst + ")"
          + "(" + xsec + ","
          + ysec + ")";
}


public String drawCurve(Graphics e , float[] coords)
{
  // To do: implement code
  String cmsg = "";
  return cmsg;
}


public int Bottom
{
   get { return BOTTOM; }
}

public int Top
{
   get { return TOP; }
}
{//end class
```

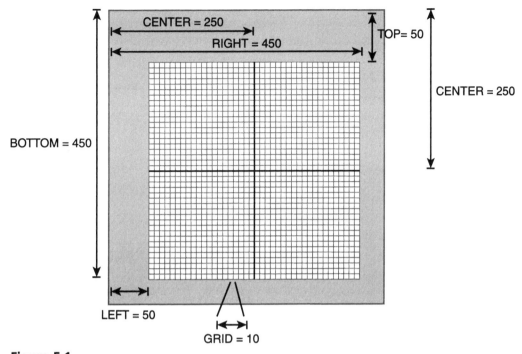

Figure 5.1
The dimensions of the window and the grid allow you to plan your programming tasks.

Planning the Grid

To set up a Cartesian grid, you must decide how you want to locate your grid in your window. As the values in Figure 5.1 indicate, on a simple basis, one that involves putting a stationary grid in place within a window, you begin by answering these questions:

- How far does the top of the grid lie from the top of the form paint area? The answer here is 50 pixels.

- How far to the left of the left edge of the paint area does the grid lie? The answer here is 50 pixels.

- How large is the grid in its pixel element measurements? The answer here is 400 × 400 pixels.

- Given its size in terms of pixel elements and the distance from the top and the left edge of the paint area, where is the CENTER field of the grid? The answer here is (250, 250).

- When you draw horizontal and vertical lines to create the grid, how many pixels apart do you want the lines to lie? The answer is 10.

In the lines accompanying comment #1, you define the fields of the CoordSystem class that address these and other questions. These fields are all constants:

```
// #1
    const int TOP  = 50 BOTTOM = 450;
    const int LEFT = 50, RIGHT = 450;
    const int CENTER = 250;
    const int GRID   = 10;
```

Figure 5.1 provides a summary view of these attributes. In addition, Table 5.1 provides a description of the attributes shown in Figure 5.1.

Calling the CoordSystem Methods from the CartForm Class for Testing

In the lines trailing comment #3 in the CartForm class, you call the pictureBox1_Paint() method. To make it so that you can work in steps as you implement the CoordSystem class, this method incorporates two calls to two methods from the CoordSystem class. The methods called directly are drawGrid() and the drawAxes(). If you choose to redevelop the code in this section, you can start by commenting out the two method calls, and then remove the comments after you have implemented them.

In this way, you can test your code in relatively small portions as you go. You can follow the same approach with the plotCTOCO2() method, which contains calls to the plotPoint() and plot-Linear() methods. To call these methods, verify that you use the construction statement associated with comment #1 of the CartForm class to create an instance (cSys) of the CoordSystem class.

Table 5.1 Fields of the CoordSystem Class

Item	Discussion
BOTTOM	This value is set at 450, the number of units from the top edge of the window.
RIGHT	This value is set at 450, the number of units to the left edge of the window.
TOP	This value is set at 50. It establishes a margin for the top of the window. The top of the Cartesian plane begins 50 units down from the top edge of the window.
LEFT	This value is set at 50. It establishes the left margin of the window. The left edge of the Cartesian plane begins 50 units over from the left edge of the window.
GRID	This value is set at 10. It establishes the number of lines that separates the horizontal and vertical lines in the grid. It does not effect the dimensions of the grid, only the distance between the lines in the grid. If the grid measures 400 units across or vertically, then there is room for 40 lines.
CENTER	The value of this field is 250. It establishes the distance from the top of the window and from the left edge of the window. You subtract LEFT to find the left edge of the grid. You subtract TOP to discover the top edge of the grid. The width and height of the Cartesian plane are twice this value (CENTER × 2 = 400).

Drawing a Grid

The drawGrid() creates horizontal and vertical lines for your grid. To draw lines, you use the C# DrawLine() method. To use this method, you must have on hand a Graphics object. As mentioned previously, the PaintEventArgs object provides you with a Graphics object. You access this method in the Graphics object (e) using the dot operator. You create a statement that uses the Graphics argument and then the name of the method in the Graphics class that you want to access. Here is the code for the drawGrid() method that contains this statement:

```
//#2
public void drawGrid(Graphics e)
{
  // Vertical lines
  for (float x = LEFT; x <= RIGHT; x += GRID)
  {
    e.DrawLine(System.Drawing.Pens.CadetBlue,
                        x, TOP,
                        x, BOTTOM);
  }
  // Horizontal lines
  for (float y = TOP; y <= BOTTOM; y += GRID)
  {
    e.DrawLine(System.Drawing.Pens.CadetBlue,
                  LEFT,  y,
                  RIGHT, y);
  }
}
```

To draw the grid, you first draw vertical lines. To draw vertical lines, you make use of the LEFT, RIGHT, and GRID fields. The LEFT field tells you the position on the x axis of the window at which you want to position the first line. The RIGHT field tells you the farthest position on the right of the x axis of the window at which you want to draw a line. The for loop allows you to traverse a range of pixel values that extends from LEFT (50) to RIGHT (450). You traverse this range in increments of GRID (10), so that you draw 41 lines. Each time you draw a line, the top coordinate of the line is x pixels from the left edge of the window and extends from a y position of TOP (50) to a bottom position of BOTTOM (450). Figure 5.2 depicts how the form appears when you implement only the for loop for the vertical lines.

Drawing horizontal lines involves an approach similar to the one you use for drawing vertical lines. In this case, you employ the for repetition statement to

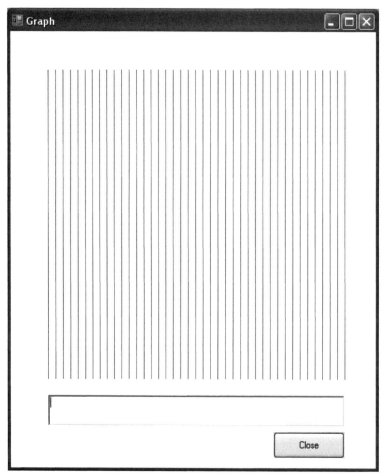

Figure 5.2
You draw grid lines using the values of TOP, BOTTOM, GRID, LEFT, and RIGHT.

traverse a range of pixels that extends from a position TOP (50) down from the top edge of the window to a position BOTTOM (450) from the top of the window. Along the way, at increments of GRID (10), you draw a horizontal line. To draw the lines, you begin at an *x* position of LEFT (50) and extend it to an *x* position of RIGHT (450). You end up with 41 horizontal lines.

You use the DrawLine() method of the Graphics class to draw the horizontal and vertical lines. This method requires five arguments. The first argument designates the color of the line you want to draw. You designate a color using a Pen object. If you use a constructor for a Pen object, you can set several Pen fields, among these is the width of the pen. Rather than using a constructor, you accept the default value for the width of a Pen. This is set at 1 Pen unit wide. For the color, you select CadetBlue from an extensive list of default colors.

The last four arguments of the DrawLine() method allow you to set coordinate values. You designate two pairs of coordinates. Each coordinate pair designates a terminal point of your line. A straight line connecting these two points results.

Adding the Axes

To create a set of *x* and *y* axes for the grid, you make use of the LEFT, RIGHT, TOP, BOTTOM, and CENTER fields in conjunction with the DrawLine() method. The procedure involves two calls to the DrawLine() method. You also make two calls to the DrawString() method to draw letters to identify the two axes. Here is the code:

```
// #3
 public void drawAxes(Graphics e)
 {
     // Draw the x axis
       e.DrawLine(System.Drawing.Pens.Red,
                          LEFT, CENTER,
                          RIGHT, CENTER);
     // Draw the y axis
       e.DrawLine(System.Drawing.Pens.Red,
                          CENTER, TOP,
                          CENTER, BOTTOM);
     // Position the X axis label
       e.DrawString("X",
                      new Font("Arial", 10),
                      System.Drawing.Brushes.Black,
                      new Point(RIGHT + GRID, CENTER - GRID));
     // Position the Y axis label
       e.DrawString("Y",
                      new Font("Arial", 10),
                      System.Drawing.Brushes.Black,
                      new Point(CENTER - GRID / 2, TOP - 2 * GRID));
 }
```

In the first call to the DrawLine() method, you use a default Pen object and set the color to Red. You then set the coordinate values for the ends of the line. For the first, you designate LEFT (50) for the *x* value and CENTER (250) for the first coordinate pair. For the second, you designate RIGHT (450) for the *x* value and CENTER (250) for the first coordinate pair. The line that results extends horizontally across the grid at a position halfway down, drawing over one of the horizontal lines you drew previously.

The second call to the DrawLine() method resembles the first, but in this case, after designating the use of a default Pen of the Red color, you set the first coordinate pair so that the *x* value is CENTER (250) and the *y* value is TOP (50). The second pair is set at CENTER (250) and BOTTOM (450). The line that results extends vertically, covering one of the lines you drew previously.

To identify the axes, you call the DrawString() method of the Graphics class. This method takes four arguments. The first argument is of the String type. For the *x* axis, you provide a string in quotes consisting of the letter "X." For the *y* axis, you provide the letter "Y." The second argument designates the font you want to use. For this argument in both calls of the DrawString() method, you employ the new keyword and a constructor for the Font class. The constructor you use allows you to designate two arguments. The first is a string in quotes that designates any font you have loaded on your system. The second argument designates the size, in points, of the font.

The third argument of the DrawString() method uses a Brush object. A Brush object is like a Pen object, but it is used to fill objects rather than draw lines. The Brush object in this instance allows you to designate the color of the text you want to draw. To designate the color, you use the dot operator to access an extensive list of default color values. From these you pick Black.

For the final argument of the DrawString() method, you provide coordinate pairs that allow you to position the text. To position the text, you designate the upper-left corner of a rectangle that contains the text you want to position. In this instance, you can use a value of the Point type. A value of the Point type consists of two integers that designate the *x* and *y* values of a coordinate pair. The approach used to set these values in this instance results from inspections of what looks right. Generally, the goal is to imagine a few extra grid squares extending above the *y* axis and to the right of the *x* axis. The CENTER, RIGHT, TOP, and GRID fields then allow you to position your coordinate identifiers. It is necessary to go two grid boxes above the TOP value, so you multiply GRID by 2. Also, to make it so that the "Y" is centered vertically on the *y* axis, it is necessary to divide the GRID field value by 2. Figure 5.3 illustrates the axes and their designations.

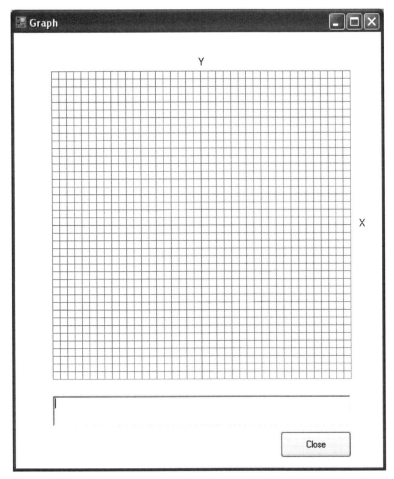

Figure 5.3
Use the DrawLine() and DrawString() methods to create the axes and their letter designations.

Creating the CoordSystem Class

When you translate values so that they correctly map to a Cartesian plane you place (or paint) in a form, you must draw your plane so you translate the coordinate values that define locations in the window to those that define locations in the plane. As Figure 5.4 shows, you must perform this action because the graphical methods C# provides employ a coordinate system that begins in the upper-left corner of the window. From the origin (0,0) of the graphical space of the window, the values on the x and y axes grow in a positive manner, so you do not employ negative values.

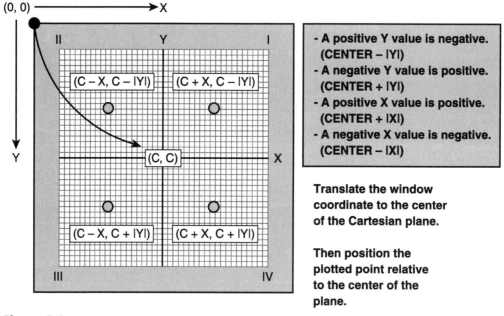

Figure 5.4
You must translate values from the upper-left coordinate set to the CENTER of your plane and then, from there, to the points in the four quadrants.

A Cartesian coordinate system works differently. Its origin lies at the CENTER of four quadrants. Values that move downward on the *y* axis are negative. Values that move to the left on the *x* axis are also negative. If you worked only with positive values, as you do in the Windows coordinate system, then you could plot values only in quadrant I, where the *x* and *y* values that describe a point, line, or curve are all positive.

As the box to the left in Figure 5.4 reveals, when you place a Cartesian coordinate system in a window, you can translate the coordinates of the Windows system to the coordinates of the Cartesian plane by arbitrarily designating the origin of the Cartesian plane in values you derive from the Windows coordinate system. You can then use fairly basic math equations to make the translations.

To make the translations Figure 5.4 illustrates, you must identify the point in your form that you want to designate as the CENTER of your Cartesian system. After you have designated this point, you can then use the four calculations given in Figure 5.4 to translate values. Here is a brief review of these calculations:

- Quadrant I of the Cartesian plane requires a positive *x* value and a positive *y* value. To obtain the Cartesian value for *y*, you subtract the absolute value

of *y* you obtain from your equation from the value you designate as the
CENTER of your plane. For the *x* value, you add the absolute value of *x*
your equation provides to the CENTER value: [(CENTER + | X |), (CENTER −
| Y |)].

■ Quadrant II of the Cartesian plane requires a negative *x* value and a
positive *y* value. To obtain the negative *x* value, you subtract the absolute
value you obtain from your equation from the value you establish as the
CENTER of your plane. For the *y* value, you subtract the absolute value
your equation provides from the CENTER value: [(CENTER − | X |), (CENTER −
| Y |)].

■ Quadrant III of the Cartesian plane requires a negative *x* value and a
negative *y* value. To obtain the negative *x* value, you subtract the absolute
value you obtain from your equation from the value you establish as the
CENTER of your plane. For the negative *y* value, you add the absolute
value your equation provides to the CENTER value: [(CENTER − | X |),
(CENTER + | Y |)].

■ Quadrant IV of the Cartesian plane requires a positive *x* value and a negative
y value. To obtain the positive *x* value, you add the absolute value you obtain
from your equation to the value you establish as the CENTER of your plane.
For the negative *y* value, you add the absolute value your equation
provides to the CENTER value: [(CENTER + | X |), (CENTER + | Y |)].

Testing Strategies

To facilitate your testing activities, you can find some lines for testing in the CartForm class. You
must create an instance of the CoordSystem class before you can call the methods the test code
names. Such an approach to testing simplifies implementation work because it allows you to deal
with isolated values. When you execute these statements, you do not use the coordSets List
field, but you must still click the Run button to populate the coordSets field.

```
private void pictureBox1_Paint(object sender,
                    PaintEventArgs e)
    // This is completely commented out to start with
    // The closing comment is at the bottom
    /*
    // Test the CoordSystem methods
    richTextBox1.Clear();
```

```
    String msg = " ";
    msg.Insert(0, "");

    // Test your points
    msg += cSys.plotPoint(e.Graphics, 0F,   0F);
    msg += cSys.plotPoint(e.Graphics, 5,   -5);
    msg += cSys.plotPoint(e.Graphics, -6.5F, -6.6F);
    richTextBox1.AppendText("\n Points: " + msg);

    // Test your lines
    richTextBox1.Clear();
    String msg = " ";
    msg.Insert(0, "");
    msg += cSys.plotLinear(e.Graphics, 0, 0, 9.0F, 7.5F);
    msg += cSys.plotLinear(e.Graphics, 0, 0, -9.0F, 7.5F);
    msg += cSys.plotLinear(e.Graphics, 0, 0, -9.0F, -7.5F);
    msg += cSys.plotLinear(e.Graphics, 0, 0, 9.0F, -7.5F);
    richTextBox1.AppendText("\n Line: " + msg);

    // Test plot your curve
    richTextBox1.Clear();
    String msg = " ";
    msg.Insert(0, "");
    float[] coords = new float[6]{-6.5F, -6.6F, 0F, 0F, 5F, -5F };
    msg = cSys.drawCurve(e.Graphics, coords);
    richTextBox1.AppendText("\n Curve: " + msg);
    */
}//end method
```

Plotting a Point

In the lines trailing comment #4 in the CoordSystem class, you implement the plotPoint() method. This method plots single points on your Cartesian plane. The method takes three arguments. The first is of the Graphics type, which is common for all the plotting methods of the CoordSystem class. This argument allows you to call methods of the Graphics class. It also allows you to paint and repaint graphical items.

To plot a point, you must first translate the coordinates your equation generates so that they can be positioned in the Cartesian plane. The accomplish this, you make use of the same operations you used when creating the grid and laying out the *x* and *y* axes. Here is the code for the method:

```
//#4
 public String plotPoint(Graphics e,
                          float x, float y)
 {
      // Adjust the value for the grid
      float xPos = (x * GRID) + (CENTER - 2);
      float yPos = CENTER - ((y * GRID) + 1);
      // Draw the points
      e.FillEllipse(System.Drawing.Brushes.Black,
                    xPos, yPos, 4, 4);
      return "(" + x + ", " + y + ")";
 }
```

To position a point, you translate the values of an *x-y* coordinate pair. To translate the *x* value, you begin with the raw value (*x*) that your equation has used or generated for the domain. You multiply this value by 10 to translate it into the GRID increments of the coordinate system. Each increment of GRID corresponds to one unit. After translating the *x* value to GRID increments, you then add this value to CENTER so that you can position it relative to the center of your plane. You also subtract 1 (representing 1 pixel) to center the point on the line that corresponds to the *x* axis.

For the *y* value, you use a similar approach. In this case, however, you first multiply the raw *y* value by GRID to translate it into units appropriate for the Cartesian plane. You then add 2 to this value to center the point on the line that corresponds to the *y* axis. You then subtract this value from the value of CENTER. In this way, a positive value moves the point upward. A negative value moves the point downward.

To draw the point, you use the FillEllipse() method of the Graphics class. This method takes six arguments. The first is a Brush object, which defines using one of the default colors provided for Brush objects. The second and third arguments are the coordinate points for the upper-left corner of the rectangle that encloses the ellipse. These are the *x* and *y* values as calculated according to the descriptions in the preceding paragraphs. The fourth argument designates the width of the ellipse. The fifth and last argument designates its height.

As a final measure, you display the coordinate values you have used to map the point. To accomplish this, you implicitly create a String object that shows the raw coordinate values enclosed in parentheses and separated by a comma.

To test your method, see the previous sidebar titled "Testing Strategies." Here is how you can implement the code for this method within the CartForm class:

```
private void pictureBox1_Paint(object sender,
                                PaintEventArgs e)
{
  // #3 Create a local version of the graphics
    cSys.drawGrid(e);                        // dependency
    cSys.drawAxes(e);                        // dependency
  // plotCTOCO2(e);
    String msg = " ";
    msg.Insert(0, "");
  // Test your points
    msg += cSys.plotPoint(e, 0F, 0F);
    msg += cSys.plotPoint(e, 5, 5);
    msg += cSys.plotPoint(e, 5, -5);
    msg += cSys.plotPoint(e, -6.5F, -6.6F);
    richTextBox1.AppendText("\n Points: " + msg);
}
```

Figure 5.5 illustrates the results you see when you call the plotPoint() method in the pictureBox1_Paint() method.

Plotting a Line

In the lines accompanying comment #5 of the CoordSystem class, you define the plotLinear() method. This method allows you to plot linear functions. This method requires five arguments. The first argument is of the Graphics type, and as with the other CoordSystem methods, this argument allows you to repaint graphical images. The last four arguments of the method define two pairs of coordinates that designate the beginning and end points of a line that represents a linear function. Here is the code for the plotLinear() method:

```
// #5
  public String plotLinear(Graphics e,
                        float xfrst, float yfrst,
                        float xsec,  float ysec)
    {
      // Adjust the coordinate values for the grid
        float xfrstPos = (xfrst * GRID) + CENTER;
        float yfrstPos = CENTER - (yfrst * GRID);
        float xsecPos  = (xsec *  GRID) + CENTER;
```

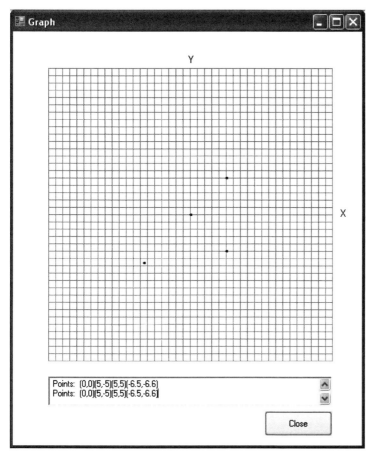

Figure 5.5
The FillEllipse() method is wrapped in the plotPoint() method.

```
        float ysecPos  = CENTER - (ysec * GRID);
        // Draw line
        e.DrawLine(System.Drawing.Pens.Black,
                        xfrstPos, yfrstPos,
                        xsecPos,  ysecPos);
        return "(" + xfrst + ","
                 + yfrst + ")"
                 + "(" + xsec + ","
                 + ysec + ")";
    }
```

Essentially, the plotLinear() method is a wrapper method for the DrawLine()
method of the Graphics class. The DrawLinear() method takes five arguments.

Table 5.2 Translation of Coordinate Values

Item	Discussion
xfrstPos	The translated value of *x* for the first pair of coordinates you use to draw the line in the Cartesian plane. You multiply the value of *x* you obtain from your equation by GRID and add the product to CENTER.
yfrstPos	The translated value of *y* for the first pair of coordinates you use to draw the line in the Cartesian plane. You multiply the value of *y* you obtain from your equation by GRID and subtract the product from CENTER.
xsecPos	The translated value of *x* for the second pair of coordinates you use to draw the line in the Cartesian plane. As with the first *x* coordinate, you multiply the value of *x* you obtain from your equation by GRID and add the product to CENTER.
ysecPos	The translated value of *y* for the second pair of coordinates you use to draw the line in the Cartesian plane. As with the first *y* coordinate, you multiply the value of *y* you obtain from your equation by GRID and add the product to CENTER.

The first argument is a Brush object that determines the color of the line. You use the dot operator to set the brush using Black, which is one of the many default Brush values C# provides.

The remaining four arguments represent the arguments of the function translated so that they map to the Cartesian plane. To translate these values, you use calculations that involve adding the raw values to or subtracting them from the CENTER value of the coordinate system. Table 5.2 provides a summary of how you calculate the four coordinate values. Calculation of these values extends the work you performed to draw lines for grids. In this case, you take into consideration plotting of points in all four quadrants of the Cartesian plane.

Here is code you can use to test the plotLinear() method:

```
private void pictureBox1_Paint(object sender,
                              PaintEventArgs e)
{
    //Test your lines
    richTextBox1.Clear();
    String msg = " ";
    msg.Insert(0, "");
    msg += cSys.plotLinear(e.Graphics, 0, 0,  9.0F,  7.5F);
    msg += cSys.plotLinear(e.Graphics, 0, 0, -9.0F,  7.5F);
    msg += cSys.plotLinear(e.Graphics, 0, 0, -9.0F, -7.5F);
    msg += cSys.plotLinear(e.Graphics, 0, 0,  9.0F, -7.5F);
    richTextBox1.AppendText("\n Line: " + msg);
}
```

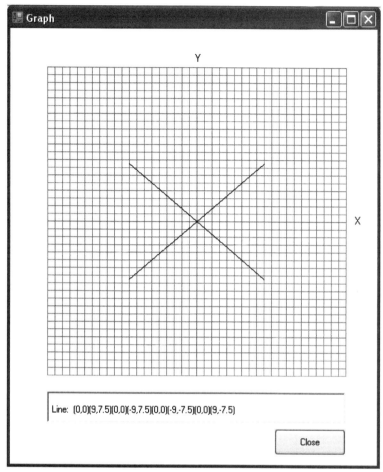

Figure 5.6
Plotting lines involves using only the coordinates for the two points that define the ends of the lines.

To display the values for the function you have plotted, you use the con-catenation operator of the `String` class and submit the resulting line to the `AppendText()` method. Figure 5.6 depicts the lines that result when you use the data from the previous set of test code.

Plotting a Curve

In the lines accompanying comment #6, you implement the `drawCurve()` method. This method is a wrapper for the `DrawCurve()` method of the `Graphics` class. It takes two arguments. The first of the arguments is the `Graphics` object used by the other methods of the `CoordSystem` class. The second argument is an array of values of the float type that you use to draw a curve. To be effective, the array you use must contain at least six values. The six values define three coordinate pairs. Using these three pairs, the DrawCurve() method automatically generates a curve. Here is the code for the method:

```
// #6
public String drawCurve(Graphics e , float[] coords)
{
    Pen curvePen = new Pen(Color.DarkBlue, 2);
    // Create a Point array
    Point[] curvePoints = new Point[coords.Length / 2];
    String cmsg = "";
    // Multiply by 10 (GRID) to increase precision
    int ctr = 0;
    while (ctr < coords.Length)
    {
        // 6.5 becomes 65, for example
        coords[ctr] = coords[ctr] * GRID;
        cmsg += " (" + (coords[ctr]).ToString() + ","
                    + (coords[ctr]).ToString() + ")";
        ctr++;
    }
    //Populate the Point array with coordinate values
    ctr = 0;
    while (ctr < coords.Length)
    {
        curvePoints[ctr / 2] = new Point(CENTER + (int)(coords[ctr]),
                                    CENTER - (int)(coords[ctr + 1]));
        ctr += 2;
    }
    //Draw curve to the chart
    e.DrawCurve(curvePen, curvePoints);
    return cmsg;
}
```

Immediately after the signature line of the drawCurve() method, you vary the routine used with the other methods in the CoordSystem class and create a Pen object. The constructor for the Pen class requires two arguments. The first is the Color value that you want to assign to the pen. The second is the point width of the pen. The Pen object appears in this code as an inducement for you to explore. Its width value is set to 2, but if you want to see a thinner or thicker line for the curve, set it to 1 or 5.

Note

> The method for drawing curves that you obtain from C# is called DrawCurve(). The method you develop as a wrapper method for the DrawCurve() method is called drawCurve(). Naming methods so that they resemble built-in methods but are capitalized in a different way (with a lowercase letter instead of an uppercase letter) constitutes a common programming practice.

After creating a Pen object, you attend to working with the values you pass to the function via the coords array. Your first task involves grouping the coordinates into sets of two. To accomplish this task, you use the Length attribute of the Array class to determine the number of elements in the array. You then divide this number by 2 and use the resulting value to set the number of elements in an array of the Point type (curvePoints).

The array of the Point type is necessary because the DrawCurve() method uses an array of the Point type as one of its arguments. A Point object consists of two integer values. Using a data type that allows you to conveniently group coordinates in pairs proves convenient. However, if you can use only integer values, you cannot then use a rational number to designate the position of a coordinate. This proves to be a problem because your equations almost always generate rational values.

The solution is to consider that a rational value of 6.5 can be multiplied by 10 (or GRID) to give you a degree of precision that is suitable for the Cartesian plane you have developed for this application. Given this situation, to accommodate the Point data type (which, again, is required by the DrawCurve() method), you can make use of the fact that since you have set your lines GRID (10) pixels apart, you can easily translate rational values into integer values suitable for the Point data type by multiplying the raw coordinate values you submit to the drawCurve() method. You need only multiply by GRID (10). The value of 6.5 becomes 65 pixels.

Accordingly, to effect this transformation, you use a while repetition statement to traverse all the values in the coords array, multiply them by GRID (10), and assign them back to the coords array. They are still of the float type, but now they represent values that you can cast as integers and make suitable for use in the DrawCurve() method.

Just before you multiply the coords array values to make them suitable for use in the DrawCurve() method, you employ the ToString() method to capture the raw values of the coords array to create a string that you can assign to the msg variable. This variable allows you to use the RichTextBox field to display the values you have plotted.

To assign the coordinate pairs that reside in the coords array to an array of the Point type (curvePoints), you create a second while repetition structure. Within the while block, you call the Point () constructor to create successive Point objects. To each object, you assign an x and a y value. To obtain these values, you employ the counter (ctr) for the while block as an index for the coords array. To fetch x values, you use the current value of ctr. The fetch the y value, you use ctr+1.

As for the curvePoints array, which contains Point objects, you determine its count by taking half the value of ctr. You divide by 2 because you have half as many objects of the Point type as you do the raw values for coordinates you obtain from the coords array. To compensate for the fact that you fetch coordinate values in sets of two from the coords array, you increment the second of the while blocks by 2 for each iteration.

After you have created the curvePoints array, you can then call the DrawCurve() method of the Graphics class. The first argument to this method is the Pen object you created in the opening statements of the method. The second argument is the curvePoints array. After calling the DrawCurve() method, you then return the msg string, which allows you to see the values used to plot your curve.

Here is code you can use to test the drawCurve() method:

```
private void pictureBox1_Paint(object sender,
                              PaintEventArgs e)
{
   // Test plot your curve
   richTextBox1.Clear();
   String msg = " ";
   msg.Insert(0, "");
```

```
    float[] coords = new float[6]{-6.5F, -6.6F, 0F, 0F, 5F, -5F };
    msg = cSys.drawCurve(e.Graphics, coords);
    richTextBox1.AppendText("\n Curve: " + msg);
}
```

Figure 5.7 illustrates the resulting curve. The curve tends to flatten out because you have used only three values. The DrawCurve() method draws curves that are smoothed out relative to the information you provide to it. It also can plot curves that you do not generate in a functional manner.

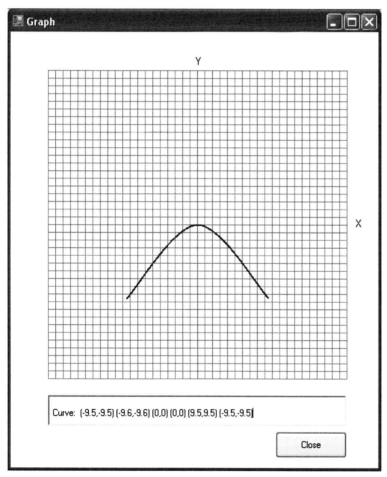

Figure 5.7
The drawCurve() method requires a minimum of three values to plot a curve.

Conclusion

In this chapter, you have extended your development efforts to include use of several methods from the Graphics class. The four primary methods are the DrawLine(), FillEllipse(), DrawString(), and DrawCurve() methods. In several instances, you have wrapped these methods in customized methods. To wrap a C# method in your own method has often involved adding code that translates the coordinates of your application into those that the C# methods can use. This translation sometimes involves compensating for differences between the coordinate system your window uses and the coordinate system given by the Cartesian coordinate system. In other cases, you have had to accommodate the differences between data types. For the DrawCurve() method, you use a Point object. To make it so that rational values can be used with the Point object, you multiply and cast values of the float data type so that they become integers. In this way, you make it so that you can plot fractional values with greater precision than would otherwise be possible.

Several other tasks arose as you proceeded with your work of graphing lines, points, and curves. You also explored the use of static List objects and how you can copy values from these and transfer them to arrays. The Values data type again enters the picture, allowing you to remove items from arrays and turn them into coordinate pairs. Working with arrays allows you to generate curves, which grow in precision as you add more coordinate pairs to them.

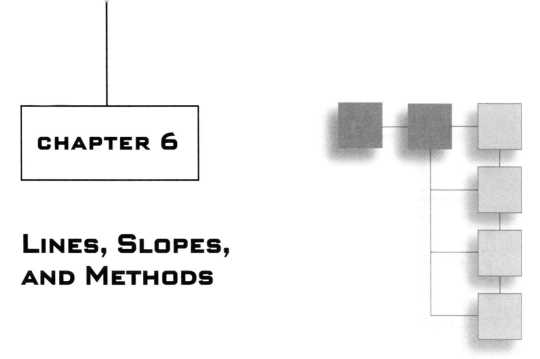

CHAPTER 6

Lines, Slopes, and Methods

In this chapter, you explore a number of topics usually associated with basic algebra. The activities you perform formalize much of the work you have performed in previous chapters. You work with formal approaches to defining linear equations. You distinguish constant equations from equations with changing values. You extend this knowledge into combining equations and joining equations through composition. Composition allows you to explore approaches to a few practical pursuits, such as predicting profits for a factor and generating graphs to make such profits easier to understand. You also work with the standard form of linear equations and the slope formula. Working in this way, you are able to extend the Lab application in a variety of ways, altering the graph so that it can accommodate more extended domain values. Here are a few of the topics covered:

- Determining whether functions are valid

- Dealing with domains

- Using composition to combine functions

- Scaling graphical output

- Implementing methods that embody functions

- Overloading constructors and methods

Valid Functions

As has been mentioned before, functions generate unique relationships between domain and range values. Some graphs show irregular relationships. In some cases, it is almost impossible to find a function to generate the line. As it is, however, those that generate straight lines are fairly predictable. The predictable functions fall into three general categories. The first category covers constant functions. Constant functions involve straight lines that run horizontally. Others fall into the category of linear functions. A third category is that of quadratic functions. All three types of functions can be applied in endless ways.

Constant Functions

The most basic type of regular function you encounter is a constant function. A constant function runs across the Cartesian plane horizontally. For every value of x, you find the same y value. The equation for a constant function takes the form of $f(x) = c$. The letter c designates a constant. The constant can be any real number. As Figure 6.1 indicates, for any value of x, you find the same value of y.

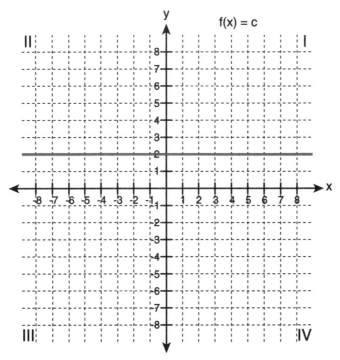

Figure 6.1
A constant function provides one value of y for all values of x.

The Vertical Line Test

This chapter discusses a number of different types of functions ranging from irregular to quadratic functions. For all of these functions, even the irregular ones, you can apply a single test to determine whether they are valid functions.

To use the vertical line approach, you draw lines vertically across your graph. Each vertical line intersects the graph only once.

Profits

Constant functions prove useful in many situations, but it remains that functions prove most useful when you use a function to process values that reveal varying relationships. To pick one such relationship, you can examine a common scenario involving cost, revenue, and profit. Suppose that you are working with a small company owned by two people. Its business is the manufacture of bicycle tires using recycled materials. If you establish that the variable x can represent the number of bicycle tires the company sells, you can lay out a set of functions that helps you understand the point at which operations become profitable. Table 6.1 elaborates this set of functions and how they can be combined to track profits.

Working from the functions you find in Table 6.1, you can proceed to deal with specific data you derive from an inspection of the operations of the tire factory. Assume that you are working with costs in terms of dollars, and you find that the partners can produce x number of tires with general costs of $510 per day. These

Table 6.1 Bicycle Tires

Function	Discussion
$C(x)$	The function $C(x)$ allows you to track the costs of producing and selling bicycle tires. The variable x designates the number of tires.
$R(x)$	The function $R(x)$ allows you to track how much revenue you generate each time you sell a tire. Again, x designates the number of tires.
$P(x)$	The function $P(x)$ allows you to determine the profit you make when you produce and sell tires. The variable x identifies the number of items you have produced and sold.
Domain	The values you can use for these three numbers can be established as real numbers, although it is likely that the tires you work with might be limited to integers. Still, as it is, if you establish $x \mid x \geq 0$, you have a reasonable domain.
Profit Generally	The function $P(x) = R(x) - C(x)$ establishes the profit function. To define this function, you pursue the idea that the profits of the tire company $P(x)$ result from the difference between the costs or expenses it incurs when it produces tires $C(x)$ and income or revenue it derives from selling tires $R(x)$.

expenses result from such items as machinery and power, not from the recycled rubber for the tires. To this general expenditure they find that the material cost for each tire is $8. Given this starting point, you can then formulate the cost function in this way:

$$C(x) = 510 + 8x \quad \text{where } x \geq 0$$

The cost function allows you to establish a perspective on the work of the factory that you can then use to determine the point at which the price the partners charge for each tire begins to bring them a profit. To accomplish this, however, you must track how much they charge for their tires. To do this, you use the revenue function. You find that they are selling their tires for $25 each, so the revenue function reads this way:

$$R(x) = 25x \quad \text{where } x \geq 0$$

You now have two functions. One tracks costs. The other tracks revenues. As Table 6.1 discusses, you can now use subtraction to bring these two functions into a relation with each other that allows you to track profit. The profit function takes this form:

$$P(x) = R(x) - C(x)$$

Generally, costs subtracted from revenues give you profits. If you then carry out the subtraction operations, you arrive at this formulation:

$$25x - (510 + 8x)$$

$$= 17x - 510 \quad \text{where } x \geq 0$$

This, then, provides you with a way to track each day's activities to discover the point at which the partners can show a profit. The profit function for the factory enables you to generate a range of values based on the number of tires the partners sell each day.

To gather data to use in this equation, you work according to the limits the domain established and audit production and sales activities. The range you work with begins with 0 and extends to 40.

To determine the point at which the partners can make a profit, you view the output of the profit function $P(x)$. The profit function allows you to determine how many tires the factory must produce each day if it is to show a profit. The point at which costs balance with revenues constitutes the *break-even point*. This is the point at which the profit $P(x)$ is equal to 0.

Coding the Function

You define the profitForItems() method in the Functions class. The sole purpose of the method is to calculate profits using a combination of costs and revenues from items (tires) sold. You define the argument for the method so that it is of the double type. The return value of the method is also of the double type. Here is the code:

```
// Calculate profit based on the number of items
    public double profitForItems(double item)
    {
       return 17.0 * item - 510.0;
    }
```

To implement the function, you first multiply the argument you pass to the method (number of tires sold) by a literal value (17.0). The compiler reads the literal value as data of a double data type. You then subtract the literal value of 510.0 from the product of this multiplication. As with 17.0, the compiler treats 510.0 as a double. You then return the result.

Generating the Table

You call the profitForItems() only once. This is in the DataForm class, in the runFunction() method. Your use of the method involves a call to the runFunction() method from the runButton_Click() method. The runFunction() method serves as a shell in which you generate calls to the methods you develop to deploy math functions investigated in this chapter.

To generate values within the domain you have designated, you define a temporary array called domain. When you designate the numbers to be included in the array, you use a comma-delimited list of integers. The compiler converts them to float values. The integer 1 becomes 1.0, for example. Here is the code for the method:

```
private void runFunction()
{
   Functions fset = new Functions();
   // Create an array of values for the domain
   float[] domain = {1, 6, 9, 20, 25, 26, 28, 30, 34, 35, 38, 40 };
   // Call the method for each item in the array
   for (int ctr = 0; ctr < domain.Length; ctr++)
   {
```

```
        coordSets.Add(new Values( (float) domain[ctr],
                     (float) fset.profitForItems(domain[ctr])));
    }
    displayTable("\n\t Items", "\t\t Profit");
}//end method
```

You use a `for` repetition block to traverse the values in the array. Within the `for` repetition block, you employ the `ctr` control variable to retrieve values from the `domain` array. To limit the control, you call the `Length` property associated with arrays. This property provides you with the number of items in the `domain` array.

Having retrieved the values representing the number of tires from the `domain` array, you provide these values as arguments to the `profitForItems()` method. The method returns the profit the items generate. To store the tire and profit values for future use, you place them in objects of the `Values` data type. The `Values` data type provides two fields of the `float` type, `X` and `Y`. You employ the `Values` constructor to assign a tire count to the `X` field and the profit figure corresponding to the count to the `Y` field. Each value must be cast to a `float`.

You use the `new` keyword to create an instance of the `Values` struct for each tire-profit pair. You then use the `ListAdd` method to store the instance in the `coordSetsList` collection. The `coordSetsList` collection is a static field in the `DataForm` class.

To print the array to the `DataForm` text area, you call the `displayTable()` method. This method retrieves the tire and profit data from the `coordSetsList` collection and formats to two decimal places using the `ToString()` method. You call the `displayTable()` method within the `runFunction()` method. This allows you to more conveniently set and track the headings for the table. Figure 6.2 illustrates the table that results. The line on which you see 00.00 as the profit represents the break-even point.

Generating a Graph

The tabular data illustrated by Figure 6.2 provides one convenient way to detect the break-even point for the bicycle tire producers. Another approach is to use a graph. Accordingly, you implement the `showData()` method in the `CartForm` class. This method serves in a capacity similar to that of the `runFunction()` method in the `DataForm` class. You remake it to accord with your needs. To preserve your work, you can comment out versions of the method you do not want to include in

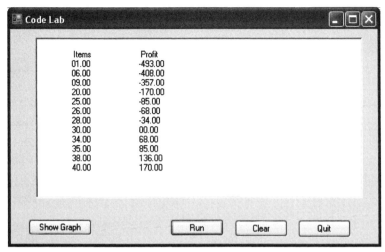

Figure 6.2
The `runFunction()` and `runButton_Click()` generate a table in the Code Lab window.

the current build. In many cases, you can use the method unchanged with different functions. Here is the implementation of the `showData()` method as rewritten to generate a graph for the break-even point for the bicycle tire data:

```
// Graph data for tires and profit
// Set YSCALE to 15 and LOCALGRID to 5
public void showData(Graphics e)
{
    DataForm tempForm = new DataForm();
    Values[] tempVals = tempForm.Vals.ToArray();
    int xFahrValA = (int)tempVals[tempVals.Length-1].X/XSCALE;
    int yFahrValA = (int)tempVals[tempVals.Length - 1].Y/YSCALE;
    int xFahhValB = (int)tempVals[0].X;
    int yFahrValB = (int)tempVals[0].Y/YSCALE;
    String msg;
    msg = cSys.plotLinear(e, xFahrValA, yFahrValA,
                             xFahhValB, yFahrValB) ;
    // Plot points
    cSys.plotPoint(e, xFahrValA, yFahrValA);
    cSys.plotPoint(e, xFahhValB, yFahrValB);

    richTextBox1.Clear();
    richTextBox1.AppendText("\n Values: " + msg);
    // Uncomment this to see the values from the DataForm table
    // showData(false);
}
```

To an extent, declaration of the local variables such as xFahrValA is redundant, but for the current chapter, use of such redundancy makes it easier to follow the activity of the method.

You begin by creating an instance of the DataForm class, tempForm. Using the tempForm object, you call the Vals property of the DataForm class. The Vals property returns a reference to the coordSetsList collection. Recall that this collection is a static field, so it comes into existence when you create the first instance of the DataForm class and stays in existence after that, shared by all instances of the DataForm class. This is the second instance of the DataForm class. Through it you can access the tire and profit data you generated previously for the table.

To retrieve isolated items from a List is not very easy to do. For this reason, you create an array and assign the elements of the List collection to it. To accomplish this, you call the ToArray() method (a member of the List class). This method copies all the items in the coordSetsList collection to a locally declared array, tempVals. The tempVals array is of the Values type.

Using the tempVals array, you access each Values item using an array index. You can then access the X (item) and Y (profit) fields of each of the Values objects stored in the array.

Note

The range of values you generate for profits extends into the hundreds of dollars. To make it so that you can map such values into the grid the Lab provides, you add two constant fields to the CartForm class. One is called LOCALGRID and has the same purpose as the GRID field in the CoordSystem class. You set LOCALGRID to 5 in this class. Another field you use to scale the values you supply to the grid is the YSCALE constant. You set YSCALE to 15. While the x axis progresses in units of 1 (each unit representing an item), the y axis then progresses in units of 15 (each unit representing $15). The use of still another constant, XSCALE, is covered later in this chapter.

To draw a line for the graph, you retrieve only two pairs of values. These two values designate the ends of the line you want to draw. To identify these pairs, you access the Values object at index 0 and at the end of the tempVals array.

As has been discussed previously, the array Length property allows you to obtain the number of items in an array. To find the index value for the last item in an array, you subtract 1 from the value you obtain from the Length property. You subtract 1 because if you take the number of items alone, then the index value you arrive at is one beyond the final index of the array. Trying to access an item in an array using an index value larger than the maximum index value of the array generates a compiler error.

To create the graph that shows you the break-even point, you call the plotLinear() method twice. Each call requires three arguments. The first is the PaintEventArgs object, which allows you to use Graphics objects. The second and third consist of the x and y coordinate values.

You follow the two calls to the plotLinear() method with two calls to the plotPoint() method. The plotPoint() method requires the same arguments you used for the plotLinear() method. As Figure 6.3 reveals, the points provide the line with more definition than it would possess otherwise.

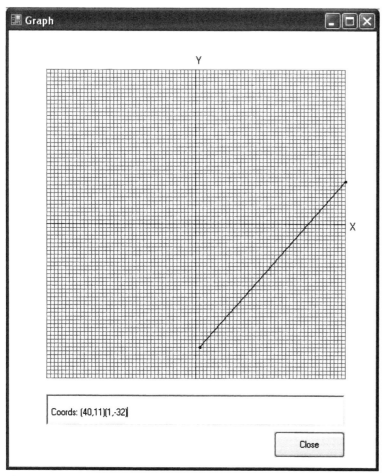

Figure 6.3
The graph shows that it is necessary to sell 30 tires before profits begin to accrue.

Grid Adjustments in the CoordSystem Class

The values you work with in this chapter exceed those you worked with in the last chapter. While the grid you have developed cannot deal readily with extremely large values, you make a few changes to the CoordSystem class to provide your grid with more lines. Toward this end, you add two constructors. One of the constructors takes no arguments. Such a constructor is called a *default* constructor. This constructor automatically sets the value of GRID to 10, as it was in Chapter 5. Here is the code that defines this constructor in the CoordSystem class:

```
public CoordSystem()
{
    GRID = 10;
}
```

The second constructor addresses the current situation, which requires a grid with more lines. This constructor takes an argument. A constructor that takes an argument is known as an *overloaded* constructor. In this case, the constructor allows you to set the value of the GRID field explicitly. Here is the code that defines this constructor in the CoordSystem class:

```
public CoordSystem(int grid)
{
    GRID = grid;
}
```

So that you can change the size of the grid using a constructor in this way, you change the way you define the GRID field in the CoordSystem class. The change is fairly simple. You make it so that it is no longer a constant (const) value. The declaration of the field now takes this form:

```
private int GRID;
```

You now use the overloaded constructor in the CartForm class when you create an instance of the CoordSystem class. Here is the statement in the constructor of the CartForm class that accomplishes this task:

```
cSys = new CoordSystem(LOCALGRID);
```

The LOCALGRID value is a constant field in the CartForm class. You set it to a value of 5. As Figure 6.3 reveals, when you set the grid size in the CartForm class using the value assigned to LOCALGRID, you see twice as many grid lines as you see with the default value, and all of the calculations for the point, curve, and line methods scale to the value you designate.

Note

The *x*-intercept is the point at which the losses (the value of the *y* axis) are zero. As the graph in Figure 6.3 shows, this value is at 30 on the *x* axis. The partners need to sell 30 items before they begin generating profits.

Note

The coordinate values you see in the text box in Figure 6.3 after you have scaled the values do not directly represent your original data. This situation receives attention later in the chapter. For now, you can uncomment the `showData(false)` call at the end of the `showData()` method to see both the scale and original data.

Composition of Functions

When you calculate a break-even point for the bicycle tire factory, you associate functions using arithmetic operations. This is one way to combine functions. Another involves making the output of one function the input of another. This approach to using functions involves *function composition*.

To explore how function composition works, you can extend the operations of the tire factory to focus on the time required to produce tires. Imagine you have a function that provides you with values representing the time the partners work in the factory to produce a given number of tires. From your previous work, you have at hand another function that relates their profit. You can list these two functions in this way:

$t(x)$ The time required to produce x number of tires

$P(x)$ The profit that results from the production of x number of tires

If you compose these two functions, you can determine how much time it takes to generate a given amount of profit. You do not only combine the output of two functions. You make the output (range values) of one function the raw data (domain values) of another function. Here is how you represent the composition:

$$P(t(x))$$

You then say that the function P is composed of the functions P and t. Another way to represent such a composition is to use the composition (o) symbol. You can equate the two ways of representing composition in this way:

$$(P \circ t)(x) = P(t(x))$$

Regardless of how you express the composition, when you proceed in this manner, the two composed functions work from a common domain. If you represent a domain with the letter **D**, the domain of the composed functions becomes $D_{P \circ t}$. All domain values for $t(x)$ must lie in D_P. If the two domains are not consistent with each other in this way, then you cannot determine a consistent range of values when you perform operations that involve the composition of the two functions.

Back to the Factory

As mentioned previously, you can formulate the time and profit composition if you consider first that you already have on hand the profit function. The function assumes this form:

$$P(x) = 17x - 510 \qquad \text{where } x \geq 0$$

This function allows you to determine the profit (P) that results if the partners manufactured a given number of tires (x) on a daily basis. Given this starting point, you can move forward to establish that, if the partners operate their factory 10 hours each day, then you can determine how productive they are. To arrive at an equation to determine how productive they are on an hourly basis, you might draw from a close analysis of the base standard textbook theory and arrive at this equation:

$$x(t) = 1.5t^2 - 0.1t^3$$

The equation allows you to assess the time involved in producing a given number of tires (x). You now move forward to relate this to the profits (P) the partners make for the tires. To accomplish this, you use composition to fold considerations of time into the profit formula. Here is how to express the relationship:

$$(P \circ x)(t)$$

Given this composition, you can now determine the time of the day that the partners cross the break-even point. You can then combine the two functions. Here is how you can proceed with this task:

$$(P \circ x)(x) = P(x(t))$$
$$= 17x(t) - 510$$
$$= 17(1.5t^2 - 0.1t^3) - 510$$
$$= 25.5t^2 - 1.7t^3 - 510$$

You substitute the equation representing productivity into the equation representing the break-even point in terms of time. The isolated equation takes this form:

$$(P \circ x)(x) = 25.5t^2 - 1.7t^3 - 510$$

You can then put the Lab to work to program this equation.

Coding the Function

To implement the function in C#, you create the `profitAndTime()` method in the `Functions` class. Here is the code for the method:

```
// Calculate profit by time
public double profitandTime(double time)
{
   return 25.5 * System.Math.Pow(time, 2)
        - 1.7 * System.Math.Pow(time, 3) - 510.0;
}
```

The `profitAndTime()` method takes a single argument: the time in hours the tire factory operates. This argument is of the `double` data type, as is the returned value of the method. To work with the time value, you use the `Pow()` method of the C# `Math` class. The `Pow()` method takes two arguments of the `double` type. The first argument provides the number you want to raise to a power. The second argument furnishes the power to which you want to raise the first argument.

Generating the Table

You call the `profitAndTime()` method in the `DataForm` class, which is in the `runFunction()` method. As you call the method, you use values you store in the `domain` array. These values designate the domain (time) values. As in the previous example, you use a comma-delimited list of integers to provide these values. The integers proceed from 1 through 10, representing the 10 hours of the work day. Here is the code for the method:

```
// Show profits each hour for the items produced
      private void runFunction()
        {
          Functions fset = new Functions();
          // Create an array of values for the domain
```

```
int[] domain = {1, 2, 3, 4, 5, 6, 7, 8, 9, 10};
// Repeat the calculation for each item in the array
for (int ctr = 0; ctr < domain.Length; ctr++)
{
    coordSets.Add(
            new Values((float)domain[ctr],
                       (float)fset.profitandTime(domain[ctr]))
                );
}
displayTable("\n\t Hours", "\t\t Profit");
}//end method
```

Within the for repetition block, you incrementally increase values of the ctr control variable to retrieve values from the domain array. For each iteration of the block, you submit a domain value to the profitAndTime() method. The domain value together with the returned value of the profitAndTime() method provide you with a pair of values you can use to create a Values object. You use the Add() method of the List class to store each such object in the coordSets List collection. To use the time and profit data to construct Values objects, you cast the two types of data to the float type. After the flow of the program exits the repetition block, you call the displayTable() method to generate the table of time and profit values. Figure 6.4 illustrates the output.

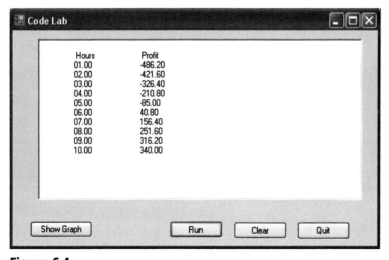

Figure 6.4
Calling the profitAndTime() method allows you to generate a table that shows the break-even point for a day's work.

Note

According to the table in Figure 6.4, profits begin to accumulate for the partners between the fifth and sixth hours of the work day.

Generating a Graph

To generate a graph for the data you generate using the composed functions, you can use the same version of the showData() method. As before, to make the values on the y axis so that they fit the grid, you scale the grid using a YSCALE value of 50. Since you are dealing with only 10 hours, you can also adjust the side of the grid to make it easier to view the values for the hours of the day. To accomplish this, as reviewed previously, you set LOCALGRID value to 12. As Figure 6.5 shows, this has

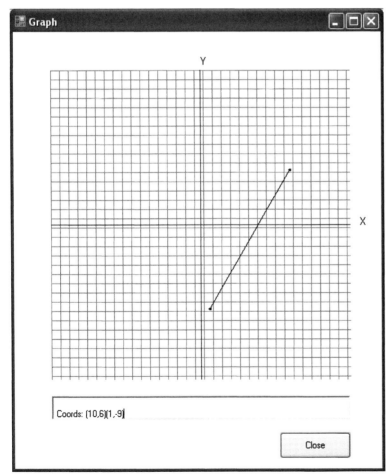

Figure 6.5
A mapping of value shows the profit on an hourly basis.

the effect of leaving the right side of the grid ragged. Still, in this way it becomes easier to see that the break-even point occurs just after the sixth hour of the day as mapped on the x axis.

Linear Functions and the Slopes of Functions

The functions relating to profit and the amount of time required during a day to break even constitute linear functions. Such functions usually imply an unchanging relationship between two values. For example, the more hours the partners work, the more tires they produce. Their productivity from hour to hour remains the same, as does the amount of revenue they acquire from the sale of each tire.

Many of the functions you deal with are linear. As has been mentioned in previous chapters, such functions generate graphs characterized by straight lines. For example, when you dealt with the function that related carbon burning to carbon dioxide added to the atmosphere, you dealt with a linear function.

One result of the accumulation of carbon dioxide in the atmosphere is that the temperature of the atmosphere increases because carbon dioxide traps heat from the sun. How the temperature of the atmosphere relates to the burning of carbon involves some fairly sophisticated math that lies beyond the current scope of discussion. Dealing with scales of temperature, however, does not. Two common scales used to measure temperatures are the Fahrenheit and Celsius scales.

If you use the Fahrenheit scale, you find that water freezes at 32 degrees and boils at 212 degrees. In contrast, you can use the Celsius scale. The Celsius scale is part of the metric system. Degrees Celsius are often referred to as degrees centigrade. Using this scale, you find that the freezing point of water is 0 degrees, while the boiling point is 100 degrees.

If you designate $C(x)$ as the function that allows you to convert Fahrenheit degrees to Celsius degrees, then you can generate this equation:

$$C(x) = \frac{5}{9}(x - 32)$$

Standard Form

You can rephrase the equation used to convert Fahrenheit degrees to Celsius degrees in this way:

$$C(x) = \frac{5x}{9} - \frac{160}{9}$$

When you rephrase the equation, you arrive at the *standard form* of a linear equation. A standard linear equation can be expressed in a way that brings together values that relate to the slope, the domain, and the point at which the line you generate using the equation intersects with the y axis. Here is how you state a linear equation (or function) in a generalized way:

$$f(x) = mx + b$$

The generalized form includes two constants, m and b. The constant m designates the slope of the function. The constant b designates the y-intercept of the function. The y-intercept is the point at which the line the function generates intercepts the y axis. A linear equation also has an x-intercept. That is the point at which the line you generate with the equations intersects the x axis.

In this form, you see distinctly that slope (m) of the equation that converts the Fahrenheit to Celsius degrees is $\frac{5}{9}$. Then comes the domain value (x). After that, you see the y-intercept value ($-\frac{160}{9}$). The y-intercept value tells you that if you set the x value (Fahrenheit) of the equation to 0, the line you generate crosses the y (Celsius) axis at $-\frac{160}{9}$, which is roughly 17.78 degrees Celsius. You express the resulting coordinate pair as $(0, -\frac{160}{9})$.

Coding the Function

To program a method that converts values from the Fahrenheit scale to the Celsius scale, you work with the standard math operators. You define the method so that it takes a value of the float type and also returns a value of the float type. To implement the math, you use literal float values (9.0F, 160.0F, 9.0F). It remains important to use rational numbers (as opposed to integer values) if you want to generate results that are precise enough for your purposes. If you use integers, your calculations are likely to be accurate only to plus or minus 1. Here is the code for the fahrToCel() method from the Functions class:

```
// Convert Fahrenheit to Celsius
public float fahrToCel(float fahrTemp)
{
    return (5.0F * fahrTemp) / 9.0F - (160.0F / 9.0F);
}
```

To avoid difficulties that can result from the order in which C# and most other programming languages perform math operations, it is best to use parentheses to group your operations. You first multiply the value for Fahrenheit degrees (fahrTemp) by the constant 5.0F. You then divide the product of this multiplication by 9.0F. You can then subtract the quotient given by 160.0F /9.0F from the result of the division.

Generating the Table

You call the fahrToCel() method in the runFunction() method of the DataForm class. As mentioned previously, the runFunction() method serves as a shell in which you can generate calls to any method you develop. To create Fahrenheit values, you define the domain array. In this instance, you define the array to be of the float type. You provide a comma-delimited list of integers, which the compiler converts to float values. Here is the code for the runFunction() method:

```
// Generate values of Fahrenheit converted to Celsius
private void runFunction()
{
    Functions fset = new Functions();
    // Create an array of values for the domain
    float[] domain = {-3, 0, 4, 10, 32, 34};
    // Repeat the calculation for each value in the array
    for (int ctr = 0; ctr < domain.Length; ctr++)
    {
        coordSets.Add(new Values( domain[ctr],
                            fset.fahrToCel(domain[ctr])));
    }
    displayTable("\n\t Fahr", "\t\t Celsius");
}// end method
```

You use a for repetition block to traverse the values in the array, and the ctr control variable allows you to retrieve domain values from the domain array. To limit the control, you call the Length property of the domain array. This property provides you with the number of items in the array.

You furnish the Fahrenheit values you retrieve from the domain array as arguments to the fahrToCel() method. The method returns the Celsius degree values for each of the Fahrenheit values. To store the values, you use the coordSetsList collection. This collection holds objects of the Values data type. The constructor for the Values data type takes two arguments. For the first argument, you use the Fahrenheit values, which the constructor assigns to the X field of the Values object. To the second you assign the Celsius argument, which the constructor assigns to the Y field of the Values object. You employ the new keyword to create a

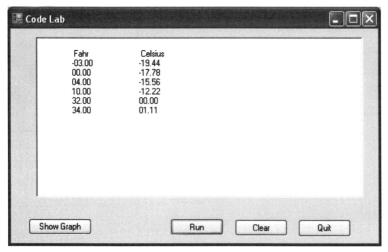

Figure 6.6
runFunction(), fahrToCel(), and runButton_Click() generate a table in the Code Lab window.

new Values object for each pair. You then use the ListAdd method to store the Values objects in the coordSetsList collection.

Your last bit of activity in the definition of the runFunction() method involves a call to the displayTable() method. This method displays the domain and range values you have assigned to the coordSetsList collection. Figure 6.6 illustrates the table that results.

Generating a Graph

To retrieve the values from the fahrToCel() method to generate a graph, you use the showData() method in the CartForm class. It is not necessary to alter the method from its previous form. However, you must alter the YSCALE and LOCALGRID field values in the CartForm class definition. In this case, you set YSCALE to 1 and LOCALGRID to 5. For a specific discussion of the lines of the showData() method, see the previous section "Generating the Table."

As Figure 6.7 reveals, the graph provides enough coordinate positions that you can view where the graph for the Fahrenheit-to-Celsius function crosses both the x and y axes. Where it crosses the x axis, as mentioned before, you see the x-intercept. This indicates that when Celsius is at 0, then the Fahrenheit equivalent is 32. Where the graph crosses the y axis you see the y-intercept. The

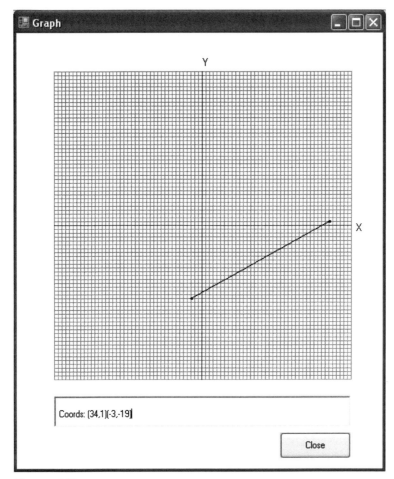

Figure 6.7
A graph allows you to relate Fahrenheit and Celsius scales.

y-intercept lies at roughly -17.78 (the temperature Celsius). The corresponding Fahrenheit value is 0.

Rise and Run

In the generalized expression of a linear equation, you represent the slope using the letter m. As the previous discussion has emphasized, the generalized equation takes this form:

$$f(x) = mx + b$$

If you investigate the meaning of the slope, you find that it is the ratio of the number of units the graphed line moves along the x axis to the number of units

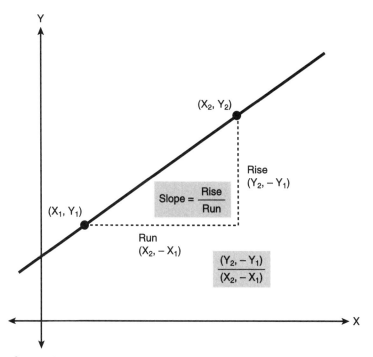

Figure 6.8
The slope represents rise over run.

the graphed line moves along the y axis. If you consider in this the ratio for the Fahrenheit-to-Celsius equation, $\frac{5}{9}$ means that for every 9 units you move along the x axis, you move 5 units up the y axis.

Figure 6.8 portrays the relation between the rise and run of a line. You determine the values for the rise and run of a line if you use any two coordinate pairs along the line. The difference between the y values of the coordinate pairs divided by the difference between the x values of the coordinate pairs gives you the slope of the line.

As Figure 6.8 shows, the equation for the slope of a linear equation takes this form:

$$m = \frac{y_2 - y_1}{x_2 - x_1}$$

If the value that results from the slope equation is positive, then the line slopes upward to the right. If the value that results from the equation is negative, then the line slopes downward to the right.

More on Temperatures

The ratio that you use to define the slope of a linear equation expresses the ratio between the change in the rise of a line and the change in the run of a line. If you consider the freezing and boiling points of water on the Fahrenheit and Celsius scales, you end up with a set of data that allows you to create a ratio that converts degrees Celsius to degrees Fahrenheit. As was pointed out previously, the freezing temperature of water on the Fahrenheit scale is 32 degrees. The freezing temperature of water on the Celsius scale is 0. Likewise, the boiling point of water on the Fahrenheit scale is 212 degrees. The boiling point of water on the Celsius scale is 100 degrees.

If you use functional notation, you can summarize these ratios in this way:

$F(0) = 32$ The temperature 0 Celsius equates to 32 Fahrenheit.

$F(100) = 212$ The temperature 100 Celsius equates to 212 Fahrenheit.

If you map these coordinates on a Cartesian plane, you see that you then have two points you can use to establish the slope of a line. Figure 6.9 shows how this is so.

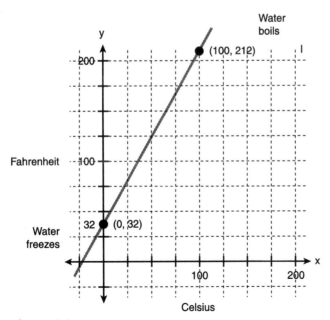

Figure 6.9
Celsius and Fahrenheit mappings of the freezing and boiling temperatures of water allow you to identify coordinate pairs.

Given the coordinate pairs depicted by Figure 6.9, you can then use the slope equation to determine the slope of the line that describes the relationship between the Celsius and Fahrenheit scales:

$$\frac{212 - 32}{100 - 0} = \frac{180}{100} = 1.8$$

This, then, becomes the slope of the line. It also stands, however that the standard form of a linear equation also allows for a y-intercept value. To determine the y-intercept value, you can set up this equation:

$$32 = 1.8(0) + b$$

You then solve the equation for b, so the result is that $32 = b$. You can then substitute the value of b into the standard form of a linear equation to provide a way to convert Celsius to Fahrenheit:

$$F(x) = 1.8(x) + 32$$

Coding a Method to Find a Slope

To program a method that allows you to discover the slope of any given set of coordinates that might lie along a line, you can proceed in much the same way that you have proceeded previously. In this case, however, you seek only to discover from a given coordinate pair the ratio that establishes the slope. Here is the code for the findSlope() method from the Functions class:

```
// Find a slope using two coordinate pairs
public float findSlope (double[] array)
{
    return (array[3] - array[1]) / (array[2] - array[0]);
}
```

The findSlope() method takes an array of the float type as its argument. When you define the array for the function, you must provide values as coordinate pairs. To use the coordinate pairs from Figure 6.9, you begin with the pairs (0, 32) and (100, 212), which you then assign to an array of the float type in this way:

```
float[] coords ={0, 32, 100, 212};
```

The equation you implement in the findSlope() method extracts the elements at the 0 and 2 indexes to set the x values. It extracts elements at the 1 and 3 indexes to set the y values. You then divide the difference of the y values by the difference of the x values, and then return the result.

Creating Output with the Slope Method

To use the method that calculates the slope for a given set of values, you can alter the `runFunction()` method in the `DataForm` class so that it contains the Celsius and Fahrenheit values shown previously. Here is the code:

```
// Show the slope and the values used to calculate the slope
private void runFunction()
{
    Functions fset = new Functions();
    // Create an array of values for the domain
    float[] domain = { 0.0F, 32.0F, 100.0F, 212.0F };
    // Calculate the slope
    float slope = fset.findSlope(domain);
    for (int ctr = 0; ctr < domain.Length -1; ctr +=2)
    {
        coordSets.Add(new Values(domain[ctr],
                                domain[ctr+1]) );
    }
    displayTable("\n\tSlope is: " + slope.ToString() + " for "
                            + "\n\t Celsius", "\t\t Fahr");
}// end method
```

The changes that you make to the `runFunction()` method involve first the use of the float data type to define the domain array. You then call the `findSlope()` method and submit the domain array as its sole argument. The `findSlope()` method returns the slope of the coordinate set you provide. The type of the returned value is float.

The use of the `for` repetition block allows you to supply arguments to the `Values` constructor. You set the increments of the counter to 2, and then provide the coordinate values from the domain array in sets of two. You must set the counter to `Length-1` to prevent the value of the counter from exceeding the maximum index value of the array.

The call to the `displayTable()` involves using two arguments. In this case, you use a line break and a tab in the first argument to create a line at the top of your output that displays the slope you calculate using the coordinates in the table that follows. To convert the slope variable to a string, you call the `ToString()` method for the float data type. Figure 6.10 illustrates the table that results.

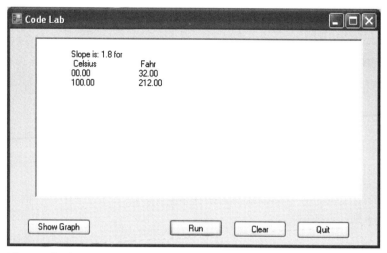

Figure 6.10
The equation for a slope allows you to calculate the slope and then show the values used to do so.

Note

You can click the Show Graph button and generate a graph of the values shown in Figure 6.10 because the coordSets collection contains enough information to generate a graph. See Figure 6.11 for the table for the Celsius-to-Fahrenheit conversion. To see the graph shown, in the CartForm class set the scaling fields as follows:

```
YSCALE = 5;
XSCALE = 5;
LOCALGRID = 4;
```

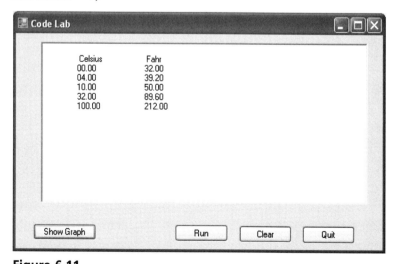

Figure 6.11
You call the celToFahr() method in the DataForm class to display a table of values showing conversion of Celsius to Fahrenheit temperatures.

Coding a Method to Convert Celsius to Fahrenheit

To create a method for the function that converts degrees Celsius to degrees Fahrenheit, you use the same approach you used when you developed the method to convert degrees Fahrenheit to degrees Celsius. The name of the method is `celToFahr()`. You implement the method in the `Functions` class. Here is the code for the method:

```
// Convert Celsius to Fahrenheit
public float celToFahr (float cTemp)
{
    // F(x) = 1.8(x) + 32
    return (1.8 * cTemp ) + 32.0;
}
```

The method takes an argument of the float type. The argument provides a value for a temperature reading in degrees Celsius. You then multiply the temperature value by 1.8 and add 32.0 to the product. The method returns a value of the float type Here is the code for the `runFunction()` method in the `DataForm` class in which you call the `celToFahr()` method to generate a table of values.

```
// Generate values of Celsius converted to Fahrenheit
private void runFunction()
{
    Functions fset = new Functions();
    // Create an array of values for the domain
    float[] domain = {0, 4, 10, 32, 100 };
    // Repeat the calculation for each item in the array
    for (int ctr = 0; ctr < domain.Length; ctr++)
    {
        coordSets.Add(new Values(domain[ctr],
                        fset.celToFahr(domain[ctr])));
    }
    displayTable("\n\t Celsius", "\t\t Fahr");
}//end method
```

To make the call to the `celToFahr()` method, you employ the same approach you have used with other methods. You assign values to the domain array. You then retrieve the values using a `for` repetition statement. With each call to the `celToFahr()` method, you assign the resulting x and y values to a `Values` object that you store in the `coordSets` collection. After that, you set the column headings using the `displayTable()` method. The `displayTable()` method retrieves values from the `coordSets` collection and prints the table.

Generating a Graph

As in previous examples, you call the celToFahr () method in the runFunction() method of the DataForm class to generate values for a table. Both the celToFahr() and findSlope() methods generate values that allow you to plot a graph. The graph that you plot is the same for both methods because the graph you generate uses the same two sets of coordinates.

The code for generating remains the same as before, except now you add a few items to accommodate a wider range of temperatures. To accomplish this task, you modify the CartForm fields so that they allow you to scale the values for the x and y coordinates. Here are the fields of the CartForm class:

```
private CoordSystem cSys;
const int YSCALE = 5;
const int XSCALE = 5;
const int LOCALGRID = 4;
private int FW = 500, FH = 600;
private PictureBox pictureBox1;
```

This set of fields represents several changes from those you worked with in Chapter 5. The additions and changes represent the need to expand the capabilities of the CartForm class to handle grid adjustments, value scaling, and an overloaded constructor. The use of the XSCALE and YSCALE constants enable you to divide the raw values from the coordSets collection so that you can plot them in your grid. The LOCALGRID constant allows you to adjust the number of lines in the grid.

Use of these values in the showData() method does not change their operations from those you have worked with before. Here are the lines in the method that the scaling constants affect:

```
int xFahrValA = (int)tempVals[tempVals.Length - 1].X / XSCALE;
int yFahrValA = (int)tempVals[tempVals.Length - 1].Y / YSCALE;
int xFahhValB = (int)tempVals[0].X / XSCALE;
int yFahrValB = (int)tempVals[0].Y / YSCALE;
```

Use of the scaling constants allows you to work with large values, but they also create some problems that emerge in the current version of the Lab application. Figure 6.12 illustrates the plotted output of the celToFahr() method along with the values used to generate the graph. While the text area at the bottom of the graph shows the values that have been plotted, they do not show you the values displayed in Figures 6.11 and 6.10.

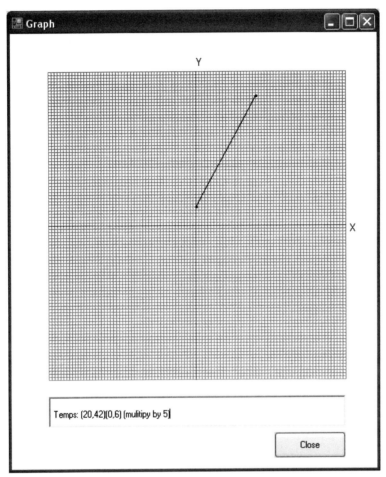

Figure 6.12
Use of the fahrToCel() method leads to the need to explain the output.

Method Overloading

To make it so that you can see the raw data used for the graph, you can implement an *overloaded* form of the showData() method. An overloaded method is a method in a given class that has the same name but a different argument list than one or more other functions of the same name in the same class. In this instance, the overloaded form of the showData() method does not perform precisely the same actions as the previous version. The overloaded showData() method does not plot the graph but instead only creates a string of raw values for the text box. Its argument allows you to display the raw values from the coordSets (or Vals) collection. You call the method from the first `showData()` method and, in this way, avoid having to rewrite other code. The call takes this form:

```
showData(true);
```

An argument of `true` causes the text area to be cleared of the scaled data so that you see only the original data. An argument of `false` allows you to see both the scaled and original data. Here is the code for the overloaded form of the `show-Data()` method as developed in the `CartForm` class:

```
// Overloaded form of the method to allow for
// the display of the original coordinate values
public void showData(bool onlyOrig)
{
    DataForm tempForm = new DataForm();
    if (onlyOrig)
    {
        richTextBox1.Clear();
    }
        richTextBox1.AppendText("\n");
    foreach (Values set in tempForm.Vals)
    {
        richTextBox1.AppendText(" ("
                          + set.X.ToString() + ","
                          + set.Y.ToString() + ") "
                        );
    }
}
```

To implement the overloaded `showData()` method, you follow the same course you follow in the original version of the method and create a local instance of the `DataForm` class (`tempForm`). After that, however, you proceed in a different direction and use the `tempForm` object to call the `Vals` property directly to use in a `foreach` repetition statement. The `foreach` statement copies the items from the `Vals` collection (which is the `coordSets` field in the `DataForm` class) to the `set` variable. The `set` variable is of the `Values` type, so it provides two fields, `X` and `Y`, that represent the Fahrenheit and Celsius temperature values that constitute each coordinate pair. From that point, you use the `X` and `Y` fields in conjunction with the `ToString()` method to create output for the text box. Since you call the `AppendText()` method, as each coordinate pair is retrieved, it is printed to the text box.

To process the argument of the method, you employ an `if` selection statement. If you supply a value of `true` as the argument to the method, then flow of the

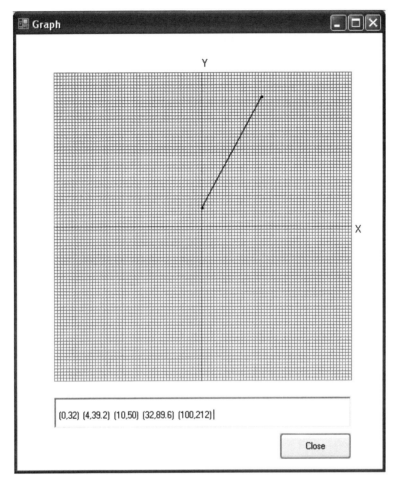

Figure 6.13
The text field displays the original data.

program includes a call to Clear() method, which removes previous data from the text box. If you set the argument to false, then the text box is not cleared. This allows you a way to see both the scaled original versions of the data. Figure 6.13 shows you the text field after you have set the argument to true, so you see only the original data. This is the output of the celToFahr() method.

Slope Characteristics

The standard form of the function for a straight line assumes this form:

$$f(x) = mx + b$$

As mentioned previously, *m* is a constant that identifies the slope of the line, and *b* is a constant that identifies the *y*-intercept. These two constants allow you to manipulate the appearance of lines in many ways. The next few sections review some of your options.

Slope Gradients and Negative Slopes

As Figure 6.14 illustrates, if the slope of an equation is negative, then the line falls from the upper left of the Cartesian plane to the lower right. If it is positive, then the line slopes upward to the right. If the absolute value of the slope is less

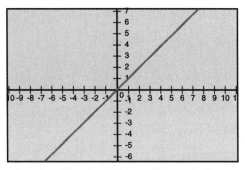

1x + 0   The slope (1) is positive, so the line climbs to the right. In this case, x = y, so the line is diagonal to quadrants it enters.

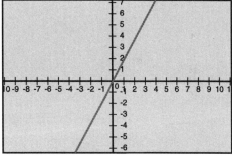

2x + 0   The slope (2) is positive, so the line climbs to the right, steeper than when the slope is set to 1.

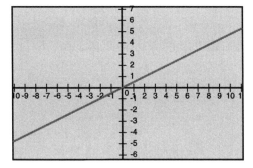

1/2(x) + 0   The slope (1/2) is positive, so the line climbs to the right. The absolute value of the slope is less than 1, so it climbs more gradually.

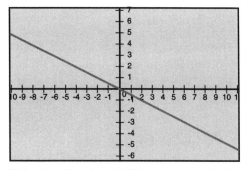

-1/2(x) + 0   The slope (-1/2) is negative, so the line falls to the right. The absolute value of the slope is less than 1, so it falls more gradually.

Figure 6.14
A negative slope falls to the right.

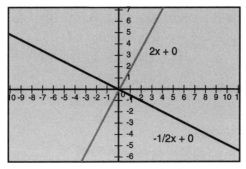

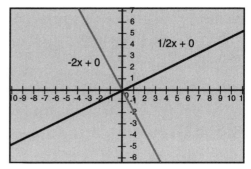

If you take the negative inverse of a given slope (2 and -1/2), then the lines are perpendicular to each other.

In this case, the line sloping up and to the right has a slope of 1/2, and the line sloping down and to the right has a slope of -2. The negative inverse generates a perpendicular line.

Figure 6.15
The negative inverse of a slope characterizes a perpendicular line.

than 1 but greater than 0, then the slope is gradual. If the absolute value is greater than 1, then the line becomes steeper.

Perpendicular Lines

If the slope of one line is the inverse and negative of the slope of another line, then the two lines are perpendicular. Figure 6.15 illustrates how this happens.

Shifting on the *y* Axis

The value of b provides the *y*-intercept of the line. A positive value for the *y*-intercept shifts the line upward on the *y* axis. A negative value shifts the line downward. Figure 6.16 illustrates a line shifted along the *y* axis.

Conclusion

In this chapter you have extended your work with the Lab in a number of ways. To the Lab you have added implementations of methods that embody functions. The functions you have worked with include standard linear equations that you combine through arithmetic operation and through the activity of function composition. Function composition allows you to deal with involved scenarios,

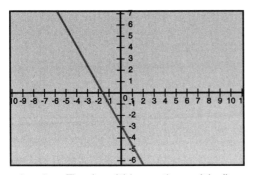

-2x – 3   The slope (2) is negative, and the line has been shifted downward 3 units on the y axis.

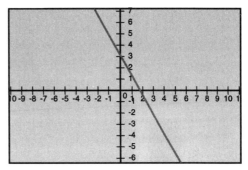

-2x + 3   The slope (2) is negative, and the line has been shifted upward 3 units on the y axis.

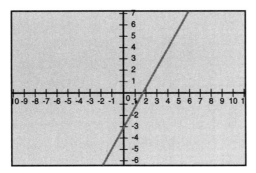

2x – 3   The slope (2) is positive, and the line has been shifted downward 3 units on the y axis.

Figure 6.16
The *y*-intercept allows you to shift a line upward or downward along the *y* axis.

such as one combining the profits a factory generates and the profitability of the work in the factory at a given hour of the day. You also explored the use of the standard formulation of a linear equation and how to use coordinate values to determine the slope of a line. For each of these explorations, you implemented methods in the Lab.

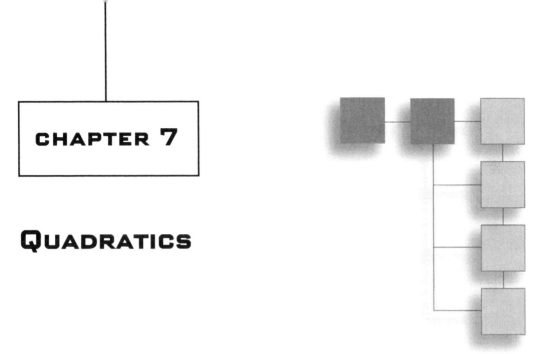

CHAPTER 7

QUADRATICS

In this chapter, you review several primary activities involving quadratic functions, functions that include absolute values, and functions that generate discontinuous lines. Quadratic equations generate parabolas, and parabolas prove useful as a way to determine minimum and maximum values. If a parabola opens downward, then the highest point or vertex of the parabola corresponds to a maximum value. If the parabola opens upward, then the lowest point or vertex of the parabola corresponds to a minimum value. Parabolas also allow you to work with tangents. Tangents have positive slopes when they climb, negative slopes when they descend, and slopes of 0 when they are associated with the vertex of a parabola. You can put these notions to work and return to the profit functions introduced in the last chapter to determine the point at which the tire factory achieves maximum productivity. To graphically represent parabolas, you make use of the methods you wrote earlier. You also implement several more methods to explore absolute values and discontinuous lines. Here are some of the topics you explore in this chapter:

- Quadratic functions and parabolas

- Completing the square of a quadratic equation

- Working with the quadratic formula

- Tangents and minimum and maximum values

- Working with absolute values and passing arrays with references

- Working with discontinuous lines

Quadratic Functions

A quadratic equation falls into the category of *nonlinear*. A nonlinear equation is an equation that, among other things, generates a line that curves so that you find its slope changes, depending on the segment of the curve you inspect (see the sidebar, "Changing Slopes"). Quadratic functions account for some but not all nonlinear functions. A quadratic equation is an equation that tends to have fairly universal applications and can be recognized by its distinct form. Here is the characteristic form of a quadratic equation in its functional form:

$$f(x) = Ax^2 + Bx + C$$

In this representation of the quadratic function, A, B, and C represent constants. The constants can be any real number, but A cannot be equal to 0.

Changing Slopes

Figure 7.1 illustrates the graph of a function that generates a graph of a curve. When you graph such a curve, you find a slope that changes. A quadratic equation generates such a graph. If you trace the coordinates of the graph on its lower part, you find that for every 1 unit on the x axis, the lower part of the curve moves approximately 1 unit on the y axis. After the line climbs past 1 on the y axis, this situation changes. For 1 unit on the x axis, the line climbs approximately 3 units on the y axis. The slope changes. A changing slope is one of the key characteristics of the graph you generate with a quadratic equation.

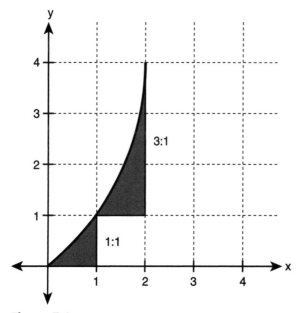

Figure 7.1
Quadratic equations generate graphs with slopes that change, depending on the portion of the curve you investigate.

The graph of a linear equation reveals a line with a slope that does not change. The graph of a nonlinear equation reveals a line with a slope that changes.

Parabolas

When you graph a quadratic equation, the curve that results is a *parabola*. To generate parabolas using quadratic equations, you can most readily manipulate the dimensions of the parabola by using a form of the quadratic equation that allows you to see its key characteristics. This is known as the *canonical form* of the quadratic equation. Here is how you express this equation as a function:

$$f(x) = p(x - h)^2 + k$$

In this form, p, k, and h are all constants. They can be any real number. The letter p controls how narrow or wide your parabola appears. The h controls how you shift it left or right on the x axis. The k determines how you shift it up or down on the y axis.

Completing the Square

It often happens that you need to make it so that a quadratic equation is in the canonical form. You can accomplish this if you use a technique for altering quadratic equations known as *completing the square.*

To complete the square of a quadratic equation, you first inspect the equation to discover whether you can rewrite so that you create a perfect square on the right side of the equals sign. Suppose, for example, that you find this equation:

$$f(x) = 2x^2 - 12x$$

This is a standard quadratic equation. As a reminder, here is the standard form of a quadratic function.

$$f(x) = Ax^2 + Bx + C$$

The 2 above corresponds to A, 12 corresponds to B, and x remains x. Missing is the last term, C. As a temporary measure, one just needs to show that you are, indeed, dealing with a standard quadratic equation, and that you assign a 0 as the coefficient of C:

$$f(x) = 2x^2 - 12x + (0)C$$

This measure equates to the first but allows you to see the standard form of the equation. To arrive at the canonical form of the equation, you must use a different approach. This one involves examining the first two terms of the equation to discover how you can transform the equation so that it has three

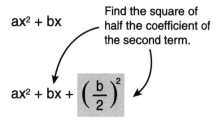

Figure 7.2
To complete the square, divide the coefficient of the second term by 2 and square the result.

terms that you can factor into a square. Figure 7.2 provides a generalized approach. For the equation at hand, consider the steps the figure shows.

Figure 7.2 reviews the general strategy you use to complete the square. The subsequent discussion reviews a specific operation.

To complete a square, you first examine the candidate equation to discern whether the terms contain common factors. By isolating the common factors, you can more easily find ways to square the terms. For the equation $2x^2 - 12x$, a common factor is 2, so you can rewrite the equation in this way:

$$f(x) = 2x^2 - 12x$$
$$= 2(x^2 - 6x)$$

At this point, you can then examine the two terms within the parentheses and apply the procedure shown in Figure 7.2 to them. To accomplish this, you begin with the second of the two terms within the parentheses. This term corresponds to Bx in the standard form of the quadratic equation. You divide B, the coefficient of x, by 2 and square the result. You then add the result to the terms. Your work proceeds along these lines:

$$f(x) = 2x^2 - 12x \qquad\qquad \text{Basic function.}$$

$$= 2(x^2 - 6x) \qquad\qquad \text{Factor out 2.}$$

$$= 2\left(x^2 - 6x + \left(\frac{6}{2}\right)^2 - \left(\frac{6}{2}\right)^2\right) \qquad \text{Divide } B \text{ by 2 and square.}$$

$$= 2(x^2 - 6x + 9 - 9) \qquad\qquad \text{Simplify.}$$

$$= 2(x^2 - 6x + 9) - 2(9) \qquad\qquad \text{Now distribute using 2.}$$

$$= 2(x - 3)(x - 3) - 2(9) \qquad\qquad \text{Just to show the squared term.}$$

$$= 2(x - 3)^2 - 18 \qquad\qquad \text{The canonical form.}$$

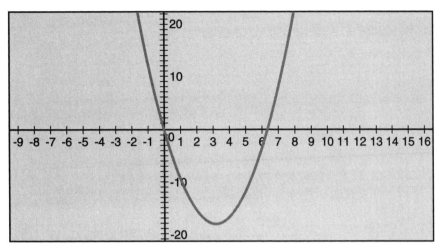

Figure 7.3
After you complete the square, you can then graph the parabola for $2(x-3)^2 - 18$ and see its primary features.

Given this form of the equation, you can then work with the quadratic equation to present it graphically or, in general, identify its terms. Using Visual Formula (see Appendix A), you can compose the equation in the equation composition area and generate the graphical representation Figure 7.3 illustrates.

Note

Visual Formula provides a way that you can check all of your linear and nonlinear equations. You can also use it to check some of the equations involving differentiation and integration.

Table 7.1 outlines some of the key features that Figure 7.3 illustrates. In the discussion that follows, you see how you can change the equation Figure 7.3 depicts to alter its positions on the x and y axes and its minimum and maximum values.

Shifting Left and Right

As mentioned previously, if the canonical equation features the difference $(x - h)$ between x and h, then your parabola shifts to the right. If the canonical equation features the sum $(x + h)$ of x and h, then your parabola shifts to the left. This explanation conforms to the model given by $(x - (-h))$. The constant h in this

Table 7.1 Features of the Standard Form

Item	Discussion
$ax^2 + bx + c$	Standard form of a quadratic equation. You can also express this as $Ax^2 + Bx + C$.
$a(x - h)^2 + k$	This is the canonical form of the quadratic equation. If the equation does not factor into terms you can square to begin with, you can create this form of the equation by completing the square.
$(x - h)$	This expression allows you to shift the parabola to the left or to the right on the x axis. The value of h represents the number of units you shift the graph. If h is negative, then, you end up with the expression $(x + h)$. The coordinate pair establishes the position of the vertex of the parabola. The expression $(x - h)$ moves the vertex of the parabola to the left of the y axis. The expression $(x + y)$ or $(x - (-h))$ moves the vertex to the right of the y axis.
a	The value of the constant a determines how sharply the parabola rises. If the value of a is greater than 1, then the parabola narrows and rises more precipitately. If the value of a is less than 1 (and greater than 0), then the parabola becomes wider and rises less precipitately. If the value is negative, then the parabola is inverted so that it opens downward.
k	The constant k establishes the y-intercept for the parabola. If the value of k is positive, then the vertex moves upward relative to the x axis. If the value of k is negative, then the vertex shifts downward.

case is a negative number. It remains, however, that your expression can be simplified as $(x + h)$.

Given this start, then, Figure 7.4 shows you the graphs that result when you use the sum of the squared terms of the canonical form of the equation. For the three curves in Figure 7.4, the starting expression is $p(x - h)^2 + k$, but k is set to 0 so that the curves are not shifted up or down on the y axis. In each instance, you can view the equation as including $(x - (-3))$ but it is just as easy to start with the simpler expression of $(x + 3)$.

In each case a negative number forces the parabola to open downward. When this number possesses an absolute value that is less than 1 but greater than 0, then the parabola widens. When the absolute value of the number is greater than 1, then the parabola narrows.

Figure 7.5 shows you the graphs that result when you use the difference of two terms of the canonical form of the equation. For the three curves in Figure 7.4, the starting expression is $p(x - h)^2 + k$, but k is set to 0. As in the previous example, this makes it so that the curves are not shifted up or down. In each

In all three instances, (x + 3) shifts the vertex of the parabola 3 units left on the x axis. This is equivalent to writing (x − (-3)).

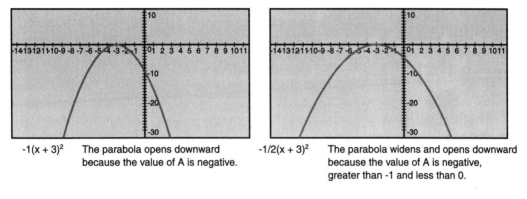

-1(x + 3)²   The parabola opens downward because the value of A is negative.

-1/2(x + 3)²   The parabola widens and opens downward because the value of A is negative, greater than -1 and less than 0.

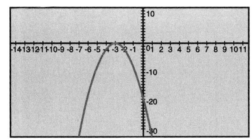

-2(x + 3)²   The parabola narrows and opens downward because the value of A is negative and is greater than 1.

Figure 7.4
If the value of h is negative, then the expression $x - h$ becomes $x - (-h)$ or $x + h$, and the vertex of the parabola shifts to the left on the x axis.

instance, you can view the equation as $(x -(+3))$. As in the previous examples, when you precede the expression with a negative number, then you force the parabola to open downward. A fraction, such as $-1/2$, widens the parabola, and values less than -1 narrow the parabola.

Flipping

The illustrations in the previous section show parabolas that open downward. Generally, if the value of a in the canonical form is negative, the parabola opens downward. When the value of a in the standard form of the quadratic equation is positive, then the parabola opens upward. Regardless of whether a is negative or positive, the same characteristics apply, as in the previous examples regarding the shifting of the vertex along the x axis. The expression $(x + h)$ shifts the vertex

In all three instances, (x – 3) shifts the vertex of the parabola
3 units right on the x axis. This is equivalent to writing (x – (+3)).

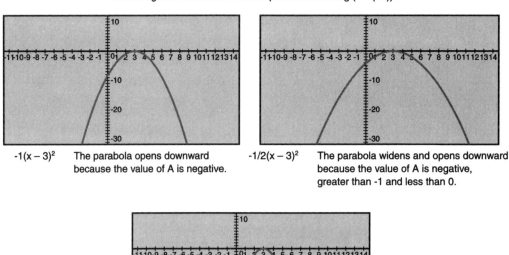

-1(x – 3)²   The parabola opens downward   -1/2(x – 3)²   The parabola widens and opens downward
              because the value of A is negative.   because the value of A is negative,
                                                                  greater than -1 and less than 0.

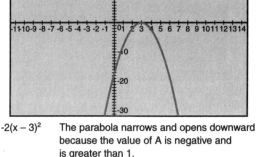

-2(x – 3)²   The parabola narrows and opens downward
              because the value of A is negative and
              is greater than 1.

Figure 7.5
If h is a positive number, then the expression $x - h$ shifts the parabola to the right on the x axis.

to the right. The expression $(x - h)$ shifts the vertex to the left. In the graphs
Figure 7.6 features, the vertexes are shifted to the left or right 3 units and all open
upward given the positive value of a.

Shifting Up and Down

The constant k in the canonical form of the quadratic equation allows you to
change the position of the vertex of the parabola with respect to the y axis. If the
value of k is positive, then the parabola shifts upward. If the value of k is
negative, then the parabola shifts downward. The parabolas Figure 7.7 illustrates
all feature positive values of a, shifting using the expression $(x - h)$, and a value
for the constant k that changes the position of the vertex of the parabola. Notice

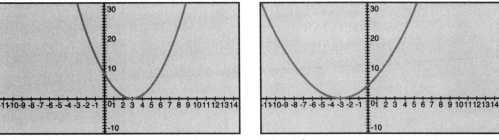

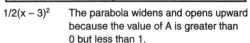

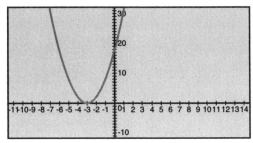

Figure 7.6
When the value of *a* is positive, the parabola opens upward.

that when you set the value of *h* to 0, you center the parabola on the *y* axis. In previous examples setting *k* to 0 positioned the vertex of the parabola on the *x* axis.

Tangent Lines

Figure 7.8 depicts a curve in a road along which automobiles are traveling. Each automobile is equipped with a laser mounted on top so that it always points straight ahead of the automobile. As the automobile rounds the corner, the laser projects straight out from the car into the area on the outside of the curve. In each instance, the result is the tangent line of the curve the path of the car describes.

The positive value of A causes the parabola to open upward, and the value of k shifts it up and down the y axis.

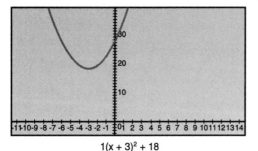

$$1(x + 3)^2 + 18$$

The parabola opens upward. It is shifted to the left 3 units. The value of k is 18, so it is moved 18 units upward on the y axis.

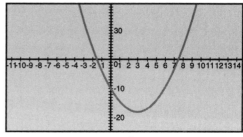

$$1(x - 3)^2 - 18$$

The parabola opens upward. It is shifted to the right 3 units. The value of k is -18, so it is moved 18 units downward on the y axis.

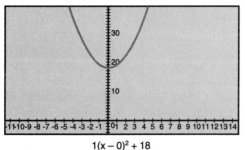

$$1(x - 0)^2 + 18$$

The parabola opens upward. If you set h to 0, then it is centered on the y axis. The value of k remains 18, so it is moved 18 units upward on the y axis.

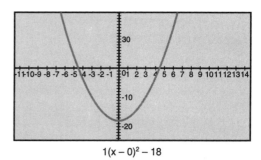

$$1(x - 0)^2 - 18$$

The parabola opens upward. If you set h to 0, then it is centered on the y axis. The value of k this time is set to -18, so the vertex moves 18 units downward on the y axis.

Figure 7.7
Changing the value of k shifts the parabola along the y axis.

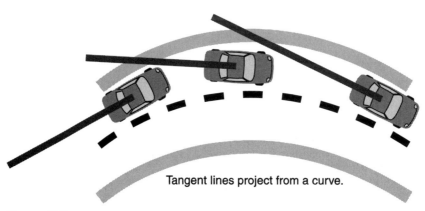

Tangent lines project from a curve.

Figure 7.8
A tangent line projects from a given point on a line.

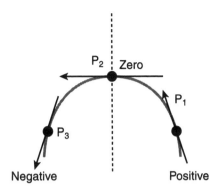

Figure 7.9
The slopes of tangent lines are positive, negative, and zero.

You refer to a *tangent line* as relative to a given point on a curve or parabola. In Figure 7.9, the points P_1, P_2, and P_3 can all be associated with a given tangent line. If you map a tangent line to each of the points Figure 7.9 identifies, then you can arrive at three generalizations:

- The slope of the tangent line is negative if the tangent follows the path of a parabola so that it falls away from the vertex of the parabola. The tangent associated with point P_3 illustrates this type of tangent.

- The slope of the tangent line is positive if the tangent follows the path of a parabola so that it climbs toward the vertex of the parabola. The tangent associated with point P_1 illustrates this type of tangent.

- If the tangent is horizontal to the point that it lies at the vertex of the parabola, then the slope of the tangent is zero. The tangent associated with point P_2 illustrates this type of tangent.

The Quadratic Formula

You can use the quadratic formula to solve a quadratic equation. Your primary goal when you solve a quadratic equation is to find the points at which it crosses the x axis. You can also determine its y-intercept. Not all quadratic equations provide such information because in many cases they do not intercept the x axis. Still, for those that do, you can use the quadratic formula to generate solutions. To use the quadratic formula, you begin with the standard form of the quadratic equation, which reads as follows:

$$ax^2 + bx + c = 0$$

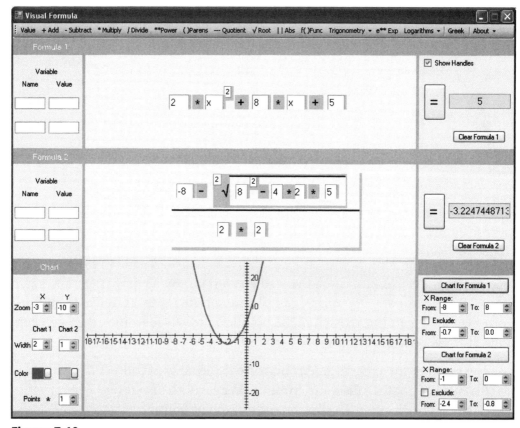

Figure 7.10
Visual Formula allows you to implement the quadratic formula and other equations with relative ease so that you can check your programming work.

Given this, you have the information you need to use the formula. You then apply the quadratic formula. The quadratic formula reads this way:

$$x = \frac{-b \pm \sqrt{b^2 - 4ac}}{2a}$$

You substitute values into each of the designated positions and then solve for both the + and − operations preceding the radical. As an example of how to proceed, consider this problem:

$$2x^2 + 8x - 5 = 0$$

For this expression, *a* equals 2, *b* equals 8, and *c* equals 5. To make your work easier, you can use Visual Formula to both solve for specific values of the equation and to implement the quadratic formula.

In Figure 7.10, the quadratic equation has been implemented in the top equation composition area. The equation generates the parabola you see in the Cartesian plane in the bottom part of the interface. The values used to generate the parabola range from −6 to 6.

In the lower equation composition area, the quadratic formula has been implemented. The value you see generated on the right represents one solution for the value of the x-intercept. If you change the plus sign preceding the radical expression to a minus sign, you see the other value for the x-intercept. In this case, the two solutions are approximately −0.775 and −3.225.

Minimum and Maximum

When you generate a parabola, if the parabola opens upward, then the vertex describes the minimum point value of the parabola. If the parabola opens downward, then the vertex describes the maximum point of the parabola.

Points that describe minimum and maximum value in parabolas prove useful for solving a large variety of problems. Imagine, for example, that you revisit the bicycle tire factory explored in Chapter 6; you can revisit the cost function to add refinements to your ability to predict profits. Suppose, for example, that you work with a cost $(C(x))$ function that reads this way:

$$C(x) = 0.1x^2 + 8x + 40$$

If the price of a tire goes to $20, what then would be the point at which the partners optimize their profits? For the profit function you combine revenue and cost functions. The basic formula for this is $P(x) = R(x) - C(x)$. Given this starting point, you then consider that if each tire sells for $20, you end up with this function:

$$P(x) = 20(x) - (0.1^2 + 8x + 40)$$
$$= -0.1x^2 + 12x - 40$$

To calculate the point at which profits equal costs, you set the equation equal to 0:

$$-0.1x^2 + 12x - 40 = 0$$

This gives you a standard quadratic equation from which you can draw values to use the quadratic formula. Accordingly, a equals −0.1, b equals 2, and c equals −40. Substituting the values into the formula, you arrive at this equation.

$$x = \frac{-(12) \pm \sqrt{12^2 - 4(-0.1)(-40)}}{2(-0.1)}$$

You find the resulting values to be approximately 3 and 116. Given these two figures, you can then generate a parabola that describes the rise and fall of profitability relative to the number of items produced. The parabola reveals that profitability peaks when the partners turn out roughly 56 tires per day.

Coding the Function

To implement a function that includes a quadratic equation that generates a graph to represent the break-even point of bicycle tire production, you work first in the Functions class. If you open the *.sln file in the Chapter 7 folder, you can find the profitCurve() method in the Functions class. Here is the code for the method.

```
// Calculate values to determine maximum profitability
public float profitCurve(float item){
    return -0.1F * (item * item) + (12.0F * item) - 40.0F;
}
```

To implement the equation, you can follow any number of approaches. As a reminder, the equation takes this form:

$$P(x) = -0.1x^2 + 12x - 40$$

The purpose of the method is to generate values in the range that you obtain when you use the quadratic formula to find the x-intercepts. As your work in the previous section shows, these two values create a domain that extends roughly between 1 and 120. This equation allows you to generate values from this domain that you can use to draw a curve.

To define the profitCurve() equation, you use an argument of the float type. You also define the returned value using the float type. Using the float type for argument and return types requires you to use the letter F to qualify the constant values; otherwise, the compiler reads them as values of the double type.

To square values, multiplying a number by itself in some ways provides an advantage over using the Math.Pow() method. A call to this method changes your method so that it assumes this form:

```
return -0.1F * (float)Math.Pow(item, 2.0)
                + (12.0F * item) - 40.0F;
```

You cast the value the Pow() method returns using the float data type. The Pow() method takes two arguments of the double type. The method implicitly converts both to the double type.

To employ the methods from the Math class in the Functions class, you can use two approaches. With the first approach, in the opening lines of the file in which you define the Functions class, you can provide a using directive to designate the System namespace:

```
using System;
```

Alternatively, if you want to leave out the using directive, you can provide the fully qualified path for the method call. Such a call takes this form:

```
return -0.1F * (float)System.Math.Pow(item, 2.0)
                  + (12.0F * item) - 40.0F;
```

Generating a Table

To generate a table of values using the profitCurve() method, you employ the same pattern you use with the linear methods. Working in the runFunction() method of the DataForm class, you alter the contents of the runFunction() method so that you create an array of the float type (domain). You can determine the values to include in the array by inspecting the results you obtain when you solve the profitability problem using the quadratic formula. As Figure 7.11 reveals, the x-intercepts indicate that the parabola the equation generates intersects the x axis at approximately 3 and 116. If your array extends across this domain, then you can generate a curve that shows you the point of maximum profitability. One goal is to use enough values to provide a fairly smooth curve and to show you generally where profitability peaks.

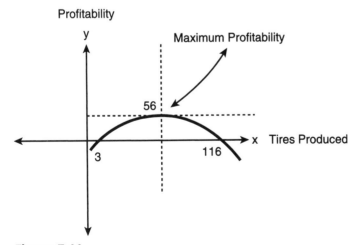

Figure 7.11
A conceptual view of the profitability of bicycle tires helps you orient your development efforts.

```
private void runFunction()
{
    Functions fset = new Functions();
    // Create an array of values for the domain
    float[] domain = {1, 10, 20, 30, 40, 50, 60,
                        70, 80, 90, 100, 110, 120};
    // Repeat the calculation for each item in the array
    for (int ctr = 0; ctr < domain.Length; ctr++)
    {
        coordSets.Add(new Values( (float) domain[ctr],
                (float) fset.profitCurve(domain[ctr])) );
    }// end for
    displayTable("\n\t Items", "\t\t Profit");
}// end method
```

After defining the domain array, you then implement a for repetition statement that allows you to populate the coordSets List container. For each iteration of the for block, you call the profitCurve() function. As an argument of the function, you retrieve a value from the domain array using the ctr variable. As the profitCurve() method returns the profitability data, you create item-profit pairs and assign them to a Values object. You then assign these to the coordSets container. You then call the displayTable() method to show the coordinate pairs you have generated. Figure 7.12 depicts the table that results. Notice that the

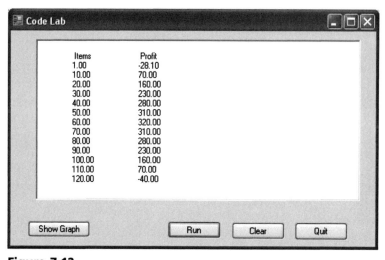

Figure 7.12
Calling the profitCurve() function for the data set allows you to identify the approximate figure for maximum profitability.

profitability figure grows to 320 when the item count reaches 60. When the item count reaches 70, the figure declines to 310 and continues to decline from there.

Generating a Graph

As with the data you worked with in Chapter 6 using linear equations, when you generate data using a quadratic equation, you assign the results to the coordSets List container. This field of the DataForm class is of the Values type and is a static, or class, field. Because it is a class field, it exists for all objects of the DataForm type. Given this situation, you can create an instance of the DataForm class in the CartForm class and retrieve data you have assigned to the coordSets collection as you create the table Figure 7.12 illustrates. Most of your work in this respect occurs within the showData() method. Here is the code for the showData() method.

```
// Set XSCALE and YSCALE - -
// YSCALE 25, XSCALE 5, LOCALGRID 5
public void showData(Graphics e)
{
    DataForm tempForm = new DataForm();
    Values[] tempVals = tempForm.Vals.ToArray();
    // Get the total number of coordinates
    int number = tempVals.Length * 2;
    // Create an array for all the coordinates
    float[] curvePoints = new float[number];
    int ctr = 0;
    // Assign the coordinates to the array
    foreach (Values coord in tempForm.Vals)
    {
        curvePoints[ctr] = coord.X / XSCALE;
        curvePoints[ctr + 1] = coord.Y / YSCALE;
        ctr += 2;
    }// end foreach
    String msg;
    // Use the coordinates to draw a parabola
    msg = cSys.drawCurve(e, curvePoints);
    richTextBox1.Clear();
    richTextBox1.AppendText("\n Coords: " + msg);
    // View values from the DataForm table
    showData(true);
}//end method
```

Most of your activity in the `CartForm` class involves rewriting the `showData()` method to generate a profitability parabola. To scale the graphical representation of the data so that it can accommodate the values you work with, you set the `YSCALE` field to 25 and the `XSCALE` and `LOCALGRID` fields to 5.

In the `showData()` method you create an instance of the `DataForm` class, `tempForm`, and you employ the `ToArray()` method of the `List` class to copy the coordinate pairs you have assigned to the `Vals` (or `coordSets`) collection to a local array, `tempVals`. You then use the `Length` property for arrays to identify the number of items in the `Vals` collection. After multiplying this number by 2, you assign the result to the `number` variable. You then use the `number` variable to create an array, `curvePoints`, which is of the `float` type.

You require the `curvePoints` array as the third argument to the `drawCurve()` method. This method is a wrapper for the `Graphics DrawCurve()` method. The `DrawCurve()` method requires an array of the `Point` type to draw a curve, and to create an instance of the `Point` type, you use values of the `float` type. The `curvePoints` array provides a list of all points that make up the coordinate pairs for the profitability values.

To retrieve values from the `Vals` collection, you employ a `foreach` repetition statement. By iterating through the `Vals` collection one `Values` object at a time and assigning it to the `coord` variable, you can use the X and Y properties to retrieve production and profit figures to assign to the `curvePoints` array. As you retrieve this data, you use the `XSCALE` and `YSCALE` fields to scale the values as you assign them to the array.

As you assign production and profitability data to the `curvePoints` array, you use the `ctr` variable, which you initialize to 0. Since you retrieve items in pairs, you use the value of `ctr` alone to retrieve the first item of the pair. To retrieve the second item, you use `ctr + 1`. With each repetition of the block, you increment `ctr` by 2.

Drawing the curve involves calling the `drawCurve()` method using an object of the `CoordSystem` class (`cSys`) that you create as a class field for the `CartForm` class. As a first argument to the method, you provide a reference of the `Graphics` type. As a second argument, you provide the `curvePoints` array. After calling the `drawCurve()` method, you also call the overloaded version of the `showData()` method. You supply this method with an argument of the `bool` type. A value of `true` indicates that you want to see only the original values used

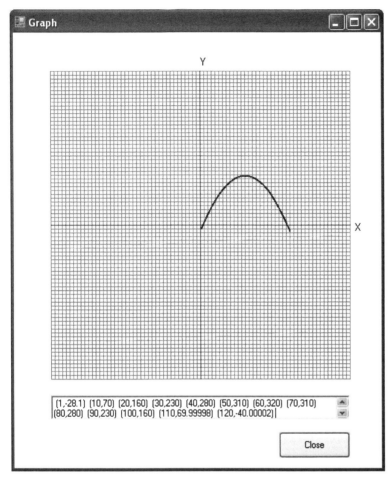

Figure 7.13
Rewriting the showData() method allows you to generate a graph of the profitability data.

to generate the graph, not the scaled values. Figure 7.13 illustrates the curve that results.

Absolute Values

Absolute values prove useful in a variety of contexts. You have already gained a sense of their usefulness when plotting values on a Cartesian plane. If you examine the situation using a number line, an absolute value is the distance of a given number, positive or negative, from zero. Because it encompasses both

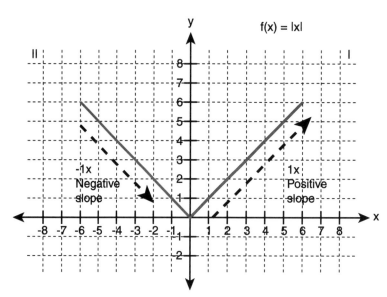

Figure 7.14
An absolute value generates positive and negative slopes.

positive and negative possibilities, the absolute value of any number must be stipulated in two ways. Here is a common representation of an absolute value:

$$x = |x| = x \qquad \text{for } x \geq 0$$
$$x = |x| = -x \qquad \text{for } x < 0$$

This definition of an absolute value defines x so that it has two slopes. You can identify one slope as 1. You can identify the other as −1. Figure 7.14 illustrates the situation that results.

Figure 7.15 explores some of the graphical variations you can achieve when you employ absolute values. You can shift the vertex of the intersecting lines left or right on the x axis or up and down on the y axis, and you can vary the angle of the lines by increasing or decreasing the value of the slope. If you employ a negative slope, then you invert the lines.

Coding a Method for an Absolute Value

When you graph an absolute value, you must accommodate both its negative and positive manifestations. Positive and negative numbers map the two possible distances of the absolute value from zero or the point at which the mapping of the distance begins.

m(|x + h|) + k

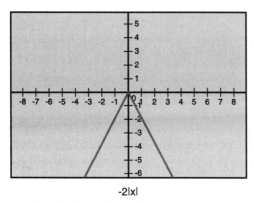

-2|x|

An absolute value provides you with
negative and positive slopes. A negative
slope inverts both slopes.

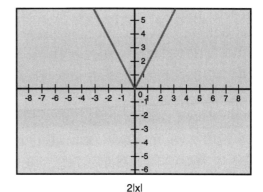

2|x|

An absolute value provides you with
negative and positive slopes.

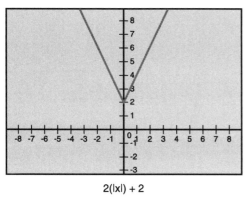

2(|x|) + 2

You can shift the graph up or down
on the y axis.

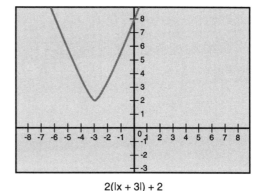

2(|x + 3|) + 2

In other respects, an absolute value
can be shifted right or left on the
x axis.

Figure 7.15
An equation that incorporates absolute values can be shifted and inverted.

With the abValues() method in the Functions class, you implement a method
that allows you to work with absolute values. Here is the code for the method:

```
// Translate a given value so that it has both positive
// and negative forms
public Values abValues(float item)
{
    return new Values(item, item * -1);
}
```

The abValues() method accepts one argument, item, of the float type. It calls the constructor of the Values struct and assigns values to it. To create the values, the method converts a negative value by multiplying the value assigned to item by −1. If the value of item is negative, then multiplication by −1 makes it positive. The returned value is of the Values type, so you return an object that stores the negative and positive versions of item. In this way you cover both manifestations of the absolute value of a given number.

To make it easier to work with absolute values, you enhance the definition of the Values struct in a way that does not adversely affect previously developed program functionality but at the same time makes it easier to comprehend and manipulate absolute values. Here is the new definition of the Values struct in the DataForm class:

```
public struct Values
{
    public float X, V1;
    public float Y, V2;
    // Two-value Constructor
    public Values(float xVal, float yVal)
    {
        X = xVal;
        Y = yVal;
        V1 = xVal;
        V2 = yVal;
    }
    // Extended constructor
    public Values(float xVal, float yVal, float v1, float v2)
    {
        X = xVal;
        Y = yVal;
        V1 = v1;
        V2 = v2;
    }

}
```

As extended, the Values struct now provides two additional fields. These two fields allow you to store two more values of the float type. In addition to adding two fields, you update the existing constructor so that it sets the values of the two new fields using the values you provide to the constructor for the X and Y fields. Initializing the fields in this way at this point provides a convenience measure.

You use the constructor in an exclusive way with either the X and Y or V1 and V2 fields as your primary pairs. In other words, the value you assign to X you also assign to V1. The value you assign to Y, you also assign to V2. This activity makes it possible to use the names of fields to "interpret" the same field values in different ways. You use this approach in your implementation of the showData() method in the CartForm class.

In addition, you add a constructor that takes four arguments. This constructor receives no use in the current version of the Code Lab, but it is in place for future use if you want to set all four fields when you create a Values object.

Note

> As an experiment, you can rewrite the runFunction() and showData() methods that deal with absolute values so that you use one Values object for each coordinate set rather than two.

Generating a Table

Although it represents a limited project, one use of the abValues() method might involve creating a table of values that shows you *x* and *y* values for a set of coordinates that includes an absolute value. Such a set of coordinates involves an *x* value that generates two *y* values. The implication is that you begin with |*x*| and then must process the two possibilities that arise from this as you process your data.

Accordingly, you revisit the runFunction() method in the DataForm class. Here is the code for the method:

```
// Create a table for absolute values
private void runFunction()
{
    Functions fset = new Functions();
    // Create an array of values for the domain
    float[] domain = { 60,    0,   50,
                      -60,    0,   50,
                        0,   -6,  -60,
                        0,   12,   70,
                      -60,  100,   70,
                       60,  100,   70};
    // Repeat the calculation for each item in the array
    displayTable("\n\t Number of coord sets "
            + domain.Length.ToString(), " ");
    for (int ctr = 0; ctr < domain.Length; ctr+=3)
```

```
        {
            coordSets.Add( new Values(domain[ctr], domain[ctr+1]) );
            coordSets.Add(fset.abValues( domain[ctr + 2] ) );
        }// end for
        displayTable("\n\t X or V1", "\t\t Y or V2");
}// end method
```

To create a table of values you can use to generate graphical representations of absolute values, you define the domain array so that it provides values in sets of three. The first two values of each set define *x* and *y* values for the vertex of a figure that represents an absolute value. The third coordinate represents an absolute value. In this respect, then, for the first set of coordinates for the domain array, you see these values:

60   0   50

Given this set of coordinates, you can interpret them as follows:

(60, 0) (| 50 | , {-50 and 50))

In this respect, then, the third number in each set represents an absolute value, so you must work with it in its positive and negative manifestations.

To accomplish this task, you create a for repetition statement that traverses the array in increments of 3. Increments of 3 allow you to work with the sets of values that characterize the domain array. The first two elements constitute literal values for the coordinate pair that defines the vertex of an angle. These you retrieve from the domain array using ctr and ctr+1 to identify indexes. Employing the retrieved values, you create a new instance of the Values struct and use the Add() method to assign it to the coordSets List collection.

Next, you attend to the generation of the two values that represent the positive and negative possibilities of the third term of the three-value set. Toward this end, you use the fset instance of the Functions class and call the abValues() method. To retrieve the number designated as an absolute value, you use ctr + 2 to identify the index of the number in the domain array.

You then have two Values objects stored sequentially in the coordSets array. Cleary, you could do things differently, using the four-argument constructor of the Values struct and assigning all the values to one Values object; but in this case, creating two objects in succession simplifies activities. Each two objects designate two coordinates of a line. For each line, you have two Values objects. The first of the Values objects designates the vertex of an angle (60.00, 0.00). The

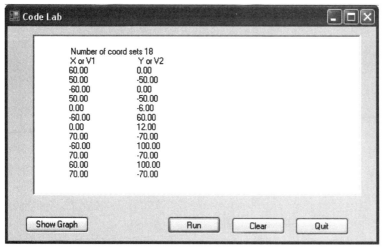

Figure 7.16
You make use of two Values objects for each graph of an absolute value.

second the end of a line you extend from the vertex (50.00, –50.00) or (–50.00, 50.00). In this way, if you follow the first column in Figure 7.16, you see that each set of vertex coordinates appears twice. On the other hand, the coordinates that accompany the vertexes are reversed. In this way, you anticipate the lines you draw using the positive and negative versions of the absolute value. (Figure 7.18 shows you the angles that result.)

Generating a Graph

To generate graphical representations of the data Figure 7.16 provides, you rewrite the showData() method in the CartForm class. To implement this method, you retrieve the values from the two Values objects you created in the DataForm class. You then extract the values from these objects to use as arguments to the plotLinear() method. Here is the code for the showData() method:

```
//Graph lines to show the vertices of
//lines that are defined using absolute values
   public void showData(Graphics e)
   {
       String msg = "";
       DataForm tempForm = new DataForm();
       Values[] tempVals = tempForm.Vals.ToArray();

       for (int ctr = 0; ctr < tempVals.Length; ctr += 2)
```

```
    {
    // Line to the right
        msg = cSys.plotLinear(e, tempVals[ctr].X / XSCALE,
                                tempVals[ctr].Y / XSCALE,
                                tempVals[ctr + 1].V1 / XSCALE
                                    + tempVals[ctr].V1 / XSCALE,
                                tempVals[ctr + 1].V1 / XSCALE);
        // Line to the left
        msg = cSys.plotLinear(e, tempVals[ctr].X / XSCALE,
                                tempVals[ctr].Y / XSCALE,
                                tempVals[ctr + 1].V2 / XSCALE
                                    + tempVals[ctr].V1 / XSCALE,
                                tempVals[ctr + 1].V1 / XSCALE );
        }// end for
        showData(ref tempVals);
}// end method
```

To retrieve the values from the Vals (or coordSets) collection, you create an instance of the DataForm class and use the Vals property in conjunction with a call to the ToArray() method to copy the Values objects in the collection to an array of the Values type. You then implement a for repetition statement that includes a counter that increases in increments of 2.

Recall that the plotLinear() method takes five arguments. The first argument is a reference to a Graphics object, which allows you to refresh graphical images as you draw them. The second and third arguments define a coordinate pair for one end of a line. The fourth and fifth arguments define a coordinate pair for the other end of a line.

With each repetition of the for block, you draw two lines. To draw the two lines, you call the plotLinear() method twice. With each call, you employ the first Values object of each vertex to establish the vertex (maximum or minimum) end of the two lines you need to draw. To retrieve these values, you provide the current value of the ctr variable to identify the index of the Values object you want to retrieve, and then access the X and Y fields of the Values object to retrieve the x and y coordinate values.

For the last set of coordinate pairs for each line, you retrieve values from the second of the two Values objects. The only difference between the two lines in this respect is that the coordinate pair that defines the lines are mirrored. To make this possible, you access the values you have stored in the second of the two Values objects.

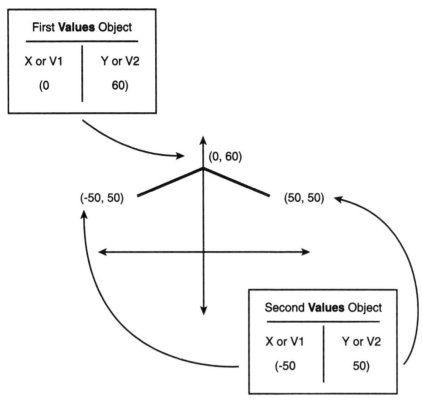

Figure 7.17
The Values object provides you with fields that you can use to interpret data in different ways.

The constructor for the Values object allows you to assign the same values to the X and V1 fields. This also applies to the Y and V2 fields. This makes it possible, then, to access the numbers you have assigned to the Values object as V1 and V2, as well as X and Y. V1 might be read, then, as "version 1" of the absolute value. V2 might be read as "version 2" of the absolute value.

As Figure 7.17 shows, given this situation, when you access the Values objects, in the first Values object, you retrieve a coordinate set for the vertex (0, 60). In the second Values object, you find negative and positive versions of the same number that you can use to plot the coordinates of a given absolute value. In Figure 7.17, you see 50. If x equals 50, and x is an absolute value, then it generates two coordinate sets (50, –50) and (50, 50).

When you generate lines, your first call to plotLinear() generates a line that rises or falls to the right. The second call to plotLinear() generates a line that rises or falls to the left. When you retrieve the values from the second object, you do so

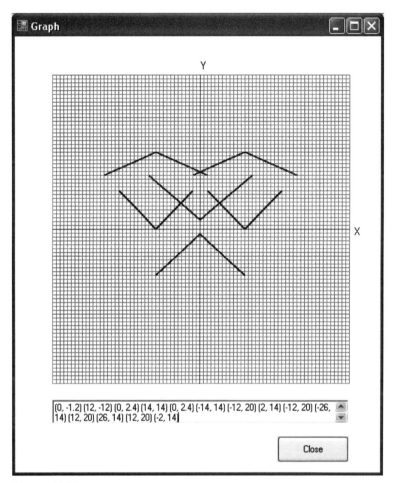

Figure 7.18
Absolute values allow you to generate symmetrical figures.

twice. As you do so, you reverse the order of the values to account for both of the points you need to plot the absolute values. For this reason, you see only one change in the two calls to plotLinear(). In the second call, rather than access the V1 field, you access the V2 field.

Figure 7.18 illustrates the vertices you create using absolute values. To allow for vertical and horizontal shifting of the figures you generate, you add the Values of the V1 field to itself and the V2 field. In this way, you shift both coordinates relative to the vertex. All of the vertices in Figure 7.18 have been shifted in this manner. As the later section titled "Reference Arguments" discusses, you employ the same approach to create strings to show the coordinate in the text area.

Translating Coordinate Values

To understand the values shown in Figure 7.18, comment out all of the numbers in the domain array definition in the DataForm class except the first line:

```
float[] domain = { 60,    0,   50,
          // -60,    0,   50,
          //   0,   -6,  -60,
          //   0,   12,   70,
          // -60,  100,   70,
          //  60,  100,   70
                        };
```

This leaves you with this set of values, which you store in the coordSets array:

60, 0, 50

Used alone, you arrive at this figure when you generate a graph:

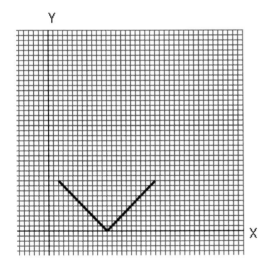

Additionally, you see the following values in the text area below the graph:

(12, 0) (22, 10) (12, 0) (2, 10)

To trace the path from the coordSets values to the graph, you begin with the returned values of the abValues() method in the Functions class. This method allows you to transform the original set of three values into a set of four:

(60, 0)(50, -50)

Given this set of values, you translate the position of the vertex 60 units to the right on the *x* axis. This gives you the starting values for the coordinates for the two lines:

(60, 0) (50 + 60) (60, 0) (-50 + 60)

or

(60, 0) (110) (60, 0) (10)

If you examine the first few lines of the CartForm class, you see that the XSCALE variable is set to 5, and this is the scale used in this instance to scale all the coordinates. Given this scaling of values, then, the values are as follows:

(60/5, 0/5) (110/5) (60/5, 0/5) (10/5)

(12, 0) (22) (12, 0) (2)

When you then consider the coordinates as plotted, you simply insert the adjusted values for the *y* axis to see the result, which is as follows:

(12, 0) (22, 10) (12, 0) (2, 10)

Moving from left to right, the points plotted are not in the order shown. Here is how they are used to plot the lines:

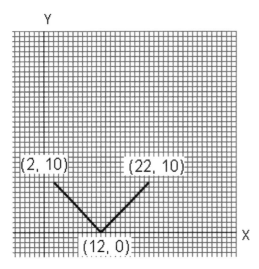

Reference Arguments

To display the coordinate values for the vertices shown in Figure 7.18, you create an overloaded version of the showData() method that takes a reference to an array of the Values type as an argument. Here is the call to the overloaded version of the showData() method. You make this call within the primary showData() method. The argument allows you to distinguish the overloaded from the primary version.

```
showData(ref tempVals);
```

There are two basic ways to pass arguments to functions. One involves all of the arguments in all of the methods you have implemented to this point in this book. You have passed arguments by values. When you pass an argument by a value, you make a copy of the argument when you pass it. The copy is temporary. It lasts only as long as your program is processing the lines of code in your method.

The second way to implement arguments involves a reference. When you use a reference, you do not create a copy of the object you are using as an argument. Instead, you are more or less directing the method to the place in memory in which the argument you are using resides. Figure 7.19 illustrates how values and references work as arguments to methods.

When you pass an object such as an array by a value, your program has to copy the entire array to a temporary argument. This can take time. It also uses up additional memory. To overcome this problem, you can use a reference. To pass

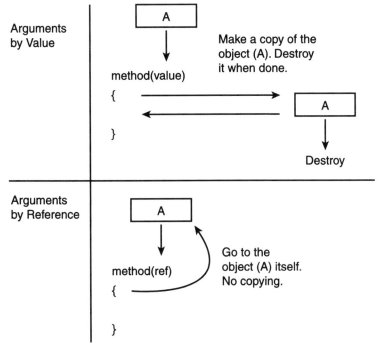

Figure 7.19
You can save time and space if you pass arrays as references instead of copying them.

an argument as a reference, you use the keyword `ref` prior to the formal definition of the argument. Here is the code for the overloaded version of the
`showData()` method that employs a reference to an array:

```
// Overload the method so you can pass a reference to
// an array and display absolute value coordinates
public void showData(ref Values[] vals)
{
    richTextBox1.Clear();
    for (int ctr = 0; ctr < vals.Length; ctr += 2)
    {
        //Line to the right
        richTextBox1.AppendText(" ("
                    + (vals [ctr].X / XSCALE).ToString() + ", "
                    + (vals [ctr].Y / XSCALE).ToString()
                    + ") ("
                    + (vals [ctr + 1].V1 / XSCALE
                    + vals [ctr].X / XSCALE).ToString() + ", "
                    + (vals [ctr + 1].V1 / XSCALE).ToString() + ")");
        richTextBox1.AppendText(" ("
                    + (vals [ctr].X / XSCALE).ToString() + ", "
                    + (vals [ctr].Y / XSCALE).ToString()
                    + ") ("
                    + (vals [ctr + 1].V2 / XSCALE
                    + vals [ctr].V1 / XSCALE).ToString() + ", "
                    + (vals [ctr + 1].V1 / XSCALE).ToString() + ")");
    }// end for
}// end method
```

Passing the `tempVals` argument as a reference allows you to use the collection
itself just as you would a copy of the collection. One difference is important,
however. Your changes to the object you pass to your method affect the original
object. In other words, the `vals` argument in the overloaded version of the
`showData()` method takes you directly to the `tempVals` object. You work with the
original object itself.

In the overloaded form of the `showData()` method, you employ the `vals` reference
to the `tempVals` object to access the data you originally assigned to the
`coordSetsList` collection. You use this data to create text (string) objects that
provide you with the adjusted values of the coordinates as they appear the
Cartesian plane. These values have been scaled for the plane, so the values you see
depend on the scale settings you have designated.

Discontinuous Lines

Some functions generate values that are not continuous. Such functions are known as *bracket functions*. The values of such functions generate plagues of values. The basis of this exercise is a set of literal definitions of line segments. Each line segment conforms to the same model. The model assumes the following form.

- To start a line segment, begin with x_n. To define the point that marks the beginning of the first line segments, you assign an arbitrary value to x. To determine the value of y in the coordinate pair, you use the equation $y = x - 1$.

- To end a line segment, you use the expression $x_n + 19$. The elevation remains at $x - 1$.

- For each line segment, beginning at x, to determine the starting point of the subsequent line, you can use the equation $x_{n+1} = x_n + 10$.

Figure 7.20 illustrates the progression of the segments.

Writing the Method

To write a method that can generate a set of values that describe the line segments shown in Figure 7.20, you create the makeSegment() method in the Functions

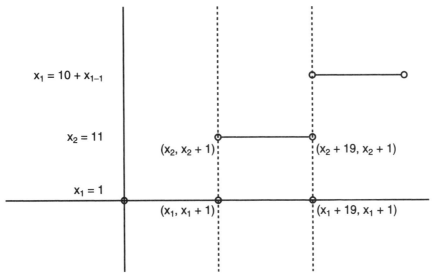

Figure 7.20
Discontinuous lines can move in steps.

class. This method takes one value of the float type. You then make use of the overloaded constructor for the Values struct to generate the values that describe each line segment. You accomplish this by inserting an expression in each of the positions the constructor provides for its fields. For the value of the X field, you use the argument x. For the value of the Y field, you use the expression x − 1F. For the value of the V1 field, you use x + 19F. For the value of the final field, you again use x − 1F. You then return the Values object you have created. Here is the code for the makeSegment() method:

```
// Take a sequence of values and make them discontinuous
// Creates a segment using value of x
public Values makeSegment(float x)
{
    Values segment = new Values(x, x - 1F, x + 19F, x - 1F);
    return segment;
}
```

Generating a Table

To generate a table of values using the makeSegment() method, you rewrite the runFunction() method in the DataForm class. To generate a set of values, you use the domain array and a for repetition statement. The values you assign to the domain array begin at 1 and then progress in steps of 10 until you reach 51.

To generate Values objects that hold the coordinate sets that define the segments, you traverse the domain array and call the makeSegment() method for each value in the array. The Values objects that result you assign to the coordSets collection. Here is the code for the rewritten runFunction() method:

```
// Create a discontinuous function
private void runFunction()
{
    Functions fset = new Functions();
    // Create an array of values for the domain
    float[] domain = { 1, 11, 21, 31, 41, 51};
    // Repeat the calculation for each item in the array
    displayTable("\n\t Number of segments "
            + domain.Length.ToString(), " ");
```

```
    for (int ctr = 0; ctr < domain.Length; ctr++)
    {
        Values tempVal = fset.makeSegment(domain[ctr]);
        coordSets.Add(tempVal);
    } end for
    // Overloaded version for 4 values
    displayTable("\n\t X \t\t Y", "\t V1 \t\t V2", true);
}// end method
```

To display the values of the array, you make use of yet another overloaded version of the displayTable() method. This time around, you make a minor change to a previously developed version to include an if selection block. If the user provides a third argument to the method of true, then the method creates four columns instead of two. You can use the first two arguments to provide text for the column headings. This overloaded version of the method uses the V1 and V1 fields of the Values struct. Here are lines from the method that prove central in this activity:

```
if (show == true)
{
    displayArea.AppendText("\t " + valSet.V1.ToString("0.00")
                            + "\t\t"
                            + valSet.V2.ToString("0.00"));
}
```

The show variable is taken from the argument list of the method. It is of the bool type. If true, then you see the data from the V1 and V2 fields. You retrieve these values by traversing the coordSets array. The variable valSet represents an instance of a Values item retrieved from the array. Figure 7.21 illustrates the output of the method.

Generating a Graph

To graph the discontinuous lines, you create a version of the showData() method that retrieves the Values objects you have assigned to the Vals (coordSets) collection. You use a foreach statement to retrieve the values and use them as

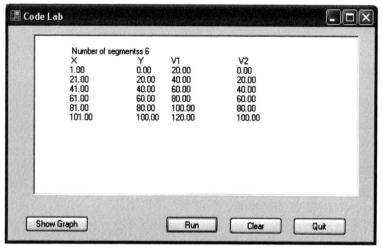

Figure 7.21
Discontinuous functions do not allow overlapping lines.

arguments in the plotLinear() method. To scale the values, you us the XSCALE field, which you set to a value of 5.

```
// Graphing a discontinuous output
// Set XSCALE and YSCALE - -
// YSCALE 25, XSCALE 5, LOCALGRID 5
public void showData(Graphics e)
{
    String msg = "";
    DataForm tempForm = new DataForm();
    foreach( Values tempVals in tempForm.Vals)
    {
        msg = cSys.plotLinear(e, tempVals.X / XSCALE,
                              tempVals.Y / XSCALE,
                              tempVals.V1 / XSCALE ,
                              tempVals.V2 / XSCALE);
    }
    richTextBox1.Clear();
    richTextBox1.AppendText("\n Coords: " + msg);
    // Overloaded version for 4 values
    showData(false, true);
}
```

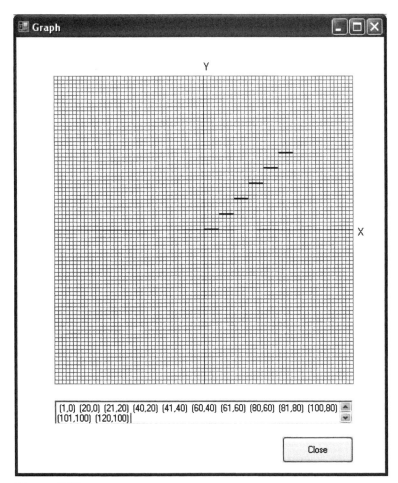

Figure 7.22
The graph shows lines that do not overlap.

You call an overloaded version of the showData() method so that you can display the numbers assigned to each of the four fields of the Values struct. Figure 7.22 illustrates the results.

Conclusion

In this chapter, you have explored how to work with quadratic equations and the methods you can use to create graphs of parabolas. In addition, you explored graphs for absolute values and discontinuous functions. The features of quadratic equations and equations involving absolute values share several features.

When you write methods to generate tabular values and graphs for such equations, you can make use of common features to make your work easier. Investigating common features also allows you to investigate ways to extend existing code in new directions. One such direction encompasses the `Values` data type. By adding two more fields to this struct, you are able to use it to store the positive and negative values associated with an absolute value and to conveniently generate lines that represent discontinuous functional relationships.

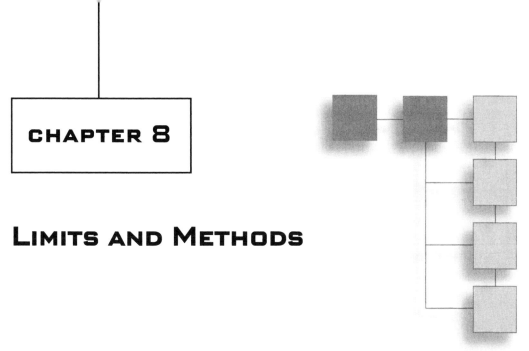

CHAPTER 8

LIMITS AND METHODS

In this chapter, you work extensively with code that allows you to graph limits. Limits can involve almost any function. In some cases, the functions generate values that approach a given limit from the right. In other cases, the functions generate values that approach a given limit from the left. In still other cases, the values generated approach a given limit from both directions, and this is known as an unrestricted limit. When a function generates values that approach a definitive point, the limit is finite. Other functions generate values that diminish or increase infinitely. The topics dealt with in this chapter include the following:

- How limits represent intervals of values

- Programming a method to generate a graph that represents a limit

- Dealing with a set of functions

- Limits to the right and limits to the left

- Inclusive and exclusive plotting

- Approaches to infinity

Talk of Limits

When you examine the thinking that underlies calculus, one of the first notions that comes to mind involves the correspondence between the inputs and outputs of functions. The preceding chapters have returned to this theme time and time again, and you have used a multitude of C# methods to implement functions so that you can produce tabular and graphical outputs of functions. Such activities allow you to experiment with the correspondences between the domain (the starting values) and the range (the output values) of functions.

Calculus provides you with a way to formally investigate how range values change. At the basis of much of this activity is the notion that when you apply a function to a given domain of values, the values you generate change in a given way. In some cases, the values you generate increase. In other instances, they decrease. Whether they increase or decrease, however, you can view their values as approaching a specific maximum or minimum. The point that marks the minimum or maximum value is called a *limit*. Experimentation with limits leads to a way to understand the derivatives of functions.

Programming to Define a Limit

To gain a basic idea of what a limit is about, consider a situation in which you work with a linear equation. Here is such an equation:

$$f(x) = 3x + 2$$

You employ this function to generate the line that Figure 8.2 illustrates. This equation constitutes a standard linear equation of the type *mx* + *b*. It is a linear equation. It also generates a continuous line. To program the equation for use in the Lab, you implement the showLimit() method in the Functions class. Here is the code for the method:

```
// From the Functions class
public float limitValues(float point)
{
    return 3.0F * point + 2.0F;
}
```

To call this method in the DataForm class, you define the domain array with a set of values ranging from 1 to 13. Here is the code from the runFunction() method in the DataForm class in which you define the domain array.

```
/Generate values to show a limit
    private void runFunction()
    {
```

```
Functions fset = new Functions();
// Create an array of values for the domain
float[] domain = { 1.0F, 2.0F, 3.0F, 4.0F, 5.9F, 6.0F,
                   6.1F, 7.0F, 8.0f, 9.0F, 10.0F, 12.0F};
// Repeat the calculation for each item in the array
for (int ctr = 0; ctr < domain.Length; ctr++)
{
    coordSets.Add(new Values((float)domain[ctr],
                  (float)fset.limitValues(domain[ctr])));
}
// displayTable("\n\t  X ", "\t\t  Y");
// Show the values in descending order
displayTableReverse("\n\t  X ", "\t\t  Y", false);
}//end method
```

Figure 8.1 illustrates the output of the runFunction() method as implemented for the limitValues() method. To generate the values, use a for repetition statement and call the limitValues() method iteratively for each value you have assigned to the domain array. You assign the Values pairs to the coordSets collection. You call the displayTableDescending() method to display the values of the array in reverse. Implementation of the displayTableDescending() method involves assigning the Values pairs of the coordSets collection to an array and then traversing the array backward. The values are generated by *x* for *y* as you descend from 12.00 to 1.00.

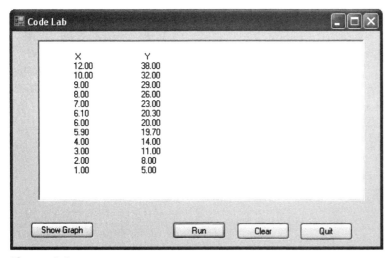

Figure 8.1
Use the Lab to see the values you generate using the function.

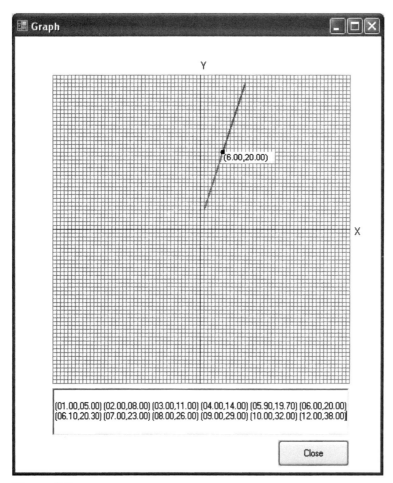

Figure 8.2
A graph of $f(x) = 3x + 2$.

Figure 8.2 depicts a graph of $f(x) = 3x + 2$. To plot the equation, you modify the showData() method in the CartForm class. Implementation of this method proceeds in three general phases, which correspond in part to the conceptual framework that characterizes limits. Here is the code for the showData() method in the CartForm class:

```
// Set XSCALE and YSCALE - -
// YSCALE 1, XSCALE 1, LOCALGRID 5
// Explore a limit
public void showData(Graphics e)
{
// #1
```

```
float LIMIT = 6.0F;
float ABOVE = LIMIT + 0.1F,
      BELOW = LIMIT - 0.1F ;
DataForm tempForm = new DataForm();
Values[] tempVals = tempForm.Vals.ToArray();
    // #2 The line moves toward 6 from the lowest number
    for (int itr = 0; itr < tempVals.Length-1; itr += 1)
    {
        if (tempVals[itr].X > BELOW && tempVals[itr].X < ABOVE)
        {
            break;
        }
        cSys.plotLinear(e, Color.Chocolate, tempVals[itr].X,
                          tempVals[itr].Y ,
                          tempVals[itr + 1].X ,
                          tempVals[itr + 1].Y );
    }// end for
    // #3 The line moves toward 6 from the lowest number
    for (int itr = tempVals.Length-1; itr > 0; itr -= 1)
    {
        if (tempVals[itr].X > BELOW && tempVals[itr].X < ABOVE)
        {
            cSys.drawCoordinates(e, tempVals[itr].X * LOCALGRID,
                    tempVals[itr].Y * LOCALGRID, LOCALGRID);
            cSys.plotPoint(e, tempVals[itr].X, tempVals[itr].Y);
            break;
        }// end if
        cSys.plotLinear(e, Color.Green, tempVals[itr].X,
                          tempVals[itr].Y,
                          tempVals[itr - 1].X,
                          tempVals[itr - 1].Y);
        // The limit is not graphed
    }// end for
    showData(true);
}// end method
```

In the first line of the showData() method, you define a variable of the float type named LIMIT. To this variable you assign a value of 6.00F. The value designates a limit. In addition, you define two other variables. One is called ABOVE, and you assign a value of 6.00 + 0.1 to it. This value lies slightly above the limit. The other variable is called BELOW, and to it you assign a value of 6.00 − 0.1. This value lies slightly below the limit.

You then make use of the ABOVE and BELOW variables to control how you traverse the tempVals array to retrieve coordinate sets to draw lines. To accomplish this, you employ two for repetition blocks. In one of the blocks, you start at the highest index of the array and decrement until you reach the limit. In the other, you start at the lowest index of the array and increment until you reach the limit.

In both repetition blocks, you call the plotLinear() method to draw lines. As Figure 8.2 reveals, these lines are of different colors. If you compile and run the Lab application for this chapter, you see that the lower part of the line is brown while the upper part is green. (The book shows slightly different shades of gray.) The upper portion of the line represents *descending* values of x and y. The lower portion represents *ascending* values of x and y.

To control the coordinate pairs you access as you draw the graph, you use subsets of the coordinates in the tempVals array to draw each portion of the graph. Toward this end, in the lines trailing comment #2, for the first of the for blocks you use an if selection statement to detect the limit. To test for the limit, you successively use the counter (itr) to access the X field of each coordinate pair in the tempVals array. If you detect the limit, then you invoke the break keyword to exit the for block.

To create the selection statement, you use a compounded Boolean expression. Both selection statements employ the same expression. It reads this way:

```
tempVals[itr].X > BELOW && tempVals[itr].X < ABOVE
```

With this expression, you identify the limit value without actually naming it. Such a procedure reflects the activities involved in working with limits because a limit is a number that you move toward in your operations but do not, in fact, reach. Since the value of BELOW lies 0.1 below the limit and the value of ABOVE lies 0.1 above the limit, the expression excludes the value of the x coordinate that equals the value assigned to the LIMIT variable.

With each iteration of the for block, you call the plotLinear() method to draw a segment of the line. For the block associated with comment #2, you begin at (1.00, 6.00). As the values increase, you draw the line and define its color using a Pen object associated with the Chocolate (brown) value. When the selection statement determines that the limit has been reached, then you invoke the break keyword to force the action of the for block to terminate and stop the drawing of the line.

In the lines associated with comment #3, you implement a second for repetition statement that performs actions similar to those performed by the first. Instead of incrementing the counter, however, you decrement it. As depicted in Figure 8.2, as the count in the second block decreases, you draw the upper line of the graph. To color the line green, you supply the plotLinear() method with a Pen object you define using the Green Color value.

As Figure 8.2 illustrates, you also plot a point and the coordinate values that define the point. The point is the limit. The selection statement tests true when the value of the X field of the coordinate pair you access in the tempVals array equals the value of the point. You then use the X field value and its complementary Y field value to supply as arguments to the plotPoint() method. You also use this coordinate pair to call the drawCoordinates() method. This method paints the coordinate pair in a white rectangle adjacent to the plotted point.

New and Overloaded Methods

In this chapter, you add the drawRectangle(), drawCoordinates(), and drawLine() methods to the CoordSystem class. These methods contain calls to members of the Graphics class that you have not seen before. The discussion of the drawCurve() method in Chapter 7 covers the details of implementation for the drawLine() method. In addition to the new methods, you also overload the drawLinear() method so that it offers an additional parameter. The additional parameter, of the Pen type, allows you to designate the color of the line the method draws.

You also overload the plotPoint() method in the CoordSystem class. In many of the graphs that show limits, you work with exclusive point values. Consider this set of domain definitions:

$$0 \le x \le 9$$
$$9 < x < 20$$

The first definition includes 0 and 9 in the domain. To show inclusion, you use a filled point on a number line. The second definition excludes 9 and 20. To show exclusion, you use hollow points on a number line. Here is how you represent the two domain definitions on a number line:

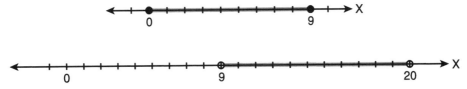

To accommodate the need for exclusive and inclusive points as you graph limits, you overload the plotPoint() method so that it can plot both exclusive and inclusive points. Here is the code for the overloaded method:

```
// Plot exclusive or inclusive points
    public String plotPoint(Graphics e,
                        float x, float y, bool typeOfPoint)
    {
```

```
// Adjust the value for the grid
float xPos = (x * GRID) + (CENTER - 3);
float yPos = CENTER - ((y * GRID) + 3);
// Draw the points
Pen linePen = new Pen(Color.DarkBlue, 1);
// Filled if true
if (typeOfPoint == true)
{
    e.FillEllipse(System.Drawing.Brushes.Black,
                            xPos, yPos, 6, 6);
}
else //Not filled
{
    e.DrawEllipse(linePen, xPos, yPos, 6, 6);
}
return "(" + x + "," + y + ")";
}
```

Overloading the method involves adding a fourth parameter (typeOfPoint) to the method's parameter list. The type of the parameter is bool. If you set the argument for the parameter to true, the if selection statement evaluates to true, and the flow of the program then calls the FillEllipse() method. This method renders an inclusive (filled) point. If you supply false as an argument, the flow of the program enters the else block and calls the DrawEllipse() method. This method renders an exclusive (hollow) point.

Formal Definitions

As Figure 8.3 illustrates, in one of its cycles, your method generates values starting at a high point and decreasing until they reach 6.1. Another cycle generates values that begin at a low point and increase in value until they reach 5.9. In both instances, you can discern a relationship between the way that the value of y increases or decreases and the way that the value of x increases or decreases. Drawing from terms characteristic of the language used to discuss limits, you can say that "As the value of x approaches 6.00, the value of y approaches 20.00." To state the case specifically, include the name of the function and say that "As x approaches 6.00, the output of the function $3x + 2$ approaches 20.00."

In formal terms, you express "As x approaches 6, y approaches 20" in this manner:

$$\lim_{x \to 6} f(x) = 20$$

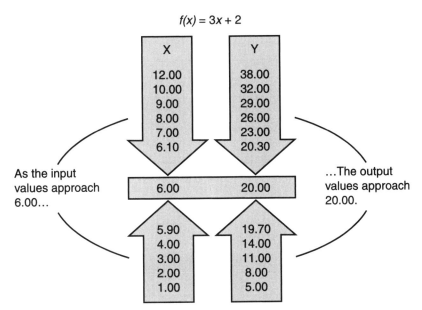

Figure 8.3
As the value of x approaches 6, the value the function generates approaches 20.

Later sections of this chapter qualify this statement, but for now the statement serves to represent the function $f(x) = 3x + 2$. When you express a limit in this way, you express what is known as an *unrestricted* limit. As Figures 8.2 and 8.3 reveal, the values the function generates are continuous and approach the limit from both directions (the green and the brown ends). This quality characterizes an unrestricted limit. More remains to be said on this topic when the discussion turns to limits from the right and limits from the left. For now, however, it is enough to understand only the general operation of a limit.

A limit is a way to characterize how the input and output of a function relate to each other. As Figure 8.4 shows, a limit allows you to relate a succession of input values to a succession of output values.

Limits and Bicycle Tires

To investigate how a limit applies to the input and output of a function, imagine returning to the bicycle tire factory the partners have set up. Business is good, and they now have contracted the services of a chemical engineer. The partners have taken an interest in developing different types of tires that address different consumer needs. They seek the services of an engineer to develop specialized tires to market to specific consumer groups.

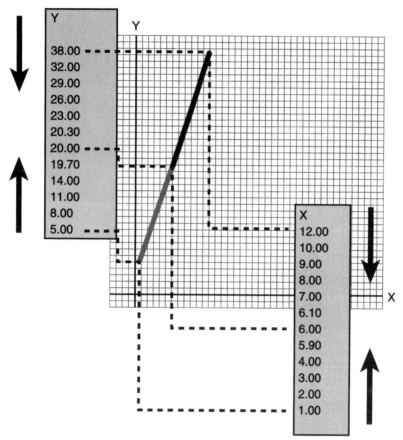

Figure 8.4
A limit defines a relationship between input and output.

The engineer informs the partners that they can add a chemical compound to the rubber of their tires to harden the tires. After mulling over this information, the partners decide that if they can harden the tires they produce, then they can appeal to the needs of at least three specific consumer groups. Figure 8.5 illustrates the three groups and their tire preferences.

One group, riders who ride long distances and often competitively, seek a tire that is hard and allows them to move fast. Such riders tend to carry no baggage. The weight they exert on the tire varies little. A second group consists of urban commuters who often wear backpacks or attach racks or satchels to their bicycles. The weight placed on the tire varies with the items they carry. Such bicyclists require a flexible, slower, and more durable tire.

At the extreme of flexibility lies the group that engages in off-road or trail bicycling. Such bicyclists use bicycles that are heavier, and they subject them to

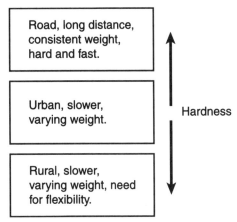

Figure 8.5
Hardened tires appeal to three specific consumer groups.

rough treatment. Such bicyclists seldom carry packs or attach satchels to their bicycles. Speed tends to be of little importance. The capacity to withstand grueling treatment is foremost.

The partners find that the hardened tires are suitable for commuting in urban areas or on paved surfaces. The harder the tire, the more suitable they find it is for long-distance riding. On the other hand, too much hardness for city dwellers is not productive, for varying loads mandate durability. In other respects, however, the softer the tire, the better it performs in off-road settings.

The engineer conducts some tests and after a time offers two equations to describe the behavior of the tires after the chemical has been added:

$$y = T(x) = \begin{cases} \dfrac{5}{81}\, x^2 + 1 & 0 \le x \le 9 \\ x - 3 & 9 < x < 20 \end{cases}$$

The equations show that if you add the chemical compound to the tire rubber, the effect is not constant. With reference to the line Figure 8.6 illustrates, when you add the compound, the hardness increases in a nonlinear way. When you reach 9 percent, however, the change in hardness becomes linear. On the other hand, as you near 20 percent, the hardness of the rubber continues to increase in a constant way. After 20, the rubber becomes unacceptably brittle, so the graph does not go beyond 20.

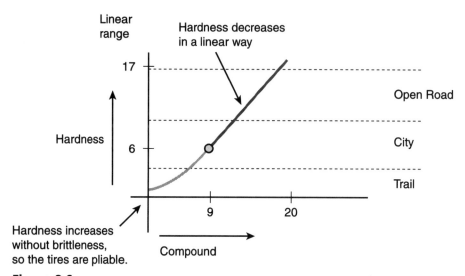

Figure 8.6
The limit establishes a point at which you can discern a change in the rate at which the compound affects the pliability of the rubber.

Together, the two ranges provide data that you can combine to form a single graphical representation of how the hardness of the tire increases as you add the chemical compound to the tire rubber. Using this graph, it becomes possible to make a generalization about how to produce tires for the three consumer groups.

In the most general terms, the partners can use the graphical representation they have of the data to begin assessing how to produce tires. The lower on the y axis their readings, the softer the tire. In light of this, they can then conclude that at a given point, they reach what they can view as the middle point of pliability. In the Trail range, the hardness of tires can be determined using a quadratic equation. When they move into the tires that are suitable for the city, however, the situation becomes more complex. When the composition of the rubber of a tire consists of less than or equal to 9 percent, the hardness of the tire must be calculated using a quadratic equation. When the composition of the tire includes more than 9 percent of the hardening compound, however, it is necessary to use a linear equation to calculate the hardness.

To determine how the hardness of the tire affects the experiences of those who use the tires, the partners conduct tests that involve having people ride and report their experiences. The absolute scale of hardness begins at 0 on the y axis and progresses to around 17. As for the tire rubber, the maximum amount of compound they can use is around 20 percent. They find after many such tests that the composition of tires for trail use must be less than roughly 4 on the *y* scale. City tires can be anywhere from around 4 to around 10 on the *y* scale. From 10 to 17 seems to be the best range for the road tires.

Coding the Functions

This exercise differs from those of previous chapters because here you program a single method that processes two functions. The functions work in tandem to allow you to generate values that you use to create a single line in a graph. To implement this method, you begin with the domains that you define for the two functions that characterize the hardness of the tire rubber after the compound has been added. Here is the set of equations and their domains:

$$y = T(x) = \begin{cases} \dfrac{5}{81}\, x^2 + 1 & 0 \le x \le 9 \\ x - 3 & 9 < x < 20 \end{cases}$$

You develop the `tireHardness()` method in the `Functions` class. To develop it, you anticipate three scenarios:

- Values that correspond to the first domain. These are the values defined by the domain $0 \le x \le 9$.

- Values that correspond to the second domain. These are the values defined by the domain $9 < x < 20$

- Values the fall outside the first and second domain. These are all values less than 0 or greater than or equal to 20.

Here is the code for the method:

```
// Generate data for tire hardness (in Functions.cs)
public float tireHardness(float point)
{
   float ret = 0;
   if (point <= 9 && point >= 0)
   {
      ret = ((5.0F * (point * point)) / 81.0F) + 1;
   }
   else if (9 < point && point < 20)
```

```
        {
          ret = point - 3.0F;
        }
        else
        {
          throw new System.ArgumentException(
                      "One or more of your domain values starting with "
                      + point.ToString() +
                      "\n is less than 0 or greater than or equal to 20.\n" +
                      "Check the values you set in DataForm.");
        }
        return ret;
}
```

To process the ranges for the two domains that are specific legitimate values, you use relational and Boolean operators to define the expression of selection statements. The significant difference between the two forms of expression lies in the fact that you must repeatedly specify the relationship you want to test. To define the first domain in C#, for example, you create a Boolean expression that joins to relational expressions: point <= 9 && point >= 0. If the point is both less than or equal to 9 and if the point is greater than or equal to 0, then the compound expression evaluates to true. The AND (&&) operator stipulates that both constituent expressions must be true if the compound expression is to be true.

The form of selection you employ to implement this method is known as a *cascading* selection structure. If the first selection expression finds that the value of the argument (point) is greater than or equal to 0 and less than or equal to 9, then the flow of the program enters the first block. After the statement in this block executes, the flow of the program skips the other two tests and goes to the next statement after the structure. If the value of the argument is greater than 9 and less than 20, then the flow of the program enters the second (else if) block. Again, after the statement the block contains is executed, the flow of the program exits the selection structure. If neither of the first two test statements proves true, then the flow of the program goes automatically to the default block and executes the statement you provide there.

This first block contains a quadratic equation. As in previous examples, you multiply the denominator of the fraction by the square of x prior to carrying out the division. To shift the value, you then add 1. You can replace the point * point approach to squaring the argument of the method with a call to the Math.Pow()

function, but if you do so, then you must cast the value the `Pow()` method returns. Here is the form your statement then assumes:

```
ret = ((5.0F * (float)Math.Pow(point,2.0)) / 81.0F) + 1;
```

The second selection statement processes a linear expression. To process this expression, you subtract the value of the argument from 3 and return the result.

The approach used to return results reflects a principle of structural programming. This principle requires that a method possess one point of return. In this instance, you calculate the value of `ret` in two places, but you return it in only one, at the end of the method.

To process argument values that fall outside the domains the two selection statements stipulate, you throw an exception of the `ArgumentException` type. The constructor for this exception allows you to include a customized body of text. As a courtesy to the user, you use the `ToString()` method to include the offending value in the string. As the discussion in Chapter 3 emphasizes, you now implement a `try. . .catch` block in the `DataForm` class to process the exceptions this method throws.

Generating a Table of Values

To generate a table of values for the tire data functions, you redevelop the `runFunction()` method in the `DataForm` class. While the approach you use to define the domain array follows the pattern previous examples establish, in this instance, you diverge from the standard implementation technique for the `runFunction()` method because you implement a `try. . .catch` block to process exceptions of the `ArgumentException` type that the `tireHardness()` method throws if you include in your data set values that rest outside the permitted domains. Here is the code for the method:

```
// Generate values for tire hardness (in CartForm.cs)
private void runFunction()
{
    Functions fset = new Functions();
    // Create an array of values for the domain
    // Some values commented out for variety
    float[] domain = { 0.0f, 1.0F, 2.0F, 3.0F, 4.0F, 5.9F,
                       6.0F, 6.1F, 7.0F, 8.9F, 8.9f,
```

```
                        9.0F, 9.1F, 11.0f,
                        //-11.1f,
                        12.0F, 13.0F, 14.0F,
                        15.0F, 16.0F, 17.0F, 18.0F, 19.0F,
                        // 19.1f, 19.2F, 19.3F, 19.4F,
                        // 19.7f, 19.8F,
                        19.9F, 19.99F};
    try
    {
       // Repeat the calculation for each item in the array
       for (int ctr = 0; ctr < domain.Length; ctr++)
       {
          coordSets.Add(new Values((float)domain[ctr],
                        (float)fset.tireHardness(domain[ctr])));
       }
       // displayTable("\n\t X ", "\t\t Y");
       displayTable("\n\t X ", "\t\t Y", false);
    }
    catch (System.ArgumentException ex)
    {
       MessageBox.Show(this, ex.Message.ToString(), "Error");
    }
}//end method
```

After defining the values of the domain array, you implement a try. . .catch block and include in the try block the code for the for repetition statement that generates the coordinate pairs you store in the coordSets collection. If you include a value outside the defined domains in your data set, then the tireHardness() method throws an exception, and the action of the runFunction() method terminates. Prior to terminating, however, it allows you to call the MessageBox.Show() method, which constructs a modal dialog.

The first argument to the Show() method identifies the parent form. You supply the this keyword to designate the DataForm form. For the second argument, you access the Message field of the ArgumentException object to retrieve your customized message. For the third message, you provide a title for the dialog, "Invalid Domain Value." To test the error processing, remove the comment from the -11.1F value that you use to define the domain array. When you click the Run button after compiling, you see the dialog Figure 8.7 illustrates.

With this set of methods, you can enter as many values as you want to generate a graph. The use of two decimal places allows you to use test values such as 8.99

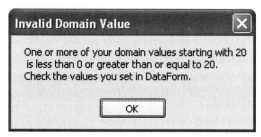

Figure 8.7
The exception generates a modal dialog.

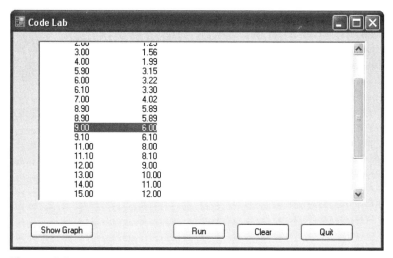

Figure 8.8
You can include any number of values within the defined domains.

and 9.01, which allow you to gain a greater sense of what a limit involves. A limit is a number you can approach infinitely. You approach but do not actually arrive at the limit. Figure 8.8 provides a view of some of the values you use as you define the domain for the functions relating to tire hardness. The darkened value is the limit.

Generating a Graphical Representation

You redevelop the showData() method in the CartForm class to generate the graph Figure 8.6 features. This implementation of the method proves to be more challenging than other implementations of the showData() method because you work with two sets of data that you retrieve from the Vals array, based on the definitions of domains that the equations for the tire-hardening compound provide. To separate the domains, you begin by ascertaining the total number of coordinate pairs you have to work with. You then traverse the Vals array to find the pair that contains the limit. You then create two new arrays and store the values from pairs that lie above the limit in one array and the values from the pairs that lie below the limit in the remaining array. You then use the two arrays as arguments to the drawCurve() method to graph the values.

Note

Much of the development of the showData() method has received attention in the previous section. However, because the method involves refining the approach used to accessing specific sets of values in the Vals (or coordSets) collection, the code in the project folder for this chapter contains several lines that are not shown in the book. These lines allow you to view information about the arrays you use to generate the graphs. You can employ these lines to help with your own development efforts. To view the output of the test code, change the argument of the overloaded version of the showData() method that appears on the final line of the primary showData() method so that its argument is false rather than true.

Here is the code for the showData() method you use to graph the data for the hardness of rubber relative to the amount of hardening compound used. This is a long method and clearly might be refactored into different methods to take care of the different phases of the graph.

```
// Set XSCALE and YSCALE - -
// YSCALE 1, XSCALE 1, LOCALGRID 8
// Explore data for tire hardness (in CartForm.cs)
public void showData(Graphics e)
{
    float LIMIT = 9.0F;
    float ABOVE = LIMIT + 0.01F, BELOW = LIMIT - 0.01F;
    DataForm tempForm = new DataForm();
    Values[] tempVals = tempForm.Vals.ToArray();
    // Number of coordinates
    int number = tempVals.Length;
    // #1 Find number coordinates up and including the limit
    number *= 2;
    int ctr = 0;
    while (tempVals[ctr].X <= LIMIT) { ctr++; }
    // Create arrays for the two sets coordinates
    int firstNumber = ctr * 2;
    float[] firstSet = new float[firstNumber];
    int secondNumber = number - firstNumber;
    float[] secondSet = new float[secondNumber];
```

```
ctr = 0;
// #2 Assign <= coordinates to the first array
foreach (Values coord in tempForm.Vals)
{
  if (ctr < firstNumber)
  {
      if (coord.X <= LIMIT)
      {
       firstSet[ctr] = coord.X / XSCALE;
       firstSet[ctr + 1] = coord.Y / YSCALE;
       ctr += 2;
      }// end inner if
  }// end if
}// end for
 ctr = 0;
// #3 Assign > coordinates to the second array
foreach (Values coord in tempForm.Vals)
{
  if (ctr < secondNumber)
  {
    if (coord.X > LIMIT)
    {
        secondSet[ctr] = coord.X / XSCALE;
        secondSet[ctr + 1] = coord.Y / YSCALE;
        ctr += 2;
    }// end if
  }// end if
}// end for

// #4 Draw the line and the curve
Pen cPen = new Pen(Color.Red, 2);
cSys.drawCurve(e, firstSet, cPen);
cPen = new Pen(Color.Blue, 2);
cSys.drawCurve(e, secondSet, cPen);

//#5 Plot and identify the point used for a limit
for (int itr = 0; itr < tempVals.Length - 1; itr += 1)
{
  if (tempVals[itr].X == LIMIT)
  {
    cSys.drawCoordinates(e, tempVals[itr].X * LOCALGRID,
                            tempVals[itr].Y * LOCALGRID,
                                          LOCALGRID);
```

```
            cSys.plotPoint(e, tempVals[itr].X, tempVals[itr].Y, true);
               break;
         }//end if
      }//end for
      // Plot the top point (or upper limit)
      cSys.drawCoordinates(e, 20 * LOCALGRID,
                           17 * LOCALGRID, LOCALGRID);
      cSys.plotPoint(e, 20, 17, false);
      // Change to false to see the test code output
      showData(true);
}//end method
```

In the lines associated with comment #1 in the version of the showData() method you use to generate a graph for the compound used to harden rubber, you define a variable to designate the limit (LIMIT). You then define the ABOVE variable with a value of LIMIT + 0.01 and the BELOW variable with a value of LIMIT - 0.01. Given this star, you then proceed to discover the number of coordinate pairs the Vals collection provides to you. To obtain this number, you first use the ToArray() method of the List class to copy the Values objects to the tempVals array. You then call the Length field associated with the tempVals array to obtain the number of pairs. You assign this value to the number variable, which is of the int type. To obtain the total number of coordinates, you multiply the value you have assigned to the number variable by 2. To accomplish this, you use a compound multiplication operator (number *= 2).

You then use a while repetition statement to traverse the Value items in the tempVals array. As you go, you compare the value stored in the X field of each Values object to determine whether it is less than or equal to the value assigned to LIMIT. Each time the statement evaluates to true, the while block repeats, and the value of the control, ctr, increases by one. In this way you learn the number of coordinate pairs less than or equal to LIMIT. This gives you the coordinates for the first domain. To obtain the total number of values the pairs contain, you multiply the value of ctr by 2 and assign it to the variable firstNumber.

To obtain the number of coordinate pairs in the second domain, you subtract the value you have assigned to the firstNumber variable from the value you have assigned to the number variable. You assign the difference to the secondNumber variable.

You can then use the firstNumber and secondNumber variables to define two new arrays, firstSet and secondSet. To populate these arrays, you set up two for repetition statements. For both of the for statements, you use the same approach to selecting values for assignment to the new arrays. You use a set of selection statements.

For the set of selection statements that follows comment #2, you assess whether the value of the counter for the block (ctr) is less than the length of the array. If this expression evaluates to true, you perform a second evaluation to discover whether the value of the X field of the current Values object is less than or equal to the value assigned to LIMIT. If this proves true, then you assign the values in the X and Y fields of the current Values object to successive positions in the firstSet array.

You repeat this routine for the secondSet array in the lines following comment #3. In this instance, you determine whether the counter is less than the number of elements created for the secondSet array. If this is true, then you determine whether the value assigned to the X field of the current Values item is less than the value assigned to LIMIT. If this is so, then you assign the values of the X and Y current Values object to successive positions in the secondSet array.

In the lines associated with comment #4, you use the firstSet and secondSet arrays to draw the lines Figure 8.9 illustrates. To draw the lines, you call the drawCurve() method of the CoordSystem class, which requires three arguments. As a first argument, you employ the graphics object to be used for drawing. For the second argument, you use one of the two arrays containing the coordinate values, firstSet or secondSet. For the final argument, you provide Pen objects. One you define using the Blue Color value. The other you define using the Red Color value.

You also call the drawCoordinates() and plotPoint() methods. These allow you to render points that correspond to the limits and to position rectangles next to the points in which you provide the coordinate values of the points. Figure 8.9 shows you the result.

Differing Forms of Limits

Some limits are characterized by values that both ascend to the limit and descend to the limit. The first example this chapter discusses concerns such a limit. It is called an unrestricted limit. Two other forms of limit also commonly occur. One is called a limit from the left. The other is called a limit from the right. The next few sections discuss such limits as they apply to the data for the addition of the hardening compound to tire rubber.

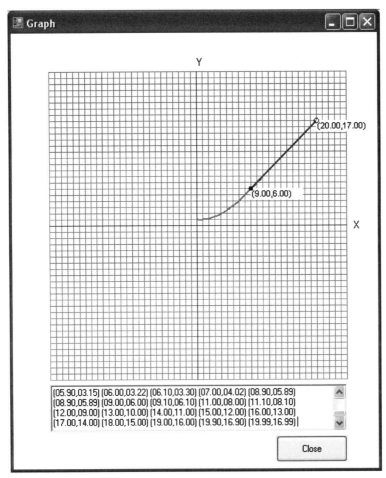

Figure 8.9
The graph shows the limit as a point of continuation and convergence.

Left-Hand Limits

As Figure 8.10 illustrates, as the amount of hardening compound tracked on the x axis approaches 9, the hardness of the tire tracked on the y axis approaches 6. The arrow in Figure 8.10 that points from the lower left toward the first point (9, 6) indicates a limit that is said to *approach from the left*. When you want to indicate that you are following the activity of the limit as it approaches 9 from the left, you use the subscript $x \to 9^-$. Here is the full form of the notation:

$$\lim_{x \to 9^-} f(x) = 6$$

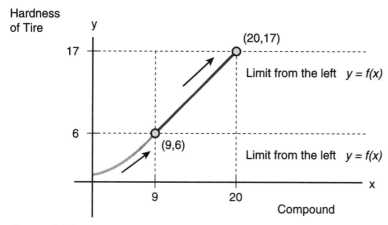

Figure 8.10
Limits can be viewed as approaching from the left.

When you programmed the `tireHardness()` method in the `Functions` class, you excluded the point (17, 20) from the primary data. The exclusion of the points constituted an expediency to make it easier to focus on the central limit. It remains, however, that this point provides important information. It shows when the addition of the chemical compound to the rubber begins to yield undesirable results. Above this point, the engineer has found that the addition of the compound to the rubber yields an unpredictable result. For this reason, you use an exclave point to indicate that 20 is not part of the domain. To express this upper limit mathematically, you use this expression:

$$\lim_{x \to 17^-} f(x) = 20$$

The expression reads, "As x approaches 17 from the left, y approaches 20."

Right-Hand Limits

If you comment out the line that plots the lower of the two lines Figure 8.10 illustrates and change the final arguments for the `plotPoint()` method so that they are false, you end up with the single line as shown in Figure 8.11. The point defined by (20.00, 17.00) remains exclusive, but in the new version of the graph, the lower of the two points (9.00, 6.00) also becomes exclusive.

The domain definition for this line is given by the expression $9 < x < 20$, and as Figure 8.12 shows, the values you generate using the equation $f(x) = x - 3$

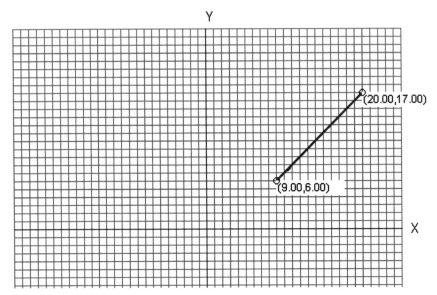

Figure 8.11
The two end points are exclusive.

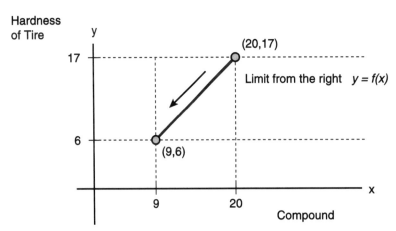

Figure 8.12
The values approach from the right.

approach the lower limit (9, 6) *from the right.* That the values descend to the lower limit is reflected in your use of the for statement that decremented the value of the counter when you implemented the code for the showData() method. The values you deal with decrease, but at the same time, the graph that results shows them approaching the limit from the right.

To show that you are dealing with a limit from the right, you employ the subscript $x \to 9^+$. Here is the full form of the notation:

$$\lim_{x \to 9^+} f(x) = 6$$

The expression reads, "As x approaches 9 from the from the right, y approaches 6."

Note

To modify the `showData()` method so that you can see only the top line as shown in Figure 8.10, you comment out the call to the `drawCurve()` method that directly follows comment #4. You also use `false` as a fourth argument in the call to the `plotPoint()` method that plots the point that the value of `LIMIT` defines. Here is the code:

```
Pen cPen = new Pen(Color.Red, 2);
// #4 First change
// Do not draw the lower line
// cSys.drawCurve(e, firstSet, cPen);
cPen = new Pen(Color.Blue, 2);
cSys.drawCurve(e, secondSet, cPen);

//#5 Plot and identify the point used for a limit
for (int itr = 0; itr < tempVals.Length - 1; itr += 1)
{
    if (tempVals[itr].X == LIMIT)
    {
        cSys.drawCoordinates(e, tempVals[itr].X * LOCALGRID,
                             tempVals[itr].Y * LOCALGRID,
                                            LOCALGRID);
        // # Second change
        // Use false as the final argument to make
        // the point exclusive
        cSys.plotPoint(e, tempVals[itr].X,
                       tempVals[itr].Y, false);
        break;
    }//end if
}//end for

cSys.drawCoordinates(e, 20 * LOCALGRID,
                              17 * LOCALGRID,
                                  LOCALGRID);
cSys.plotPoint(e, 20, 17, false);
// Change to false to see the test code output
showData(false);
```

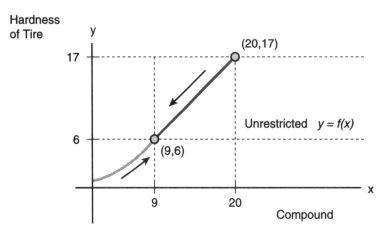

Figure 8.13
Values converge from both the left and the right when the limit is unrestricted.

Unrestricted Limits

As Figure 8.13 illustrates, when a limit can be approached from both the left and the right, then it is known as an unrestricted limit. The first example in this chapter represented an unrestricted limit. The limit defined by (9, 6) with respect to the two equations given for the tire data can be regarded as unrestricted. The tireHardness() method allows you to generate values from both the left and the right. The values that you generate converge consistently on the limit.

To show that you are dealing with an unrestricted limit, you employ the subscript $x \to 9$. Here is the full form of the notation:

$$\lim_{x \to 9} f(x) = 6$$

The expression reads, "As x approaches 9, y approaches 6."

Continuity

In the graph depicted in Figure 8.14, as you process the values of x that proceed from 0 to 9, the values you deal with constitute an *interval*. A limit is characterized by an interval of domain values. When the interval of domain values generates a continuous interval of range values, then you are dealing with a continuous function.

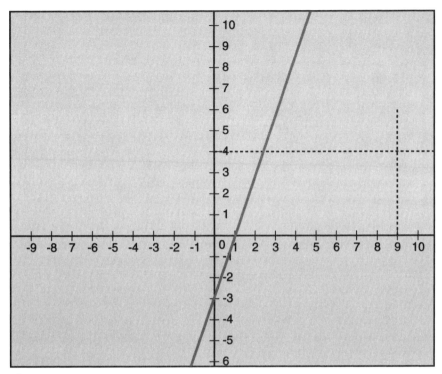

Figure 8.14
To determine a limit, solve for a given value.

If a function is continuous, then you can solve it for any given limit. To solve a function for its limit, you substitute the value you want to use as a limit. For example, consider this equation:

$$f(x) = 3x - 3$$

To express this equation as a limit, you use this approach:

$$\lim_{x \to 4} (3x - 3) = 3(4) - 3 = 9$$

The limit of x as x approaches 4, then, is 9. Figure 8.14 depicts the graph of this equation so that it shows the interval investigated and the limit.

What applies to limits also applies to quadratic equations. If the function is continuous, then you can use substitution to find the limit. Consider this equation:

$$\lim_{x \to 4} (x^2 - 2x^3 + x^2 - 8)$$

To arrive at the limit, you substitute into the equation the value you use to set the interval. Here is how you proceed:

$$= ((4)^2 - 2(4)^3 + (4)^2 - 8)$$
$$= (16 - 2(64) + 16 - 8)$$
$$= (16 - 128 + 16 - 8)$$
$$= -104$$

Infinity

Some limits involve functions that generate infinitely large or infinitely small values. When a limit involves infinitely large values, it assumes this form:

$$\lim_{x \to 0} f(x) = \infty$$

With this limit, the value of $f(x)$ grows larger without bound in a positive way as x approaches x_0. As examples of how this works, consider the equations $d(x) = 4/x$ and $d(x) = 4/x^2$. Figure 8.15 illustrates the graphs of these functions. As the value of x increases, the value of y decreases. The curve approaches but never merges with the y axis. When this happens, the line curve extending upward or downward and appearing to merge with the y axis is known as the *vertical asymptote*. The line extending to the right or left is known as the *horizontal asymptote*. Figure 8.15 illustrates the graphs of two functions that generate infinite positive values.

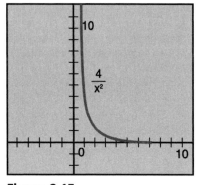
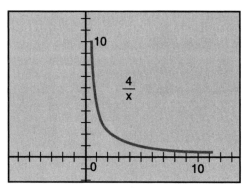

Figure 8.15
These functions generate values that create horizontal and vertical asymptotes.

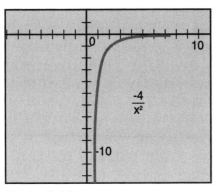 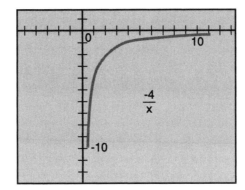

Figure 8.16
Some functions generate values infinitely in a negative direction.

You can carry out any number of operations to generate different types of graphs. When the limit involves infinitely negative values, it assumes this form:

$$\lim_{x \to 0} f(x) = -\infty$$

With this limit, the value of $f(x)$ grows larger without bounds in a negative way as x approaches 0. Figure 8.16 illustrates the graphs of two functions that generate infinite negative values.

When you are dealing with an equation in which the domain values generate range values that approach infinity, you can determine the limit by creating a table of values or by generating and inspecting a graphical version of the values the function generates.

You can deal with limits involving infinite values using an algebraic approach. Consider an expression that involves setting a limit that extends into infinity. To accomplish this, you use the subscript $x \to \infty$, which translates to "As x approaches infinity." As with the previous equations, a limit that approaches infinity might proceed in a positive or negative direction ($-\infty$ or ∞).

$$\lim_{x \to \infty} \left(\frac{4x - 1}{x} \right) = 3$$

With this equation, you can reason that as $x \to \infty$, $b/ax^n \to 0$ as long as the value of the integer n is positive.

Given this situation you can multiply by 1 in the form of $\frac{1/x}{1/x}$. When you multiply by 1 in this way, you are in effect dividing the numerator and the denominator by the value of x. Here is how you proceed:

$$\lim_{x \to \infty} \left(\frac{4x - 1}{x} \right)$$

$$= \lim_{x \to \infty} \left(\frac{4x - 1}{x} \right) \times \frac{\frac{1}{x}}{\frac{1}{x}}$$

$$= \lim_{x \to \infty} \frac{(4x - 1)\frac{1}{x}}{(x)\frac{1}{x}}$$

$$= \lim_{x \to \infty} \frac{(4x)\frac{1}{x} - (1)\frac{1}{x}}{1}$$

$$= \lim_{x \to \infty} \left(4x \frac{1}{x} \right) = 4 - 0 = 4$$

Conclusion

In this chapter, you have explored basic notions relating to limits and how you can implement methods to generate values for them and to create graphical representations of them. Much of your effort involved working with unrestricted limits, but you also worked with limits from the right and limits from the left. In addition to such explorations, you also touched briefly on limits involving infinite values. Writing methods to address limits involves considering that almost any function can be used to generate values that can be understood in the context of limits. A limit allows you to examine values as they approach a given point, and from this you can see that relationships between the succession of values you supply to a function and succession of values you generate using the function create a way to understand change.

To plot values relating to limits, you added several new methods. Among the methods you added were those that allow you to show inclusive and exclusive points. To implement a set of functions that shows the changing hardness of rubber used for bicycle tires, you developed a cascading selection structure based on the domains you defined for the constituent functions. To work with an array in which you stored values generated by different functions, you implemented code that automatically assessed intervals. Such activities put you in a position to investigate rates of change and other topics that lead from limits to differentiation.

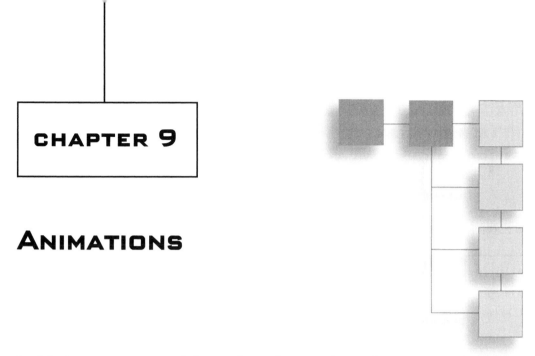

CHAPTER 9

ANIMATIONS

In this chapter, you extend the work you have performed in previous chapters to encompass building collections of data that allow you to implement animations. To create an animation, you create a new form, AniForm. To this form you add an object of the NoFlickerPanel type that you derive from the Panel class. To make it possible for the animation to occur, you create a timer. The timer allows you to control the activity of your infinite loop on the basis of system ticks. You then implement a number of different types of methods based on the output of linear equations that allow you to control the movement of a point in the panel. To create a path for the point, you generate data using methods you implement in the Functions class. You store this information in the coordSets collection, and then retrieve it as needed in function calls you make inside an infinite loop you set up in the AniForm class. Here are some of the topics covered in this chapter:

- Adding another form to the Code Lab application

- Using the Timer class to create a way of controlling animation

- Dealing with flicker using the NoFlickerPanel class

- Implementing code to sustain continuous animation

- Revising the CoordSystem method for animation effects

- Triggering and handling events

Graphs and Animation

Here is a procedure you can use to add a form for animation:

■ To add a form that you can use to work with animations, select Project > Add Windows Form. In the Templates area, click on the Windows Form icon. In the Name field, type AniForm, for "animation form." Click Okay.

■ Then select View > Full Screen. If you have not done so, click the tab for Aniform [Design].cs. Then select the Properties field of the AniForm form. In the Text field, type Animation. This changes the text you see in the title bar to Animation.

■ Then use the cursor to pull out the size of the AniForm form until it is approximately 590 by 640 pixels in size.

Adding a Text Area and Buttons

After selecting Toolbox from the View list, select RichTextBox. Drop the Rich-TextBox icon on the AniForm form.

In the Properties pane of the RichTextBox, leave the default of richTextBox1 as the name.

Then position the RichTextBox object in the lower part of the widow with its upper corner at roughly (35, 440). Press the Shift key and the left and down arrow keys to expand the panel until it is approximately 100 pixels high and 500 pixels wide (see Figure 9.2).

Then add two buttons to the bottom of the AniForm form. In the Name field of the Properties panel, name one button show. In the Text field for the show button, type Start. Name the other button close, and in the text field for the close button, type Close. Position the Start button at coordinate (140, 555). Position the Close button so that it is at (340, 555). See Figure 9.2.

Double-click the Close button. When the AniForm.cs code file opens, type a statement to close the form in the method. Here is the code:

```
private void close_Click(object sender, EventArgs e)

{
    this.Close()
}
```

Anticipating Development

To make it easier to work with the code in this chapter, before going further, you make a few changes and additions to the DataForm class that allows you to exert greater control over your work. Accordingly, you create a new layer of functions. Now, instead of rewriting the runFunction() method each time you want to work with a new set of data, you instead write a specialized method that contains the code for this activity, and then call it in a selection structure you implement in the runFunction() method. Here is the new code for the runFunction() method:

```
private void runFunction(int f)

{

  if(f == 1)
  {
      Function1();
      // Use with AniForm
  }
  else if(f == 2)
  {
      Function2();
      // Use with AniForm2
  }
  else if(f == 3)
  {
      Function3();
      // Use with AniForm3
  }
  else if(f == 4)
  {
      Function4();
      // Use with AniForm4
  }
  else
  {
      / /No action
  }
}
```

The code you start with allows you to work with all of the exercises in this chapter. Since you are in the process of developing the first of a series of animation forms, you start with option one.

You call the runFunction() method in the runButton_Click() method. To change the way the runFunction() operates, you comment out or remove comments from lines of code in this method. For starters, uncomment the first line, which invokes Function1(). This is a function you used in a previous chapter and allows you to experiment with your timer. Here is the code for the runButton_Click() method:

```
private void runButton_Click(object sender, EventArgs e)

    {
        runFunction(1); //Use with AniForm
        // runFunction(2); // Use with AniForm2
        // runFunction(3); // Use with AniForm3
        // runFunction(4); // Use with AniForm4
        // lines left out
    }
```

Invoking the Animation Form

In addition to working the runFunction() method, you also need to add a few lines elsewhere. To accomplish this, select the DataForm designer form. Then select View Toolbox and place a button in the DataForm window beneath the text area. For the Name field of the button in the Properties panel, type animation. For the Text field of the button, type Animate. Figure 9.1 illustrates the Lab with the new button.

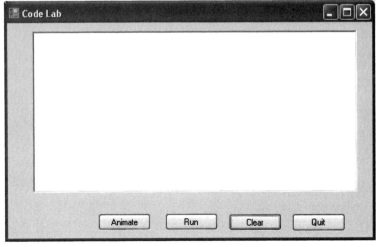

Figure 9.1
Add and activate a new button.

Click the new Animate button and to the `animation_Click()` method add code to create an instance of the Animation form. Here is the code:

```
private void animation_Click(object sender, EventArgs e)

{
    // if (run == true)
    // {
         AniForm aniForm = new AniForm();
         //lines left out
         aniForm.Activate();
         aniForm.Show();
    // }
    // else
    // {
    //     MessageBox.Show(this, "Click Run to "
    //                         + "generate a table first.");
    // }
}// end method
```

In the source file, you see several other constructors included. These constructors are for the versions of the AniForm class that you develop in this chapter. For now, you require the constructor for the first of the AniForm classes.

Also, for now, comment out the lines that create a selection statement. Leave only the three lines that create an instance of the AniForm class and that call the Activate() and Show() methods.

Compile the Lab project and click the Animate button. The Animation form opens, as shown in Figure 9.2. No data appears in the field. After inspecting the Animation form, click Close.

Adding a Timer

A timer is an object that allows processes to run in a form. To add a timer, click your AniForm [Design] tab so that the Animation form is active. Then click the Timer icon in the Toolbox. Drop the Timer icon into the Animation form.

When you drop the icon into the Animation form, you see a clock icon in the bottom of the work area. The timer is associated with the form. Figure 9.3 illustrates the Timer icon. The timer is named timer1 by default. Naming timers tends to make them easier to track, so do not change the default name.

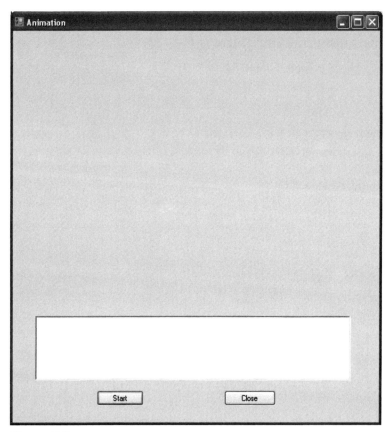

Figure 9.2
The Animation form provides a starting point for dynamic graphs.

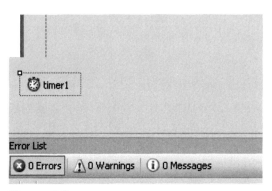

Figure 9.3
Select a timer from the Toolbox list and drop it in the panel area of the Animation form.

A `Timer` object is in essence a thread. A thread is like a swimming lane in your application. You can have several activities going on at one time by regulating them using different threads. A timer is an object that makes using a thread fairly easy.

Timer Methods

Each time you create a timer, the IDE crates a method that goes with it. If you create a `Timer` object named `timer1`, then the method for `timer1` is called `timer1_Tick()`. The method provides a place in which you can place code you want to execute at distinct intervals or for distinct duration separately from other processes you include in your application.

A timer is a component designed for forms. It initiates an event that you want to run at regular intervals. To make it so that the event runs at regular intervals, you call the code you want to run from within the method associated with the timer. You then can call the timer at any point in your class using the `Timer.Start()` method.

To stop a timer, you call the `Timer.Stop()` method. To control the rate at which the timer ticks, you assign a value to the `Intervals` property of the `Timer` class. The value you assign designates milliseconds. A millisecond is 1/1000 second, so if you want an event to occur every second, you use this notion:

```
timer1.Interval = 1000;
```

Set at 1000, the timer "ticks" every one second, and that regulates the speed at which an event unfolds in your application. You can increase the lengths of ticks indefinitely. The shortest interval of time you can use is 0001 (or just 1).

When you start a timer, it begins to run. Running means that it allows an event to occur at a given rate of ticks. Again, the rate is in milliseconds, starting at the current number of seconds from a given time. That time is the start of the current day.

After you start a timer, the timer runs indefinitely until you call the `Stop()` method. When you call the `Stop()` method, the timer is reset. If you start it again, it is initialized with a new start time and runs indefinitely from there, until you again call the `Stop()` method.

Setting Up the Basic Timer

To set up the timer for the Animation form, you can use a number of approaches. One is to start by resetting the timer when you create an instance of the AniForm class. To accomplish this, you call the Timer.Stop() method, as shown in Figure 9.4. This measure ensures that the timer resets when you open the form.

You then start the timer in a number of ways. You might start it when the form opens, calling the Timer.Start() method in the constructor. The approach used here is to allow you to be able to control the timer fairly closely, so you start it in the method associated with the Show Graph button. This allows you to restart the timer each time you click the button. You can set the interval for a timer immediately after you start it. To accomplish this, as mentioned previously, you can employ the Interval property.

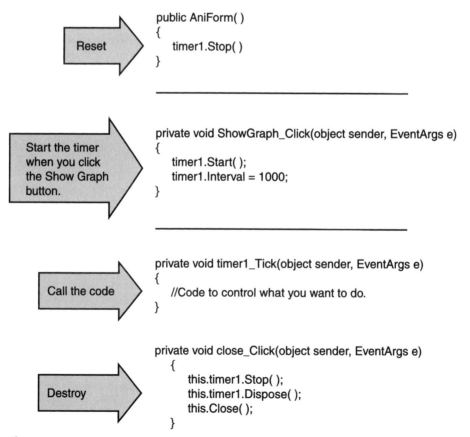

Figure 9.4
Start, Stop, Interval, and process activities are associated with a timer.

To associate actions with the timer, you place code in the Tick() method associated with the timer. As with the other activities, you can associate code with a timer either by placing it directly in the Tick() method or by calling methods that contain code. The methods that you call can contain calls to the Timer.Stop() method if the actions you invoke include a course of action that requires you to reset or terminate the timer.

When you are finished with your timer, you must destroy it. If you do not destroy it, then it can continue to run even after you close your form. If it continues to run, it can hang up your computer for an indefinite period, possibly causing your system to crash. To avoid such difficulties, you call the Stop() method to halt the action of the timer and then the Dispose() method to destroy the timer.

Attending to Preliminaries

Before you proceed with implementation of the code for the timer, review the general layout of the Lab program. Recall that the DataForm class contains the runFunction() method. For this exercise, you can use a method defined in Chapter 8, in which you called the limitValues() method. You give it a new name, however, Function1(), which you now call by using an argument of 1 for the revised version of the runFunction() method. That limitValues() method generates values for a set of limits. You assign the coordinate pair for that result to the coordSets List collection. This collection you access using the Vals property. Here is the code for the Function1() method in the DataForm class:

```
// Generate values to show a limit
private void Function1()
{
    Functions fset = new Functions();
    // Create an array of values for the domain
    float[] domain = { 1.0F, 2.0F, 3.0F, 4.0F, 5.9F, 6.0F,
                       6.1F, 7.0F, 8.0f, 9.0F, 10.0F, 12.0F};

    // Repeat the calculation for each item in the array
    for (int ctr = 0; ctr < domain.Length; ctr++)
    {
        coordSets.Add(new Values((float)domain[ctr],
                  (float)fset.limitValues(domain[ctr])));
    }
     displayTableDescending("\n\t X ", "\t\t Y", false);
}// end method
```

The data for the coordSet collection is generated when you click the runButton_ Click() method. Now you are interested in making use of this data in your Animation form. To use the data, you click the Animation button to invoke the Animation form.

To update the animation_Click () method so it can now acknowledge that you have generated data that can be used for animation activities, remove the comment from the code that checks the run flag. Here is how the code should appear:

```
private void animation_Click(object sender, EventArgs e)
  {
    if (run == true)
    {
        AniForm aniForm = new AniForm();
      // Lines left out
        aniForm.Activate();
        aniForm.Show();

    }
    else
    {
        MessageBox.Show(this, "Click Run to "
                            + "generate a table first.");
    }
  }// end method
```

Implementing the Code for the Timer Actions

Given that you have in place the DataForm code that generates a collection of values you can use as data for timer actions, you can proceed to implement the code in the AniForm class that processes the data using a timer. The general course of your work involves creating an instance of the DataForm class so that you can retrieve the values you have stored in the Vals collection (also known as the coordSets collection). You set up a timer method in the AniForm class that allows you to retrieve a Values item once each second from the Vals collection and print it to the text area of the Animation form (as shown in Figure 9.5). Here is the code for the AniForm class. Subsequent paragraphs provide detailed discussion.

```
public partial class AniForm : Form

{
    // #1
    DataForm tempForm;
    Values[] tempVals;
    int LENGTH;
    int counter;

    public AniForm()
    {
        // #2
        InitializeComponent();
        timer1.Stop();
        tempForm = new DataForm();
        tempVals = tempForm.Vals.ToArray();
        LENGTH = tempVals.Length;
        counter = 0;
    }

    private void AniForm_Paint(object sender, PaintEventArgs e)
    {
    }

    private void button1_Click(object sender, EventArgs e)
    {
        // #3
        timer1.Start();
        timer1.Interval = 1000;
    }

    private void close_Click(object sender, EventArgs e)
    {
        // #6 (not in sequence—see the comments in the text)
        timer1.Stop();
        timer1.Dispose();
        Close();
    }

    private void timer1_Tick(object sender, EventArgs e)
    {
        // #4
        // The timer executes each second, printing a Value item
```

```
if (counter < LENGTH)
{
    showData(tempVals[counter++]);
}
else
{
    timer1.Stop();
    counter = 0;
}
}

private void AniForm_Load(object sender, EventArgs e)
{
}

// #5
public void showData(Values set)
{
    richTextBox1.AppendText("("
                            + set.X.ToString(''00.00") + ","
                            + set.Y.ToString(''00.00") + ") "
                            );
}// end method
}// end class
```

To set up the timer, in the lines accompanying comment #1, you declare four class fields. The first field, tempForm, is an object of the DataForm type and allows you to access the Vals collection you generate when you click the Run button in the DataForm class. The second field is an array of the Values type, which allows you to retrieve the Values objects from the Vals collection. You also declare two fields of the int type. One (LENGTH) allows you to identify the number of items in the array. The other (counter) allows you to create an incremental counter you can use through success calls to the timer method.

At comment #2, you attend to the initialization of the class fields. To accomplish this, after resetting the timer1 object by calling the Stop() method, you construct a DataForm object and assign it to the tempForm field. You call the Vals field of the tempForm object to call the ToArray() method and assign the Values items you retrieve to the tempVals array. Given the initialization of the tempVals array, you then call the Length property of the tempVals array and retrieve the number of items in the array. This number you assign to the LENGTH field. As a final measure, you initialize the counter field to 0.

In the lines associated with comment #3, you define the button1_Click() method so that it calls the timer1 object and sets the interval of the timer to one second (1000). In the lines accompanying comment #4, you then proceed to define the actions the timer controls.

To define the actions, you provide code to the timer1_Tick() method. To accomplish this, you create an if. . .else selection statement. This statement first determines whether the value of counter is less than the value of LENGTH. If this is true, the flow of the program enters the if block and calls the showData() method. This method takes one argument, an object of the Values type. To retrieve the object, you employ the counter field incrementally to set the index value of the tempVals array. Once each second, then, the timer1_Tick() method increments the value of counter, retrieves a Values item from the tempVals array, and calls the showData() method to print the output.

When the value of counter increases to the point that it is greater than the number of items in the tempVals array, the if selection statement evaluates to false, and the flow of the program enters the else block. When it enters the else block, the first statement in the block calls the timer1.Stop() method. This method halts the timer. In the following statement, you reset the counter field to 0 so that, if you restart the timer, you can again traverse the array.

The showData() method is defined following comment #5. This method allows you to print the X and Y fields of a Values object. You have seen this method several times before. The argument allows you to retrieve the two field values of the Values struct (X and Y), and you call the ToString() method for each to format the output.

One final action remains important in the use of the timer, and that is stopping and disposing of the timer when you close your form. You place the code that accomplishes this in the close_Click() method, which is associated with comment #6. You first call the Stop() method to stop the timer. Then you call the Dispose() method to destroy the timer.

If you do not call these two methods when you close the form, if the timer is running, it continues to run. If it continues to run, even if you try to close the Lab application, you will have to wait until the timer expires. Using the Stop() and Dispose() methods stops and destroys the timer as soon as you close the Animation form.

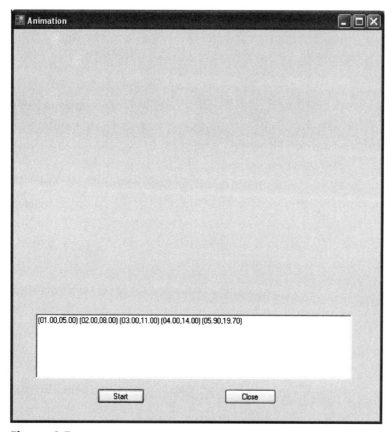

Figure 9.5
After four seconds, you see five sets of coordinates.

To execute the application, click the Run button in the DataForm form to generate a table of values. Then click the Animate button. The Animation form then appears. In the Animation form, click the Start button. The values then appear in the text area at one-second intervals. After all the values have printed, click the Start button again to see them generated again. When you click the Start button, the timer is reset, along with the value of the counter field. Figure 9.5 illustrates the text area of the Animation form after you have allowed the timer to run for four seconds.

Version Review

At this point, the work with the basic version of the AniForm class ends. The new version is called AniFormV2. To change from the first version of the class to the second, you change the code in the DataForm animation_Click() method so that it reads as follows:

```
AniFormV2 aniForm = new AniFormV2();
aniForm.Activate();
aniForm.Show();
```

Making this change amounts to removing the comment from AniFormV2. You can always switch back and forth between the AniForm and AniFormV2 classes.

In the runButton_Click() method, you now change the argument so that it is runFunction(2). This does not directly affect the functionality of your program. It merely provides you with a new set of data.

You do not need to make further changes. However, if you save a copy of the AniForm class to work with, you must make a few changes in your class so that you can use it. The changes are to the constructor and the Load and Paint methods. The constructor change involves only making the constructor possess the same name as the class. As for the Load and Paint methods, if you begin with a Load method named this way:

AniForm_Load()

Then you change it so that it reads this way:

AniFormV2_Load()

For the Load and Paint methods, you change the part of the method name that corresponds to your renamed class. For example, AniForm_Load() becomes AniFormV2_Load(), and AniForm_Paint() becomes AniForm V2_Paint().

You also make a change to the AniForm.Designer.cs file. In this file, find this line:

this.Load += new System.EventHandler(this.AniForm_Load);

If you have changed your version to AniFormV2, then you change this line so that it reads

this.Load += new System.EventHandler(this.AniFormV2_Load);

This error is easy to fix because if you do not attend to it, the compiler gives you an error that no Load method is defined. If you click on the error message, then you go directly to the line you need to fix. Just change the name of the reference to the Load method so that it corresponds to the name in your current file.

Creating a No-Flicker Panel

To make it so that you can create animations, you create a customized Panel class. In the Toolbox, you'll find a Panel object. This object is good enough for static displays of graphical items, but when you display an animated activity, you need a type of panel that prevents an annoying side effect of animation known as *flicker*. This is a momentary whitening of a display object that occurs when you repaint the object repeatedly. To prevent flicker, you create a special form of a panel that processes painting activities so that the flicker does not occur.

Deriving One Class from Another

To create the no-flicker panel, you derive a customized panel from the base `Panel` class. Your derived class is called `NoFlickerPanel`. As has been mentioned in previous chapters, when you derive one class from another, the class from which you derive your class is called the *base* class. The class you derive is called the *derived* or *child* class. The process in general is known as *inheritance*. Inheritance is based on the idea that when you derive one class from another, you reuse the features of the base class. The derived class gains access to all the methods of the base class. It inherits them.

Some limitations apply, however. It is not important for now to investigate all the limitations, but the one that counts most is that the methods and fields you inherit must be defined as either `public` or `protected`. You have seen `public` and `private` methods and fields throughout most of this book. A `public` field is one that you can access directly using the name of an object. With the `Values` struct, for example, when you made the `X` and `Y` fields `public`, you made it so that you could directly access these fields using the dot operator. If you declare a `Values` object named `coord`, for example, then you can use the statement `coord.X` to call the value assigned to this field.

The same relationship applies to methods. Methods of the `CoordSystem` class are `public`, so after you create an object named `cSys` in the `CartForm` class, you can then call methods of the `CoordSystem` class. In contrast, use of the `private` keyword makes it so that you can access methods and fields only within the class in which you define them. Several of the `DataForm` methods shown in previous chapters are `private`. Such methods are not used outside the `DataForm` class.

As for a `protected` method or field, you cannot access it using an object such as `cSys`, but you can still access it. You can access it if you derive a class from the `CoordSystem` class. Within the derived class, you can then call the `protected` method or field.

Specifics of Derivation

To define a special no-flicker panel, you derive a class called `NoFlickerPanel` from the `Panel` class. To create the `NoFlickerPanel`, select Project > Add New Item. In the Name field type NoFlickerPanel. Then click the Class item. The `NoFlickerPanel` class is added to your project. It includes the basic using directives and the shell of a class definition within the namespace definition. To the basic code, you add a using directive for `System.Windows.Forms` so that you can access the namespace for the Panel class. To derive one class from another, in the signature line of your derived class definition, you state the name of the derived class, a colon, and the name of the base class. You then add a few more lines, discussed presently. Here is the complete code for the class:

```
using System;
using System.Collections.Generic;
using System.Text;
using System.Windows.Forms;
namespace CodeLab
{
    public class NoFlickerPanel : Panel
    {
        public NoFlickerPanel()
        {
            SetStyle(ControlStyles.OptimizedDoubleBuffer, true);
            SetStyle(ControlStyles.UserPaint, true);
            SetStyle(ControlStyles.AllPaintingInWmPaint, true);
        }
    }
}
```

As you have seen many times in previous chapters, opening and closing curly braces establish the scope of the class. Within the scope of the derived class, you access public or protected methods within the base class. Additionally, you can create customized methods. You have been performing this activity all along as you have employed the wizard to create classes derived from the Form class. In this case, you create a derived class that you define wholly on your own from the Panel class.

The name of the derived class is NoFlickerPanel. Your sole activity in defining your derived class involves creating an explicitly defined constructor in which you call the SetStyle() method, which you access through the Panel class. This method allows you to define your class so that you eliminate characteristics that allow flickering to occur.

Note

The code within the NoFlickerPanel class attends to creating a *double buffer,* among other things. Double buffers lie a bit beyond the scope of the current discussion, but the essential notion is that when you change the appearance of a form through animation, the effect of your changes is to momentarily erase and then repaint the contents of the form. This creates a moment during which the form is white. The moment of white appears as a flicker. The purpose of a double buffer is to eliminate this effect. The double buffer basically fills the white space. To see what happens without a double buffer, comment out this line:

```
SetStyle(ControlStyles.OptimizedDoubleBuffer, true);
```

The effect severely diminishes the pleasure of using the application.

Adding the Panel

After you define and save the NoFlickerPanel, the C# IDE automatically adds an icon for it to the Toolbox. Click on the Toolbox panel. You find the icon beneath CodeLab Components. Figure 9.6 illustrates the icon.

To place a NoFlickerPanel object in the AniFormV2 form, click on AniFormV2 to bring it into focus. Then click on the NoFlickerPanel icon in the Toolbox and place it in the AniformV2 form. As soon as you place the NoFlickerPanel icon on the form, access the Properties pane. For the name field, type Graph. For the BackColor value, select White from the color palette.

Figure 9.6
The NoFlickerPanel icon appears at the top of the Toolbox list.

Then in the AniFormV2 Designer tab, resize the panel until it is approximately 500 pixels wide and 500 pixels tall. Position it 25 pixels from the left margin and 35 pixels from the top.

Adding the Axes

When you finish positioning the panel, you find a method called `Graph_Paint()` in the `AniFormV2` class. The name of your panel is Graph, so this method is automatically generated for it. It allows you to paint features in the panel.

To create a grid for the panel, you follow the same approach you used in previous chapters with the `CartForm` class. You add an additional field to the `AniFormV2` class. This is a field of the `CoordSystem` type, `cSys`. You also define the same fields you defined in the `CartForm` class to control the dimensions of the grid and to scale the output. Here are the fields you add:

```
CoordSystem cSys;
const int YSCALE = 1;
const int XSCALE = 1;
const int LOCALGRID = 5;
```

Within the constructor of the class, you add a line to create an instance of the `CoordSystem` class:

```
cSys = new CoordSystem(LOCALGRID);
```

You then add lines to the `Graph_Paint()` method to draw the grid and the axes for the coordinate system. Here are the lines:

```
private void Graph_Paint(object sender, PaintEventArgs e)
{
      cSys.drawGrid(e.Graphics);
      cSys.drawAxes(e.Graphics);
}
```

After your changes to the `Graph_Paint()` method, if you compile your project and click the Run and Animate buttons, you then see the graph shown in Figure 9.7.

Adding an Animated Point

The most simple animation involves painting a point that changes according to the coordinate values you select given a tick of the timer. To accomplish this,

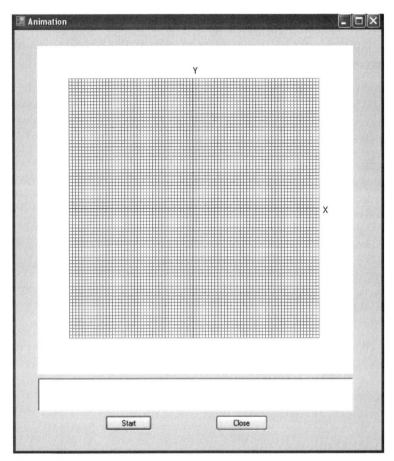

Figure 9.7
You use the Graph_Paint() method to paint the coordinate system on the panel.

you need to add only a few lines to the timer1_Tick() and Graph_Paint() methods.

To recapitulate, the Graph object is the panel object you create using the NoFlickerPanel class. When you create the Graph object, the C# Toolbox automatically inserts the Graph_Paint() method into your code. This method governs the painting of the Graph object.

In the Graph_Paint() method, you call the CoordSystem plotPoint() method. When you call this method, you first use a selection statement to determine whether the value currently assigned to the count field remains less than the length of the tempVals array. If this test proves true, then you retrieve coordinates from the tempVals array and employ them as arguments to the plotPoint() method. To set the style of the point to be plotted, you supply true as the final argument of the plotPoint() method. An argument of true designates a filled point. Here is the code for the Graph_Paint() method.

```
private void Graph_Paint(object sender, PaintEventArgs e)
{
    cSys.drawGrid(e.Graphics);
    cSys.drawAxes(e.Graphics);
    if (counter < LENGTH)
    {
        cSys.plotPoint(e.Graphics, tempVals[counter].X / XSCALE,
                                   tempVals[counter].Y / YSCALE, true);
    }
}
```

A panel, form, or other such graphical object possesses a special function that allows you to force your application to repaint it. This is the Invalidate() method. This method invokes the Paint method for the object with which you call it. The object with which you call the Invalidate() method is the Graph object. The method called is the Graph_Paint() method.

You make the call to the Invalidate() method in the timer1_Tick() method. This, then, causes the Graph object to be repainted with a new point once each second. Here is the code for the timer1_Tick() method:

```
private void timer1_Tick(object sender, EventArgs e)
{
    counter++;     // Increase by 1 for each tick
    if (counter < LENGTH)
    {
        showData(tempVals[counter]); //print the coordinates
        // Graph is the name of the NoFlickerPanel object
        Graph.Invalidate(); //invoke the Graph_Paint() method
    }
    else
    {
        timer1.Stop();  //If all items have been retrieved, stop
        counter = 0;    //reset the counter field to 0
    }
}
```

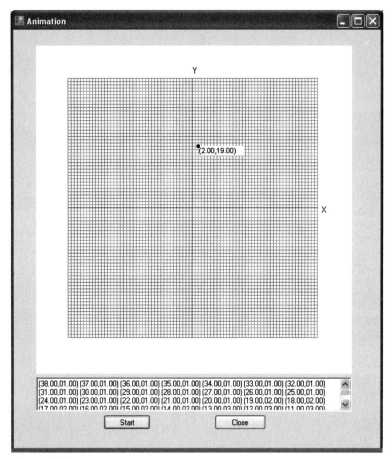

Figure 9.8
As the coordinates are displayed, the point moves.

Since counter is a class field that you incremented for any given cycle of the timer, you can also use it to retrieve a Values item from the tempVals array to supply as arguments to the showData() method, which prints the coordinate values of the current coordinate pair. Figure 9.8 illustrates how the plotted point appears after four ticks of the timer. The values used are generated by Function2() in the DataForm class.

Adding a Continuous Array

Change your Lab project so that you include the AniFormV3 class. In the DataForm class, change the animation_Click() method so that it invokes the AniFormV3 class. Here is how the code reads:

```
private void animation_Click(object sender, EventArgs e)
{
      // Lines left out
      AniFormV3 aniForm = new AniFormV3();
      // Lines left out
      aniForm.Activate();
      aniForm.Show();
      // Lines left out
}
```

Also, in the runButton_Click() class, set runFunction(3) as the current option. In order to generate animations that feature continuous motion, you require a set of continuous, sequential values that allow you to guide the object you are moving in a smooth, uninterrupted way. You can create this set of values if you use one or more for statements to create values that you assign to Values objects that you store in the coordSets List collection.

To create a set of sequential values for the coordSets collection, you can use the incremental values of a number of for repetition statements to generate hundreds of coordinate sets that cause the point to move in a variety of interesting ways. This solves the problem of creating values that allow you to move an object in a smooth, interesting fashion. Another problem remains, however.

Consider that the ticker moves in milliseconds. If you generate hundreds or thousands of values, while you can then move the point around the Cartesian plane in many ways, you still move the point only one pixel with each tick. If you allow only one tick per second, then the movement tends to be painfully slow.

To overcome this problem, you make two changes. You increase the speed of the timer, and you also increase the interval the point moves. To change the interval of movement, you can use grid units rather than pixel units. The LOCALGRID field provides you with this value. When you set it to 5, you move the object in the grid 5 units per tick. To accommodate the change of speed, you use the SPEED field in the AniFormV3 class. You can set this as small as 1/1000 of a second.

If you consider that when you set the LOCALGRID field in the AniForm class to 5 (as in Figure 9.8), then you have 40 lines to work with as you move in any direction on the graph from its origin. This is because the graph is 400 pixels wide and high. Moving it up, down, left, or right from the origin, you have 200 pixels to work with.

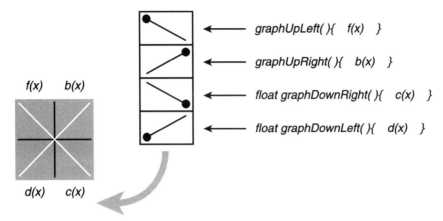

Figure 9.9
Storing the output of different methods allows you to generate patterns.

Generating Coordinates

The `AniFormV3` class provides an example of an animation that includes a line that is drawn and erased in each quadrant of the Cartesian plane (see Figure 9.11). To plot such a set of lines, in `Function3()` of `DataForm` class, you generate coordinates that define different patterns. As the discussion in Chapter 8 emphasized, you can combine the output of any number of equations and store their output in the `coordSets` collection. You can then retrieve this data and use it to guide a point as you animate it on the Cartesian plane. This approach to storing and retrieving coordinates allows you to create patterns that are more complex than those you could create using the output of one equation alone. Figure 9.9 illustrates the situation.

In the `DataForm` class, you call a set of functions that generate sets of coordinates that allow you to map lines in the four quadrants of the Cartesian plane. No math is employed for this example, just repetition statements in four methods that generate coordinate pairs in which the pairs consist of positive and negative values. If both values are positive, the line maps to quadrant I. If both are negative, then it maps to quadrant III. Combinations of negative and positive values map to either quadrant II or quadrant IV. Here is the code for the `Function3()` method in the `DataForm` class. You can see complete implementation of the code in the `DataForm` class.

```
// The left side
private void Function3()
{
```

```
        Functions fset = new Functions();
        int GRIDAT5 = 39;
        fset.graphUpLeft(GRIDAT5, ref coordSets, 1, 0);
        fset.graphUpRight(GRIDAT5, ref coordSets, 1, 0 );
        fset.graphDownRight(GRIDAT5, ref coordSets, 1, 0);
        fset.graphDownLeft(GRIDAT5, ref coordSets, 1, 0);
        displayTable("\n\t X ", "\t\t Y");
}
```

The methods you call in the Function3() class are defined in the Functions class. The definitions of the functions all assume the same form and might be collapsed into a single function. They are left separate here to carry forward the theme of using the combined output of functions to create a single animation pattern. In this instance, the actions of four linear equations are joined together. Here are the implementations of the graphUpLeft() and graphUpRight() methods. The graphDownLeft() and graphDownRight() follow the same path:

```
public void graphUpLeft(int distance, ref List<Values> coordset,
                        float slope, float shift)
{
    // Q II Start at 0, make x negative, y positive
    // mx + b
    for (int ctr = 0; ctr <= distance; ctr++)
    {
        coordset.Add(new Values((float)-1 * ctr,
                                (float)slope * ctr + shift));
    }
    // Start at distance, make x negative, y positive
    for (int ctr = distance; ctr >= 0; ctr--)
    {
        coordset.Add(new Values((float)-1 * ctr,
                                (float)slope * ctr + shift));
    }
}// end method

public void graphUpRight(int distance, ref List<Values> coordset,
                        float slope, float shift)
{
    // Q I Start at 0, make x positive, y positive
    // mx + b
    for (int ctr = 0; ctr <= distance; ctr++)
    {
```

```
        coordset.Add(new Values((float) 1 * ctr,
                                 (float)slope * ctr + shift));
    }
    // Start at distance, make x positive, y positive
    for (int ctr = distance; ctr >= 0; ctr--)
    {
        coordset.Add(new Values((float)1 * ctr,
                                 (float)slope * ctr + shift));

    }
}//end method
```

To "load" the coordSets collection with coordinates for a linear and a quadratic equation, for example, you might use runFunction(3).

To load the methods shown in Figure 9.9, you employ option 3, which calls the Function3() method. This method calls four methods in succession from the Functions class, which generate 4 sets of 80 coordinates, so you end up with 320 coordinate pairs. Figure 9.10 illustrates a few of these values. The values in Figure 9.10 map the movement of the point in quadrant III (both coordinates are negative).

To plot lines or points using these coordinate pairs, you provide code in the Graph_Paint() method in the AniFormV3 class. To work with the coordinate pairs, you declare an array of the Values type as a class field for the AniFormV3 class. In

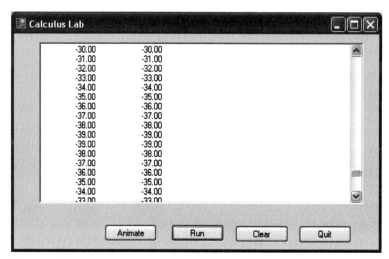

Figure 9.10
Pairs of negative coordinates generate a line in quadrant III.

the constructor of the class, you employ the `ToArray()` class to convert the `Vals` property of the `DataForm` class to an array:

```
public AniFormV3()
     {
         InitializeComponent();
         timer1.Stop();
         tempForm = new DataForm();
         tempVals = tempForm.Vals.ToArray();
         LENGTH = tempVals.Length;
         counter = 0;
         timer1.Interval = SPEED;
         // Add overloaded constructor
         cSys = new CoordSystem(LOCALGRID);
}
```

In the lines preceding the implementation of the constructor, you change the SPEED field, which you set to 10 milliseconds:

```
const int SPEED = 10;
```

In this pass, you implement an infinite loop for the application. In other words, the animation plays over and over again. To make this happen, you comment out the `timer1.Stop()` method and call in the `timer1_Tick()` method. As in the previous example, the animation occurs because the `Invalidate()` method in the `timer1_Tick()` method calls the `Graph_Paint()` method. In this case, rather than ceasing when the number of ticks reaches a given limit, the animation continues to run until you click the Close button.

All of the painting activity takes place in the `Graph_Paint()` method. When the `timer1_Tick()` method calls the `Graph.Invalidate()` method, the counter variable is increased by one. You then use the counter variable to traverse the coordinate pairs assigned to the `tempVals` array. Here is the code:

```
private void Graph_Paint(object sender, PaintEventArgs e)
{
    cSys.drawGrid(e.Graphics);
    cSys.drawAxes(e.Graphics);
    Pen drawingPen = new Pen(Color.DarkBlue, 2);
    if (counter < LENGTH)
    {
      cSys.plotLinear(e.Graphics, Color.RoyalBlue,
```

```
                              tempVals[counter].X / XSCALE,
                              tempVals[counter].Y / XSCALE,
                              tempVals[0].X / XSCALE,
                              tempVals[0].Y / XSCALE);
              cSys.plotPoint(e.Graphics, tempVals[counter].X / XSCALE,
                                  tempVals[counter].Y / YSCALE, true);
              cSys.drawCoordinates(e.Graphics, tempVals[counter].X,
                                  tempVals[counter].Y,
                                  LOCALGRID);
        }// end if
}// end method
```

To simplify the animation, you set one of the coordinate pairs to (0, 0). This makes all the lines you draw either move toward or away from the origin of the plane. Figure 9.11 provides a composite illustration of the lines that you generate with the coordinates from the coordSets collection. The animation cycles draw and then erase each line. The first line drawn extends into quadrant II. The

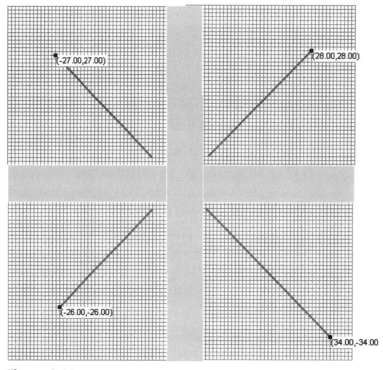

Figure 9.11
The animation runs in an infinite loop and draws and erases lines in each quadrant.

animation then moves through the quadrants of the Cartesian plane in a clockwise direction. As in previous examples, you plot the coordinate using the plotPoint() method. To create the white box that identifies the coordinates, you call the drawCoordinates() method.

Queues and Coordinates

As Figure 9.11 reveals, if you combine the output of a set of equations to generate coordinates that move a point in a continuous way, you can create complex events that can take on an infinitely varied form. Clearly, programming for games and using equations to generate output merge through this activity. Many other activities come into play, of course, but the fact that you can create "intelligent" motions of a given object by using mathematically generated data underlies much of the work of staging events in computer games. The potential of a given moment in a game depends on the potentials of the events that precede and follow the event. There are two primary ways to stage such events. One is through random interaction. The other is through programmatic intelligence. Where motion is concerned, the intelligence lies in the paths you chart mathematically.

Cardinal Directions

The easiest approach to programming methods that allow you to navigate the plane in an arbitrary way involves using linear equations that lack slopes. Figure 9.12 illustrates an arbitrary pattern of movement around the Cartesian plane. As the letters and lines indicate, the motions are all in cardinal directions.

To make it possible for the point to move in the programmed manner Figure 9.12 illustrates, you add four methods to the Functions class. You might optimize the code and use a more efficient approach, one involving only one method, but creating four methods makes it easier to study. The four methods you implement are named goRight(), goLeft(), goUp(), and goDown(). All require similar arguments. Here are the methods as implemented in the Functions class:

```
// From the left of plane to the right
public void goRight(int startX, int atY,
                    int distance, ref List<Values> coordSet)
{
    int ctr = 0;
```

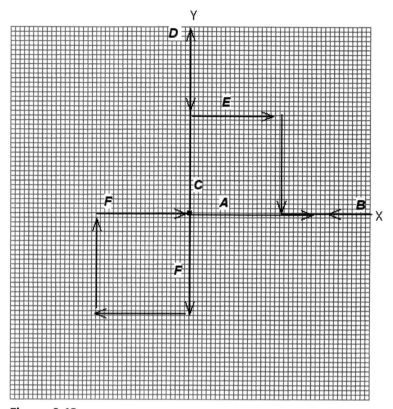

Figure 9.12
A pattern unfolds from the use of linear movements.

```
    while (ctr <= distance)
    {
        coordSet.Add(new Values((float)startX+ +,  // Reference
                                (float)atY));
        ctr+ +;
    }
}// end method

// From the right of plane to the left
public void goLeft(int startX, int atY,
                int distance, ref List<Values> coordSet)
{
    int ctr = 0;
    while (ctr <= distance)
    {
        coordSet.Add(new Values((float)startX- -,  // Reference
                                (float)atY));
```

```
            ctr++;
        }
}// end method

// From the bottom of plane to the top
public void goUp(int startY, int atX,
                int distance, ref List<Values> coordSet)
{
    int ctr = 0;
    while (ctr <= distance)
    {
        coordSet.Add(new Values((float)atX,      // Reference
                        (float)startY++));
        ctr++;
    }
}//end method

// From top of plane to bottom
public void goDown(int startY, int atX,
                int distance, ref List<Values> coordSet)
{
    int ctr = 0;
    while (ctr <= distance)
    {
        coordSet.Add(new Values((float)atX,      // Reference
                        (float)startY--));
        ctr++;

    }
}// end method
```

In each instance, you create coordinate pairs that you assign to a reference to a List object. To make activities clearer, the name of the argument is coordSet, the same as the collection in the DataForm class.

To generate coordinate pairs, you set the starting x or y coordinate value. Then you set a constant for the remaining x or y coordinate value. If the point moves to the right or left, then the value of x changes and the value of y remains constant. If the point moves up or down, then the value of x remains constant and the value of y changes. The argument for distance controls an absolute distance for the movement of the point.

Adding Equations

The cardinal functions are set up to move in horizontal or vertical directions. To change them so that they can move in other ways, then, you can use the output of an equation for the *x* or *y* value. For example, in the goRight() equation, if you substitute the output of an equation of the form *mx* + *b*, then you create a sloping line.

```
// From left of plane to right
public void goRight(int startX, int atY,
                    int distance, ref List<Values> coordSet)
{
    int ctr = 0;
    while (ctr <= distance)
    {
        // Use a linear equation - the comment shows an alternative
        coordSet.Add(new Values((float)startX+ +,
                                (float)0.5F * startX + 0 ));
                                //(float)atY));
        ctr+ +;
    }
}// end method
```

If you include linear and nonlinear equations, you can create a much richer set of patterns. As it is, however, moving the point in this way allows you to implement any number of game scenarios when you add features such as collision detection.

Generating Coordinates

To create a set of coordinates for the path shown in Figure 9.12, you call the cardinal methods from the Functions class in succession and build the path the moving point follows. While you might use more sophisticated methods to create the path, it remains that the cardinal methods provide you with the ability to create many of the scenarios offered by classical 2D games. Here is a sequence of calls that create a pattern of movement that corresponds to the pattern Figure 9.12 illustrates:

```
private void Function4()
{
    int G5 = 39;
    Functions fset = new Functions();
    fset.goRight(0, 0, G5, ref coordSets);
    fset.goLeft(G5, 0, G5, ref coordSets);
    fset.goUp(0, 0, G5, ref coordSets);
    fset.goDown(G5, 0, G5/2, ref coordSets);
```

```
    fset.goRight(0, G5/2, G5/2, ref coordSets);
    fset.goDown(G5/2, G5/2, G5/2, ref coordSets);
    fset.goLeft(G5/2, 0, G5/2, ref coordSets);
    fset.goDown(0, 0, G5 / 2, ref coordSets);
    fset.goLeft(0, -G5 / 2, G5 / 2, ref coordSets);
    fset.goUp(-G5 / 2,  -G5 / 2, G5 / 2, ref coordSets);
    fset.goRight(-G5 / 2, 0, G5 / 2, ref coordSets);
    displayTable("\n\t X ", "\t\t Y");
}// end method
```

The first argument of each of the cardinal methods designates the starting point on the axis along which the point is to move. For the goRight() method, this is the 0 coordinate on the x axis. The second argument provides what amounts to a constant. With the goRight() method, this is the constant value that determines the value of the y-intercept. The third argument is a reference to a List argument. As mentioned previously, when you employ a reference argument for a collection, you do not copy the elements in the collection. Instead, you more or less take the method to the collection, changing its elements directly. References tremendously enhance the performance of any game, especially if many thousands of items are involved. Even in this scenario, which involves only a few hundred coordinate pairs, copying the collection for each of the calls might noticeably affect performance.

Plotting the Point

You implement a code in the Graph_Paint() method to plot. Plotting the point involves calling the plotPoint() and drawCoordinates() methods of the CoordSystem class. As in previous examples, you set the number of ticks to accord with the length of the tempVals array. Here is the code:

```
private void Graph_Paint(object sender, PaintEventArgs e)
{
    cSys.drawGrid(e.Graphics);
    cSys.drawAxes(e.Graphics);
    cSys.plotPoint(e.Graphics,tempVals[counter].X,
                              tempVals[counter].Y);
    richTextBox1.AppendText(" Count " + counter.ToString());
    cSys.drawCoordinates(e.Graphics, tempVals[counter].X,
                                     tempVals[counter].Y,
                                     LOCALGRID);
    peformEvents(e.Graphics);  //Detect a few collisions
}// end method
```

As mentioned previously, with each tick of the timer, the counter field value is incremented by 1, and the Graph.Invalidate() method causes the program to invoke the Graph_Paint() method. The Graph_Paint() method follows the same pattern established in previous examples. You employ the counter variable to retrieve successive coordinate pairs assigned to the tempVals array. You use the resulting values as arguments to the plotPoint() method. Then you call the AppendText() method of the RichTextBox object to show the values in the text area. You also call the drawCoordinates() method to paint the values of the coordinates in the coordinate plane next to the plotted point. The only difference between this and previous examples is that you also deploy a method that detects when the coordinates "collide" with a given event node.

Event Detection

A call to a new method appears as the last call in the Graph_Paint() method. The new method is the peformEvents() method. This method takes a single argument, of the Graphics type, and provides you with the ability to create "events."

You can define an event in any number of ways when you implement a game. In the current scenario, an event consists of the appearance of a red point larger than the default black point. Defining the event involves using a selection statement to determine when the value of the x coordinate of any coordinate pair includes an x value of 19 and an even y value, an x value of –9, or a y value of 17. When either of these conditions is true, then the flow of the program triggers the event, and you see a flashing red dot with an orange center. Here is the code for the method:

```
private void performEvents(Graphics e)
{
    // Three event occasions
    if ( (tempVals[counter].X == (float)19
        && tempVals[counter].Y % 2 == 0 )
        || tempVals[counter].X == (float)-9
        || tempVals[counter].Y == (float)17 )
    { // begin if block
        eventCount+ +;
        // Outer ring
        cSys.plotPoint(e, tempVals[counter].X,
                        tempVals[counter].Y,
                        true, Color.Red,
                        6);
```

```
        // Inner ring
        cSys.plotPoint(e, tempVals[counter].X,
                          tempVals[counter].Y,
                          true, Color.Orange,
            3);
    }// end if block
    richTextBox1.AppendText("\t Events: " + eventCount.ToString());
}// end method
```

To track the events, you add a new field to the AniFormV4 class. This is the
eventCount field. You initialize it to 0 in the constructor and increment it each
time the selection statement in performEvents() method is true. Next to creating
an infinite loop and loading graphical objects into a game, event detection stands
as one of the three or four primary activities involved in the development of
computer games. You can implement event detection in any number of ways. As
Figure 9.13 illustrates, the basic in terms of the movement of graphical objects is
that you detect points or areas of points in which objects "collide."

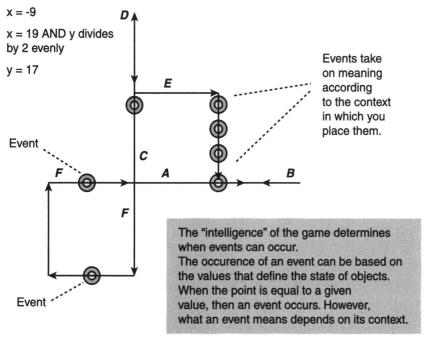

Figure 9.13
You detect points or areas of points in which objects collide.

Note

A somewhat annoying but sometimes useful event supplement appears in the code. This is the `System.Console.Beep()` method, which causes your computer to beep each time the flow of the program triggers an event. Remove the comment from the call in the `performEvents()` method to hear the beep.

You make the red-and-orange event points possible by overloading the `plotPoint()` method in the `CoordSystem` class. This method offers an argument list consisting of six items. The first is an item of the `Graphics` type. The second and third arguments provide the *x* and *y* coordinates for the point. The third argument stipulates whether the point is to be hollow or filled (true for filled). The fifth argument designates a `Color` object. The last argument provides the size of the point. Here is the code:

```
//Plot exclusive or inclusive points, color, size
public void plotPoint(Graphics e,
                      float x, float y,
                      bool typeOfPoint,
                      Color color,
                      int size)
{ // begin if block
    // Adjust the value for the grid
    float xPos = (x * GRID) + (CENTER - size);
    float yPos = CENTER - ((y * GRID) + size);
    // Draw the points
    Pen linePen = new Pen(color, 1);
    SolidBrush ballBrush = new SolidBrush(color);

    // Filled
    if (typeOfPoint == true)
    {
        e.FillEllipse(ballBrush, xPos, yPos, size*2, size*2);
    } // end if block
    else // Not filled
    {
        e.DrawEllipse(linePen, xPos, yPos, size, size);
    }// end else
    return "(" + x + "," + y + ")";
}// end method
```

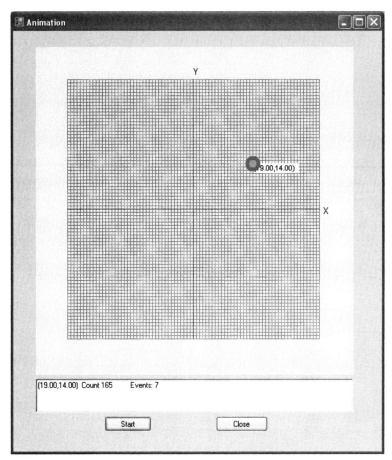

Figure 9.14
The flow of the program triggers an event based on coordinate values.

It is necessary to construct a SolidBrush object to use as a brush in the FillEllipse() method. The SolidBrush class is a *concrete* class derived from the Brush class. The Brush class is an *abstract* class. An abstract class does not allow you to create an instance of it. In the NET framework, abstract classes set patterns for other classes, as is the case with the SolidBrush class. The SolidBrush constructor allows you to use an argument of the Color type to designate the color of the ellipse. This same argument also works with the constructor for the Pen class, so in this way, you can define both the brush and the pen object you set for the two methods you call to graph ellipses. Figure 9.14 illustrates the AniFormV3 form when an event is triggered. Note that the BackColor field of the NoFlickerPanel has been set to AliceBlue.

Conclusion

In this chapter, you have extended the Code Lab application to make use of the `coordSets` collection as a device for storing coordinate values that you can use to guide an animated object. You also explored the use of a timer and a type of `Panel` object that allows you to display animations in a way that eliminates flicker. To implement animations, you can make use of a timer to play the animation for a defined interval, after which you reset your timer. Alternatively, you can remove the control from the timer and allow it to run indefinitely. This approach characterizes the "main loop" of games, in which the game plays on an indefinite basis, its duration determined by events encountered during the play. To anticipate such scenarios, you set processed events on the basis of coordinates. Using an overloaded form of the `plotPoint()` method, you created an animation in which triggered events invoked the display of flashing dots.

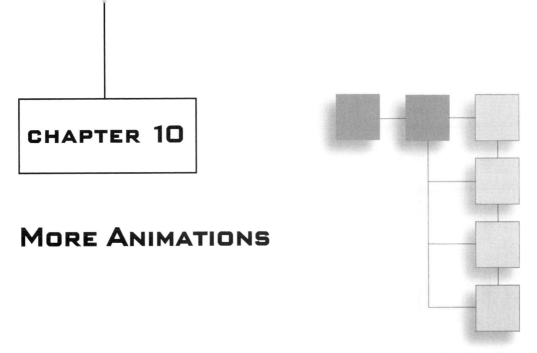

CHAPTER 10

MORE ANIMATIONS

In this chapter, you make fairly extensive changes to the code you developed in Chapter 9. You formalize the generation of random and fixed values and develop methods in the DataForm class that allow you to create distinct types of Values objects that you can later combine to create event contexts for complex events. To generate data, you make use of the Random class. You also modify the NoFlickerPanel so that it has a background that consists of a starry sky representing intergalactic space. After enhancing the background, you add code to the AniFormV5 class that makes the point you implement blink as it moves. Ultimately, you create a scenario in which you can use random and fixed values to generate events that involve two inflating points and a line between them. Such events are characteristic of any game you develop. In this instance, however, you generate such events on a wholly automated basis, using the numbered map you store in the coordSets collection. This chapter brings your work to an end for the projects in this book. On the other hand, it might provide a starting point for many other projects. Topics covered in this chapter include the following:

- Generating random numbers
- Preparing the way for random events
- Making objects glow
- Adding a background to your panel
- Understanding event nodes and transitions
- Creating event contexts

Random Numbers

Thus far, the activities you have performed have involved using definitive, predictable values. It happens, however that you can also use values characterized by chance. Such a value is known as a *random* number. Formally, a random number is a number that occurs in a set of numbers. When it occurs randomly, it stands the same chance of occurring as all the other numbers in the set. For example, suppose that you have at hand a set that consists of these numbers:

{0, 1, 2, 3, 4}

The set consists of five numbers, so if you are working on a random basis, the probability, or chance, is 1 in 5 that the number you pick will be any one of the numbers.

The C# Math library provides a class called Random that generates random numbers. To use the class, you declare an instance of the class and then draw from a number of methods it provides to generate random numbers.

A Function for Random Values

To generate random values that you can use in the context of the animation you developed in Chapter 9, you add a method to the Functions class. To implement this method, you first declare a field of the Random type, randomNum. In the constructor of the Functions class, you then create an instance of the Random class using the default Random constructor and assign it to the randomNum identifier. Here is the code for the Functions class:

```
class Functions
{
   // Lines omitted
   // Declare an instance of the Random class
   Random randomNum;
   public Functions()
     {
         // Initialize the random object
         randomNum = new Random();
     }

     // Return an indicator for a random number
     public float addRandom(int range, Values coord)
     {
```

```
        float value = 0;
        if (coord.X == randomNum.Next(range))
        {
            value = 1;
        }
        else
        {
            value = 0;
        }
        return value;
    }// end method
    // Lines omitted
}// end class
```

The method you add, addRandom(), takes two arguments. The first argument, range, is of the int type. You use the range argument in conjunction with the Next() method of the Random class. This argument allows you to designate a range of values that extends from 0 to one greater than the maximum value you want to obtain. If you seek random numbers in a range extending from 0 to 39, then, you set range to 40.

As a second argument to the addRandom() method, you supply an object of the Values type. This argument allows you to retrieve the value of the X field of a Values object and determine whether the value assigned to it equals the random number the Next() method returns. If the random value equals the value of the X field, then you assign 1 to a local variable, value, which the function then returns. If the two values are not equal, the you assign 0 to the returned value. Figure 10.1 summarizes the situation.

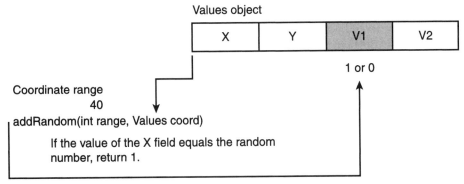

Figure 10.1
The random number you generate allows you to set the V1 field of a Values object to 1.

Generating a Table of Values

To generate values to use in your animation, you work in the DataForm class, as usual. The preliminary changes you make to the DataForm class to accommodate the needs of the current chapter involve trimming out code in the runButton_Click() method so that you call only one method. Here is the code:

```
private void runButton_Click(object sender, EventArgs e)
{
    // Generate intial values
    runFunction(5);  //Use with AniForm4
    if (run == false)
    {
        run = true;
    }
}
```

The Function5() method remains the primary method you use for generating data in this chapter. To call this method, you use 5 as an argument to the runFunction() method. As in previous chapters, a selection structure in the runFunction() method uses this argument to select the primary method to use for generating data. The code from previous chapters remains in place to preserve consistency. In this chapter, this activity is minimal. Here is the code for the runFunction() method:

```
private void runFunction(int f)
{
    if(f == 5)
    {
        Function5();
        //Use with AniForm5
    }
    else
    {
        //No action at this point
    }
}
```

As with the runFunction() method, in the animation_Click() method, your work in this chapter involves a minimal set of actions. For the first exercise, you use the AniForm5 class, so you uncomment the code that constructs an instance of this class. In the second exercise, you use the AniForm6 class, so you then comment out the code for the AniForm5 class and uncomment the code for the

AniForm6 class. Here is the code for the method with the construction for the AniForm5 uncommented:

```
private void animation_Click(object sender, EventArgs e)
{
    if (run == true)
    {
        AniFormV5 aniForm = new AniFormV5();
        // AniFormV6 aniForm = new AniFormV6();
     // Lines left out
    }
}
```

Random Events

The insertRandom() method of the DataForm class extends the activities of previous chapters in a new direction. The purpose of the insertRandom() method involves calling the addRandom() method to randomly generate values of 1 that you assign to the V1 field of Values objects stored in the coordSets container. Assigning 1 to the V1 field designates the Values object for future use in contexts requiring randomly identified entities.

To update the coordSet collection, you copy the contents of the collection into a temporary List object, tempSet, changing the values assigned to the V1 field as you do so. You might copy the coordSet values to an array and then change the values of the array, assigning them back to a List object afterward. Simply creating a new List object and then assigning objects to it simplifies things. Here is the code for the insertRandom() method.

```
private int insertRandom(int range)
{
    List<Values> tempSet = new List<Values>();
    Functions fset = new Functions();
    int randomCount = 0;
    foreach (Values item in coordSets)
    {
        // Set V1 to the random value
        tempSet.Add(new Values((float)item.X,
                               (float)item.Y,
                               (float)fset.addRandom(range, item),
                               (float)item.V2)
                               );
    } // end foreach
```

```
// Clear the first coordinate set and substitute the
// new one containing the random indicators
coordSets.Clear();
coordSets = tempSet;
// Track the number of events
foreach (Values temVal in coordSets)
{
    if (temVal.V1 == 1)
    {
        randomCount++;
    } // end if
} // end foreach
  return randomCount;
}// end method
```

To assign random designations to Values objects, you employ a foreach statement to traverse the coordSets collection. You use the items variable to retrieve
each Values object in the collection. You then use the tempSet collection to call
the Add() method and create and assign Values objects to it that incorporate the
information for each of the Values objects in the coordSets container. The only
change you make to the data involves assignment of the return value of the
addRandom() method to the V1 field.

When you complete this activity, you then have re-created all the Values objects
in the coordSets collection, changing them only to assign values to the V1 fields of
the objects. Given this situation, you then use the coordSets object to call the
Clear() method of the List class. This clears the collection of all of its elements.
After that, you assign the tempSet object to the coordSet object.

When the flow of the program leaves the scope of the insertRandom() method,
the tempSet collection is destroyed. The coordSet collection remains in existence,
however, along with the items you have newly assigned to it.

In addition to revising the elements in the coordSets collection, you also gather
some information about the number of elements in the collection you have
designated as random. To accomplish this, you use another foreach statement.
As an argument to the statement, you employ the coordSets collection. You test
the value of V1 or each element in the collection for equality with 1. If the value
equals 1, then you increment the randomCount field by 1. The randomCount variable is declared within the scope of the insertRandom() method. You employ the
value of this variable as the return value of the method.

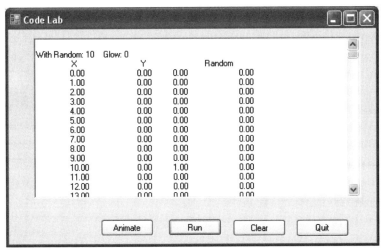

Figure 10.2
The third column from the left shows you the coordinates designated as random.

You call the insertRandom() method in the Function5() method directly following the code you implemented in Chapter 9 to generate the basic values for mapping the movement of the point. At the top of the form, you see two categories of information. One is for *Random.* The other is for *Glow.* The code to generate Glow objects remains to be implemented. The Glow objects are the red event points you implemented in Chapter 9. In this chapter, you move much of the code that relates to them to the DataForm class. The next section provides discussion of the insertGlow() method. For now, if you click the Run button, you see a table of values similar to those shown in Figure 10.2.

Restoring Glow

In Chapter 9, you implemented code in the AniForm5 class to manually invoke events that painted larger red points on the path of the moving point. Now you move that activity to the DataForm class, creating the insertGlow() method to make it so the glow points you dealt with in Chapter 9 are part of the programmed path of the moving point.

Implementing a Nonrandom Method

To implement the insertGlow() method, you follow the same approach you followed when you implemented the insertRandom() method. First, in the

Functions class, you implement a limited method that takes care of generating *nonrandom* values. For now, this method contains literal values. It could be enhanced to allow you to provide an array of values. Here is the code for the method in the Functions class:

```
public float addNonRandom(Values coord)
{
    float value = 0;
    if ((coord.X == (float)19 && coord.Y % 2 == 0)
               || (coord.X == (float)-9)
               || (coord.Y == (float)17))
    { // start of if block
        value = 1;
    } // end of if block
    else
    {
        value = 0;
    }
        return value;
}//end method
```

The addNonRandom() method includes roughly the same selection criteria you used in Chapter 9 to designate coordinates at which the moving point glows. The method takes a Values object as its argument. It returns a float value. To designate nonrandom coordinate sets, it first evaluates coordinate sets to which 19 has been assigned to the X field. If the value of the X field equals 19 and the value of the corresponding Y field is divisible evenly by 2, then the statement renders true. The selection statement also renders true if the X field value equals −9 or the Y field value equals 17. If the statement renders true, then the local variable, value, is set to 1, and this is the number the method returns.

Generating Nonrandom Values

To use the addNonRandom() method in the DataForm class, you make a call to it in the insertGlow() method. Much of the code in this method is redundant. You might eliminate it, for example, by merging the insertGlow() and insert-Random() methods and calling the addRandom() and addNonRandom() methods as part of the same foreach statement. However, in this context, maintaining the activities provides a ready way to view events in isolation. Here is the code for the insertGlow() method in the DataForm class:

```
private int insertGlow()
{
     int glowNumber = 0;
     // Create a temporary List
     List<Values> tempSet = new List<Values>();
     Functions fset = new Functions();
     // Add the definitive but arbitrary items to the List
     foreach (Values item in coordSets)
     {
          //For glow (large circle)item, set V2 to 1
          tempSet.Add(new Values((float)item.X,
                                  (float)item.Y,
                                  (float)item.V1,
                                  fset.addNonRandom(item))
                                  );
     }// end foreach
     // Clear first coordinate set and substitute the
     // new one containing the new values
     coordSets.Clear();
     coordSets = tempSet;
     //Track the number of events
     foreach (Values temVal in coordSets)
     {
         if (temVal.V2 == 1)
         {
            glowNumber++;
         } // end if
     } // end foreach
        return glowNumber;
}// end method
```

The three ways in which this method differs from the insertRandom() method begin with your declaration of a local variable called glowNumber. You employ this variable to track the number of glow items you identify. You also call the addNonRandom() method to identify the Values items you want to designate as nonrandom. You assign the nonrandom designation to the V2 field of the Values item.

As in the insertRandom() method, in the insertNonRandom() method you copy the altered values from tempSet collection to the coordSets collection. You can

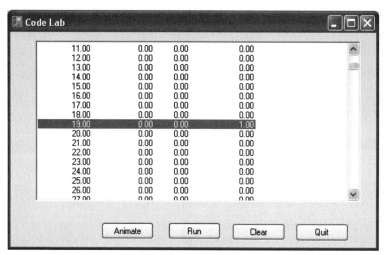

Figure 10.3
The nonrandom method generates the fixed set of values.

then traverse the coordSets collection using a foreach statement to discover the number of altered items. Figure 10.3 illustrates the table you end up with when you call this method from the Function5() method. You end up with 17 items in the current data set. As Figure 10.3 illustrates, if you scroll the window, you find the first changed value (1) in the row corresponding to the X value of 19.

Modifying AniForm5

In this version of the Code Lab application, you add a background image to the form you have used up to this point solely to display points on a Cartesian plane. The background image represents intergalactic space. Figure 10.4 illustrates the AniForm5 form after you have added the space background.

To set a file for a background to either a form or a panel, you employ the BackgroundImage field of the Properties panel. To add an image to the NoFlickerPanel object, you first select the AniForm5 form and then click on the panel area to set the focus on the NoFlickerPanel object. Then, in the Properties tab, as Figure 10.5 illustrates, you locate the BackgroundImage field.

You then click the ellipses button that appears to the right of the field. This opens a dialog that allows you to select an image for a background. In this instance, you click the Local Resource button and the Import button. These actions allow you to navigate to the bin/Resources directory in the Chapter 9 folder. This folder

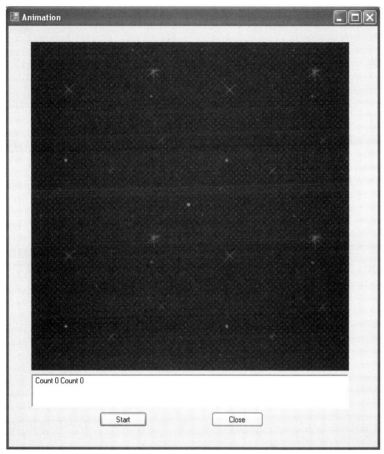

Figure 10.4
A starry background replaces your Cartesian coordinate system.

contains the stars.gif file. After you select the stars.gif file and click Open, you see the dialog Figure 10.6 illustrates. After you click OK, the background appears in the panel area.

Pattern-Driven Activities

If you open and compile the Code Lab application with its default settings for Chapter 10, you see large and small point events, in addition to the moving point, which flickers. The changes you make to the AniForm5 class to achieve these effects include adding a few new fields to track events, changing the Graph_Paint() method, and extending the performEvents() and showRandom() methods.

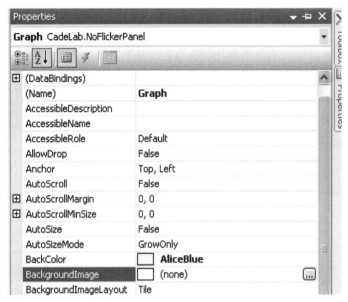

Figure 10.5
Click the ellipses button for the BackgroundImage field of the NoFlickerPanel.

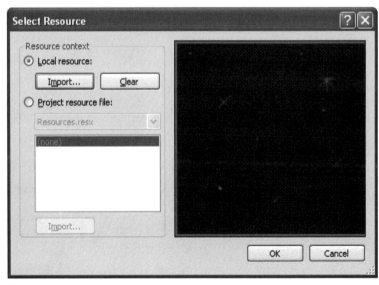

Figure 10.6
Select the background image using the dialog provided.

Fields and Initialization

To track events, you add and initialize three fields. The addition of these fields allows you to verify the execution of fixed, random, and total events. The code to define these fields is included in the AniForm5 class definition of fields and in the constructor for the AniForm5 class. Here is the code for these fields:

```
int eventCount, randomCount, fixedCount;
public AniFormV5()
{
   //lines left out
      eventCount  = 0;
      randomCount = 0;
      fixedCount  = 0;
}
```

Formal initialization of the fields is not necessary, but setting them in the constructor follows good programming practices. When the form is opened, the counts for all of the fields are set to 0.

Basic Point Events

The basic point events of the application remain much as they were in Chapter 9. However, in this chapter, you add a flickering quality to the point as it moves. To add the flicker, you use an if . . . else structure and alter the color of the point with each change in the counter field. Also, you now work without the use of the Cartesian grid. Here is the code that implements these changes:

```
private void Graph_Paint(object sender, PaintEventArgs e)
{
      // Removed to show only space background
      // Use to see coordinate positions
      // cSys.drawGrid(e.Graphics);
      // cSys.drawAxes(e.Graphics);
      Color color;
      if (counter % 2 == 0)
      {
          color = Color.Red;
      }
      else
```

```
    {
        color = Color.MintCream;
    } // end if-else
    cSys.plotPoint(e.Graphics,tempVals[counter].X,
                              tempVals[counter].Y,
                              true,
                              color,
                              3);
    eventCount++;
    richTextBox1.AppendText(" Count " + eventCount.ToString()
                              + "\tFixed\t " + fixedCount.ToString()
                              + "\tRandom\t " + randomCount.ToString());
    performEvents(e.Graphics);
    showRandom(e.Graphics);
}//end method
```

The selection structure in the first few lines of the method uses the modulus operator to determine if the value of the counter is an even number. If so, then you set the Color variable (color) to Red. If not, then you set the Color variable to MintCream. In this way, each time the counter variable increases in value, the color of the point you see changes.

To accommodate the change in the point color, you use an overloaded version of the plotPoint() method. The overloaded form of the method allows you to designate the position of the point with the first two arguments. The third argument sets the point to solid, if true. The fourth argument sets the color of the point. For this argument, you use the changing value of color. The final argument designates the size of the point. This remains what it has been in previous examples.

To track the total number of events, you use the eventCount field and increment it each time the timer method calls the Graph_Paint() method. You might just as well use the counter value at this point to count the total number of events, but a separate field for this purpose allows you to track events if you implement code that generates more than one event with each cycle of the timer.

You retrieve the values of the eventCount, randomCount, and fixedCount fields to show the status of events. The performEvents() and showRandom() methods account for incrementing the values of the randomCount and fixedCount fields.

V2 Events

You attend to fixed events in the `performEvents()` method. The V2 field of the `Values` object is set to 1 for fixed events. Such events consist of expanded points you paint over the normal path of the animated points. To determine when to paint a V2, you employ a selection statement. The selection statement determines whether the V2 value of a `Values` object in the `tempVals` collections equals 1. If it does, then you paint a point 12 pixels in diameter. Each time you paint such a point, you increment the `fixedCount` field by 1. Here is the code for the `performEvents()` method:

```
// Display basic events
private void performEvents(Graphics e)
{
    if (tempVals[counter].V2 == 1)
    {
        fixedCount++;
        // Outer ring
        cSys.plotPoint(e, tempVals[counter].X,
                          tempVals[counter].Y,
                          true, Color.Red,
                          12);
        // Inner ring
        cSys.plotPoint(e, tempVals[counter].X,
                          tempVals[counter].Y,
                          true, Color.Orange,
                          6);
        // Sound event - irritating but useful
        // System.Console.Beep();
    }
}//end method
```

To attend to random events, you implement the `showRandom()` method. The `showRandom()` method features much of the same code you see in the `perform-Events()` method, with the difference that you use a local `Random` object to generate random numbers that allow you to distribute the random events so they do not paint over the path of the mapped point. To accomplish this, you define the `tempVal` variable so that it is regularly updated with a value you generate using the `Next()` method of the `Random` class. As an argument to the `Next()` method, you use a literal value of 40, which allows you to generate numbers in the range from

0 to 39. If the value of the counter field is even for the current tick of the timer, you multiply this value by −1. You then use the resulting value as the value of the Y coordinate for the points you plot.

```
// Display the random events
private void showRandom(Graphics e)
{
    Random rand = new Random();
    if (tempVals[counter].V1== 1)
    {
        randomCount++;
        float tempVal = (float)rand.Next(40);
        if (counter % 2 == 0)
        {
            tempVal *= (-1);
        }
        // Outer ring
        cSys.plotPoint(e, tempVals[counter].X,
                          //tempVals[counter].Y,
                          tempVal,
                          true, Color.Coral,
                          tempVal/2);
        // Inner ring
        cSys.plotPoint(e, tempVals[counter].X,
                          //tempVals[counter].Y,
                          tempVal,
                          true, Color.Lavender,
                          tempVal/2);
    }
}//end method
```

To determine when to execute a random event, you test the value of the X field of the current Values object to determine if it equals 1. If it equals 1, then you execute the event. To track the number of random events, you increment the randomCount field each time a random event executes. Figure 10.7 depicts the star plane when both a random and a nonrandom event occur simultaneously.

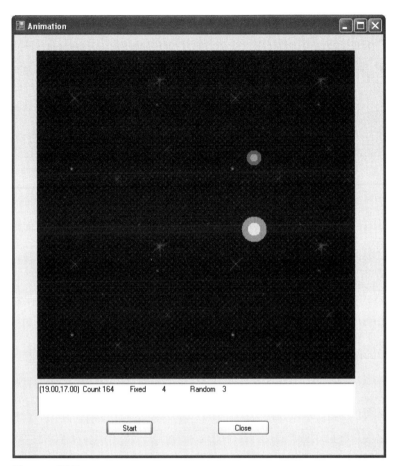

Figure 10.7
Random and nonrandom events rarely occur simultaneously.

Event Contexts

The AniFormV6 class allows you to combine basic events to form secondary, or *complex,* events. A complex event requires you implement code that constitutes the intelligence of a game. A complex event takes place in a context in which two or more primary pieces of data are evaluated to determine whether a secondary event should follow.

As Figure 10.8 illustrates, when the data you use in any given method of a game or computer application possesses distinct characteristics (such as coordinate values, or the V1 and V2 values of the Values items in the coordSet

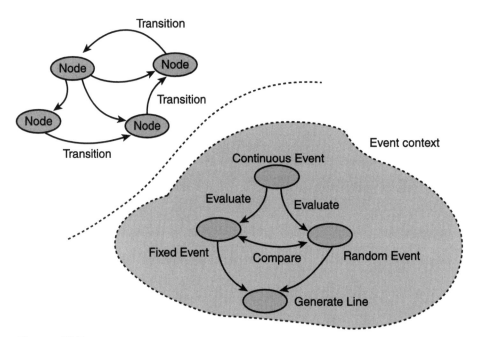

Figure 10.8
Transitions and nodes generate event contexts.

collection), they can be used to create *nodes*. A node is a point in a program when you compare or evaluate one bit of data against one or more other bits of data in a way that a secondary event results. When you bring one bit of data into relation with another, you create a transition. The existence of a transition, at the same time, transforms the two or more formerly isolated bits of data into nodes. The nodes together with the transitions create an event context.

Note

For more information on event modeling see John Flynt and Ben Vinson, *Simulation and Event Modeling for Game Developers* (Thomson Course PTR, 2005). This book offers C++ and C# programs and extended discussion of how nodes and transitions can be used to model computer game events.

Setting Events

To implement the AniFormV6 class, you modify the AniFormV5 class in three basic ways. You add a method, setTransition(), which attends to evaluating the fixed and random events so that you can create a transition between them.

To make this possible, you make use of two fields of the AniFormV6 class, pointA, and pointB. These are of the Values type. To make use of them, you assess each element in the temVals array to determine if it is a fixed or a random value. If it is a random value, you assign it to the pointA field. If it is fixed, then you assign it to the pointB field. Here is the code that accomplishes these tasks:

```
//Obtain information on the current pair of events
       private void setTransition(Graphics e)
       {
           // Identify first coordinate pair (random)
           if (tempVals[counter].V2 == 1)
           {
               fixedCount++;
               pointA.X = tempVals[counter].X;
               pointA.Y = tempVals[counter].Y;
           }

           // Identify second coordinate pair (fixed)
           if (tempVals[counter].V1 == 1)
           {
               randomCount++;
               pointB.X = tempVals[counter].X;
               pointB.Y = tempVals[counter].Y;
           }
}//end method
```

As you set up the conditions of transitions between the points, you also count them as separate events by augmenting the fixedCount and randomCount fields.

Given that you have identified two elements in the temVals array in a way that you isolate them for comparison to each other, you now have in place a way to make them into nodes of a transition. The transition involves bringing them into relation with each other and determining whether you can draw a line between them. They become nodes, then, in a context in which you generate a more complex event. The complex event involves two large points, one a fixed point, the other a random point, and a line you draw between them.

To set conditions that must be fulfilled before the complex event can unfold, you add a few lines of code to the Graph_Paint() method. First, you call the set-Transition() method to extract pointA and pointB data from the tempVals array.

Then you implement a selection statement. Here is the code for the selection statement in the Graph_Paint() method:

```
//Paint what has not already been painted
if (tempVals[counter].X == pointA.X
    && pointA.Y != oldPoint)
{
    executeContext(e.Graphics);
}
// Define the old point for the next cycle
oldPoint = pointA.Y;
```

The code first determines whether the coordinate assigned to pointA.X is equal to the coordinate field of the current Values object in the tempVals array. Additionally, it determines whether the current value assigned to the Y field of pointA is equal to the value of the Values object stored in the oldPoint field. The oldPoint field identifies the point previously painted to the panel area. You do not want to repaint the previously painted point, for then the points you see painted tend to persist, destroying the visual effect produced when the expanded points flash and then disappear.

Event Execution

Given the truth of these conditions, the event context can be invoked as a totality, and then you call the executeContext() method. This method represents a combination of the performEvents() and showRandom() methods of the Ani-FormV5 class. This method serves only to draw two points and the line that the event context encompasses. Here is the code for the method:

```
private void executeContext(Graphics e)
{
        // Small circle
        // Outer ring
        cSys.plotPoint(e, pointA.X,
                          pointA.Y,
                          true, Color.Red,
                          12);
        // Inner ring
        cSys.plotPoint(e, pointA.X,
                          pointA.Y,
                          true, Color.Orange,
                          6);
```

```
        // Large circle
        // Outer ring
        cSys.plotPoint(e, pointB.X,
            //tempVals[counter].Y,
                        pointB.Y,
                        true, Color.Coral,
                        20);
        // Inner ring
        cSys.plotPoint(e, pointB.X,
            //tempVals[counter].Y,
                        pointB.Y,
                        true, Color.Lavender,
                            10);
        // Draw a line between the coordinates
        cSys.plotLinear(e, Color.Pink,
                        pointA.X, pointA.Y,
                        pointB.X, pointB.Y);
        // Make stars flicker
        flickerStars(e, Color.LightGray);


}//end method
```

The event context calls for you to paint two enlarged points, each consisting of an inner ring and an outer ring. The same fixed event cannot be rendered twice in a row. The same random event can be rendered, however. You connect the two points using a line. The plotPoint() method allows you to render the points. The plotLinear() method allows you to draw the line. To draw the line, you use the coordinate values provided by the pointA and pointB fields.

As a final measure, you add a few cosmetic effects to the starry panel. You accomplish this by calling the flickerStars() method. The flickerStars() method paints points to the panel based on the positions of stars in it. Here is the code for the flickerStars() method:

```
private void flickerStars(Graphics e, Color color)
{
        cSys.plotPoint(e, 13, -15F, true,
                        Color.Red, 2);
        cSys.plotPoint(e, 12, 14, true,
                        color, 1);
        cSys.plotPoint(e, -11, -11, true,
                        color, 2);
}
```

To determine the values of the coordinates you supply to your calls to the plotPoint() method within the flickerStars() method, you inspect the stars in the background image. You can choose from among any stars you find interesting. If you remove the comments from the drawGrid() and drawAxes() methods, you can see the coordinate grid imposed over the background. By estimation, you can then set the coordinate positions for any stars you want to make flicker. Recall that you can supply float values to the plotPoint() method, so you can use rational numbers (fractional values) to refine the positions you designate. Also, recall that you need to allow for the scale of the grid. Figure 10.9 illustrates the event you generate using combinations of data. This is a complex event because it is composed of one or more constituent events.

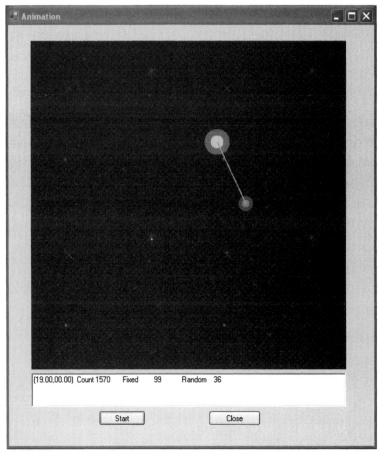

Figure 10.9
An event context allows you to join lines and enlarged and blinking points.

Conclusion

This chapter brings you to the end of the book. In this chapter, you extended the work you have performed in previous chapters to make use of the values in the `coordSet` collection in a variety of ways. You use the values to plot the course of the moving point. When you supplement these basic values with additional information relating to fixed and random designations of points, you create a way to work with complex events. To work with complex events, you changed the appearance of the `NoFlickerPanel` so that it represented a starry sky. You enhanced the moving point so that it became a blinking point. Then you added events that allowed you to increase the size of the moving point at specific places in its path. As a final measure, you made it so that the enlarged moving point could be connected using a line to a randomly generated, enlarged fixed point.

The central theme of this book has been that you can completely anticipate the events of a given computer game if you map out the values that guide the activity of a game in a definitive fashion. In this book, you have learned how to use math equations to generate numbers that you then store in a collection. You then use the collection of numbers to map out activities in a Cartesian plane.

The Cartesian plane serves largely as a formalized canvas on which you can paint events. As you have seen in this chapter, when you remove the coordinates and axes from the panel, you suddenly have in hand a game space in which you can begin crafting events that seem wholly separate from the series of numbers that ultimately makes them possible.

Complex events in games are generated using mathematical equations. This book provides only a starting point for how such activity takes place. Still, in this book, you have been able to glimpse the essentials. You first figure out how to translate the values you generate using math equations into the world space of a Cartesian coordinate system. You then figure out ways to store and retrieve sets of numbers that you create by compounding the output of different functions. You then use methods to generate events from the numbers in your collection.

From here, you can proceed to take further steps. Some such steps involve storing sets of numbers in files or databases. That activity lies beyond the scope of this book, but this book still anticipates such activity. If these numbers are generated beforehand, retrieving them and using them to guide actions can proceed in some instances much more quickly than if you regenerate them each time you use them. Likewise, the actions then made possible can become extremely complex, because they represent combinations of data generated by different methods rather than isolated actions executed just once.

In this book, you stop short of writing data to files or using a database, but if you have established a fundamental understanding of the work of a collection as a medium of intelligence in your game, then you are in an excellent position to take your work in this direction to add what might be viewed as the next component to the Code Lab application. As a starter, return to Chapter 9 and remove the comments from all of the possible calls (1 through 4) to the `runFunction()` method in `runButton_Click()` method. If you again consider Figure 1.7 in Chapter 1, you see that this marks just be beginning of any numbers of maps you might lay down as you use functions to generate patterns of data.

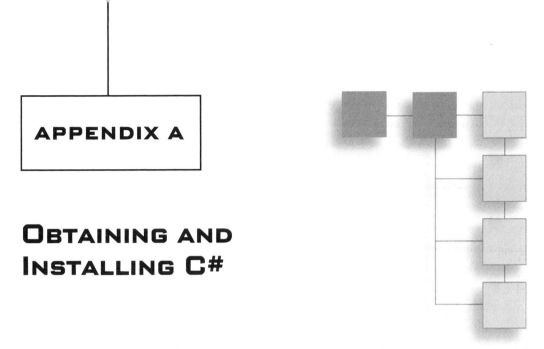

APPENDIX A

OBTAINING AND INSTALLING C#

Microsoft makes available a version of Microsoft Studio that, as of the writing of this book, you can obtain free of charge. This appendix instructs you how to obtain and install this software. If you already have Microsoft Studio, the projects you obtain from the CD or the Internet site for this book will work as long as your version is new enough.

The projects in this book have been created using Microsoft Visual C# 2005, and the version number is 8.0.50727.42. In other words, you should be okay as long as you have Visual Studio 2005 or later. If you have an earlier version, the form and code files contain code that is compatible with older versions, but you will not be able to use the project (*.sln) files.

Where to Find It

Microsoft makes available "express" editions of several of its development environments. The environment for C# is among these. To view the packages Microsoft makes available, go to this site:

  http://msdn.microsoft.com/vstudio/express/

Figure A.1 illustrates the page you see.

One detail you might note on the page is that the express packages take 30MB to 375MB of your disk space. This is not likely to create a problem for most people. If

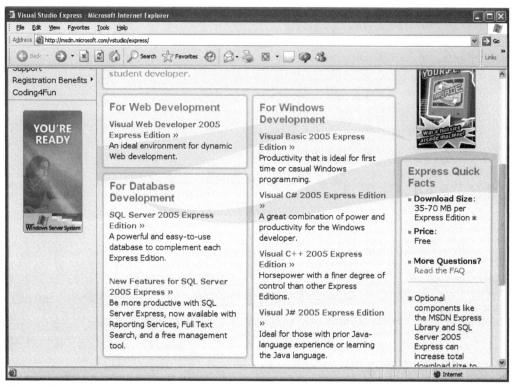

Figure A.1
Microsoft provides a list of its free express packages.

you have less than 1GB of remaining space, however, it is probably not a good idea to download and install even an express version of a development environment.

Click on the link that reads Visual C# 2005 Express Edition. The link might have changed to a different version by the time you visit the site, but if Microsoft continues the program, then a similar link should be visible.

You then see the page that discusses Visual C# specifically and allows you to begin downloading the express version. (See Figure A.2.)

Click on the link that reads Download Now. You then see the page Figure A.3 illustrates, the Download Now page. If you have a version of Microsoft Visual Studio that predates the 2005 version, you do not need to do anything. Generally, unless you have visited this site before, you can probably proceed without problems. If you have visited this site before, however, and have downloaded either the C# Express Edition or the 2005 versions of any of the named packages (particularly SQL Server 2005), then you must uninstall previous versions, as

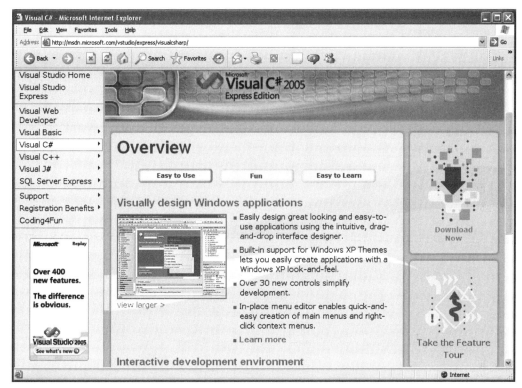

Figure A.2
Access the page for the Express Edition.

instructed. Again, note that for other versions (2004 and so on) you probably do not have to uninstall any of your software.

Note

The author has left Visual Studio 2004 and Visual Studio 6.0 installed without encountering problems.

Click on the Download link as shown in Figure A.3 You then see the File Download dialog for the vcssetup.exe file. (See Figure A.4.) Click the Save button.

You see the Save As dialog box. (See Figure A.5.) Navigate to the appropriate directory and click the Save button to save the vcssetup.exe file. The download of this file requires only a few seconds. When the download completes, you should be able to see the vcssetup.exe file in a directory you can easily identify. At this point, proceed to the next section, "Installing the Express Edition."

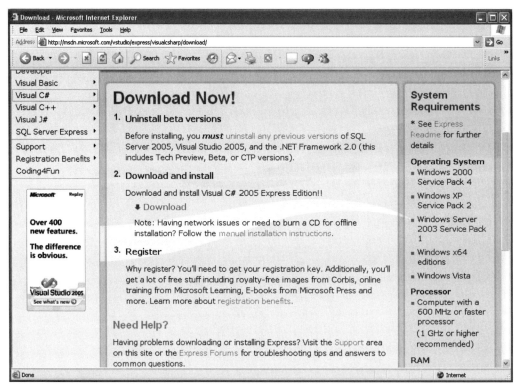

Figure A.3
Access the page to begin your download.

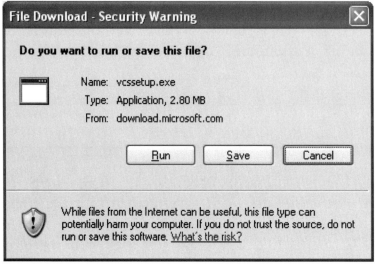

Figure A.4
Click the Save button.

Figure A.5
Save the installation package to a convenient location on your hard drive.

Installing the Express Edition

The instructions in this section assume that you have accessed the Microsoft site and downloaded the setup package for the Microsoft Visual C# 2005 Express Edition. If you have not completed this task, go to the previous section of this appendix, "Where to Find It" and perform the activities documented there.

To install the express edition of C#, click the vcssetup.exe file. You see the dialog shown in Figure A.6. Click the Run button to begin the installation.

A series of dialogs inform you that the installation package is being configured. If you are installing for the first time, you then see the Welcome to Setup dialog Figure A.7 illustrates.

Leave the default options and click the Next button in the Welcome to Setup dialog. You then see the End-User License Agreement that Figure A.8 illustrates. To accept the terms of the user agreement, click the check box. Then click the Next button.

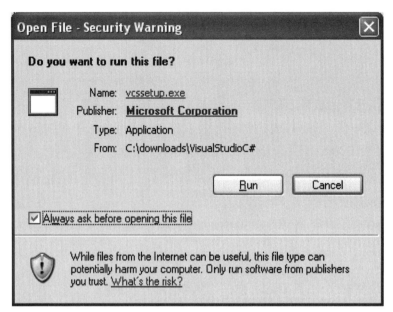

Figure A.6
Click Run to begin the installation.

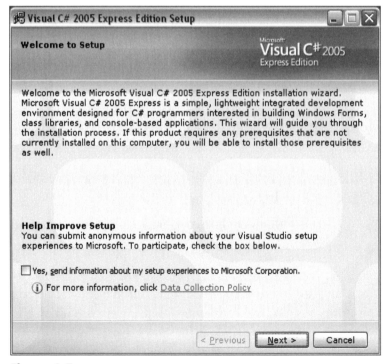

Figure A.7
Click the Next button.

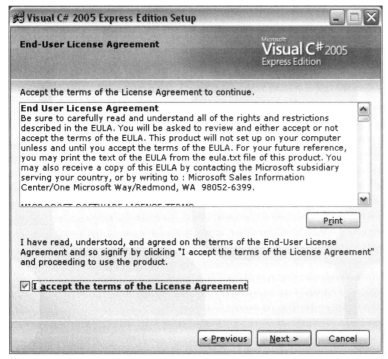

Figure A.8
Click the check box and the Next button.

After you click Next in the End-User License Agreement, you see the Installation Options dialog, illustrated by Figure A.9. It is not necessary to use either the MSDN or SQL resources for this book. At this time, leave the options unchecked and click the Next button.

Note

You can install the Microsoft Development Network (MSDN) files or the SQL Server files at a later time. To accomplish this task, use the installation routine this appendix documents. The dialogs you see when you update your software differ from those shown here, but after having seen the installation process once, you should find it familiar and easy to use. At that point, you can choose the option to install the MSDN or SQL Server software as additions to your primary C# Express installation.

You then see the Destination Folder dialog, as shown in Figure A.10. This dialog identifies the location on your disk drive to which the installation package

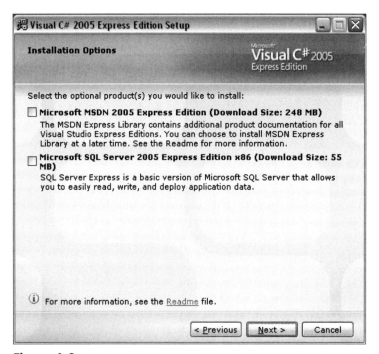

Figure A.9
Leave the check boxes unchecked and click the Next button.

Figure A.10
Accept the default location and click the Install button.

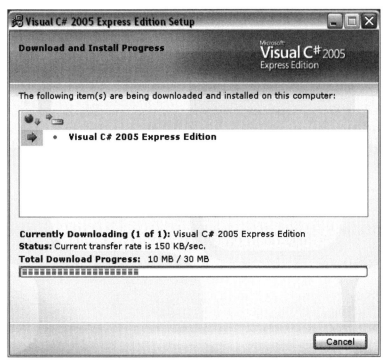

Figure A.11
The dialog for Download and Install progress is visible for several minutes.

transfers the files for the Express Edition. Do not change the default setting. Click Install.

You then see a dialog for Download and Install Progress. As Figure A.11 reveals, this dialog tells you the status of the download, along with the size of the software package. You do not need to respond to this dialog.

As the download progresses, the dialog changes to reflect the status of the download and installation. Figure A.12 illustrates the dialog as it tracks installation activities. You do not need to respond to this dialog.

When the download and installation activities finish, you see the Setup Complete dialog, as shown in Figure A.13.

Note

Microsoft requests that you register your software within 30 days. It is suggested that you do so at this point, but you can still work with all of the software in this book without registering. To register your software, click the Register Now link.

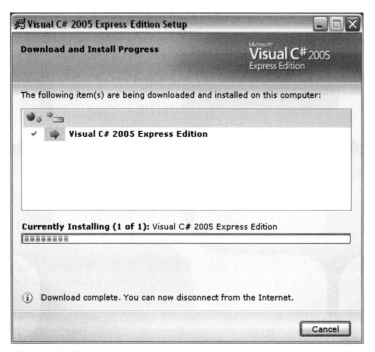

Figure A.12
The dialog changes to reflect installation activities.

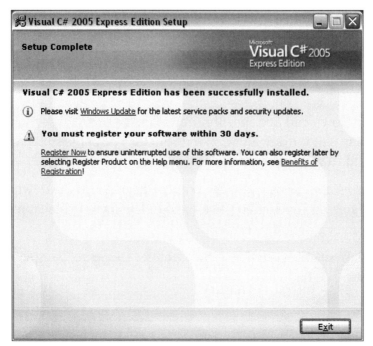

Figure A.13
Click the Exit button in the Setup Complete dialog.

Click Exit in the Setup Complete dialog.

After you exit the Setup Complete dialog, you can then go to the Start menu and select Start > All Programs > Microsoft Visual C# 2005 Express Edition.

Alternatively, navigate to the Chapter 1 folder and click on the *.sln file. The project file for Chapter 1 opens. You can then press F5 to compile and run the Chapter 1 project.

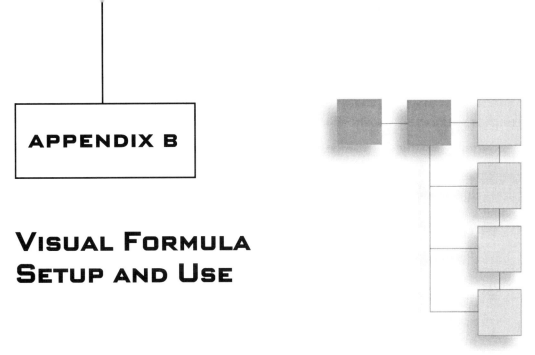

APPENDIX B

VISUAL FORMULA SETUP AND USE

To install Visual Formula, you copy it from the book's CD. The installation does nothing more than copy a single program file to your hard drive.

One approach to installing Visual Formula is as follows:

1. On your C: drive (or the main drive of your computer), navigate using Windows Explorer to your C:\Program Files directory.

2. Create a directory called Visual Formula.

3. Copy the Visual Formula program file into this directory. The name of the Visual Formula program is Visual Formula.exe. Then create a shortcut for the Visual Formula program and copy it to your desktop. See Figure B.1.

If you have the appropriate .NET Framework software on your computer, you can then click on the icon on your desktop to execute Visual Formula. See Figure B.2.

Note

When you click to activate Visual Formula, if you see a dialog that tells you that you require additional software from Microsoft, see the supplemental document provided on the CD. It is called "Microsoft Software Advisories." This document explains how to download the .NET support software that allows you to run applications developed with C# and other Microsoft development tools. The software is a standard part of the Microsoft platform, presents no danger to your current software configuration, and requires minimal disk space.

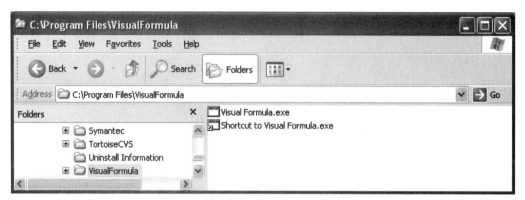

Figure B.1
Copy Visual Formula to your disk drive and create a shortcut.

Figure B.2
A desktop icon provides convenient access.

Visual Formula Overview

Visual Formula provides you with two general capabilities. The first is to quickly implement equations and generate their solutions. The second involves generating graphical representations of equations.

The use of Visual Formula received attention in several chapters of this book. Figure B.3 provides a summary of its primary features. Table B.1 discusses specific features.

Linear Graphs

A linear function generates a graph characterized by a slope that does not change. The line-slope-intercept equation provides a way to experiment with linear equations. Here is the line-slope-intercept equation as you have seen it in previous chapters:

$$f(x) = mx + b \quad \text{or} \quad y = mx + b$$

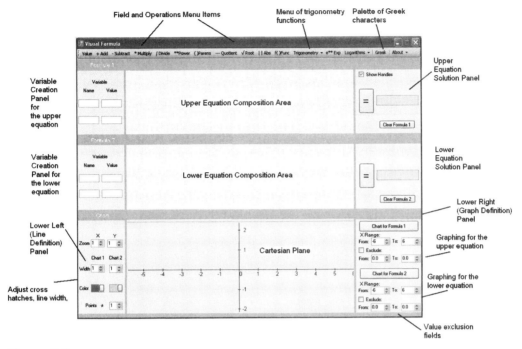

Figure B.3
Visual Formula keeps most of its functionality in view.

Table B.1 Visual Formula Features

Feature	Discussion
Clear Formula 1	This button deletes everything you have implemented in the upper equation composition area. It also deletes the graph that corresponds to the equation in the upper equation composition area.
Clear Formula 2	This button deletes everything you have implemented in the lower equation composition area. It also deletes the graph that corresponds to the equation in the lower equation composition area.
Color	This field opens a palette from which you can choose the colors of the lines you generate for the equations in the upper and lower equation composition areas.
Equals Button	The Solution panels of the upper and lower equation composition areas offer buttons with equals signs on them. When you click the button with the equals sign, you execute the equation you have created in the corresponding equation composition area.
Equation Composition Area	One of the two areas Visual Formula provides in which you can compose equations.

continued

Table B.1 (continued)

Feature	Discussion
Exclude	This check box appears in the lower-right panel. One Exclude check box applies to each of the equations you compose in the equation composition areas. Click the Exclude box and then the Range controls associated with it to prevent a given range of values from being used in your calculations.
Lower Equation	This refers to any equation you create in the lower composition area.
Lower-Right Panel	Also known as the Graph Definition panel. It contains the Chart Formula 1 and Chart Formula 2 buttons. It also contains fields for the upper and lower equations that allow you to exclude values used by the equations.
Lower-Left Panel	Also known as the Line Definition panel. You find controls to allow you to change the width of lines, the color of lines, and the density of cross hatches on lines. You also find the Points control.
Points	This control is in the lower-left panel. It allows you to smooth lines by increasing the number of points used to calculate them.
Shift + Left Mouse Button	This action deletes any specific item you have placed in the lower or upper composition areas. Use it to correct details. Do not click the Clear Formula buttons unless you want to delete everything.
Show Handles	When you place a field in the equation composition areas, by default you see shaded borders that allow you to adjust their sizes using the mouse cursor. If you do not want to see these handles, deselect the Show Handles check box in the upper-right panel.
Solution Panel	Either of the two panels to the right of the equation composition areas.
Upper Equation	This refers to any equation you create in the upper composition area.
Variable Creation Panel	This panel provides you with two fields. In the Name field, you type the name of a variable you want to use when you compose an equation. You can use any name you want, but Visual Formula reserves x and z for special purposes. You can set a value in the Value field as a constant to associate with any variable name you create.
x	When you supply x in any Value field you create in the composition area, Visual Formula generates a set of values for your equation. In this way, you can generate continuous lines when you graph the output of your graphs.
z	Use z in the lower equation composition area. It provides the output of the equation you create in the upper equation composition area.
Zoom	This field allows you to increase the number of cross hatches you see on the x or y axis.
Width	This field allows you to increase the thickness of the lines used to graph your equations.
X Range	This field allows you to extend the number range of the x axis in the Cartesian plane. You can either click the Range controls to decrease or increase the values, or you can activate the field and enter numbers from the keyboard.

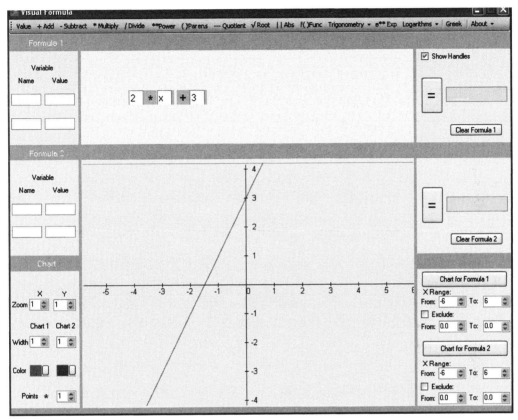

Figure B.4
Create and graph a linear equation.

Drawing from Table B.1, you can use this equation to generate a line with a positive slope of 2 and a *y*-intercept at 3:

$$y = 2x + 3$$

Refer to Figure B.4 as you go, and implement this equation in Visual Formula using the following steps:

1. Select Value from the menu bar. To position the field the Value item activates, click in the top equation composition area. This creates a field for constants that corresponds to the *m* constant. This constant defines the slope of the equation. In the Value field, type 2.

2. Select Multiply from the menu bar. Then click to place the multiplication symbol immediately after the Value field.

3. Following the multiplication sign, double-click to create a second Value field. Type an x in this field. The x represents a range of values you use to generate the graph of a line.

4. After setting up the Value field for x, click Add from the menu bar. To place the plus sign in the equation composition area, click just after the x Value field.

5. Click Value from the menu bar. Then click in the composition area after the plus sign to place the Value field for the y-intercept constant. Type 3 in this field.

See the equation composition area of Figure B.4 for the appearance of the equation after you have implemented it. To test your work, click the button on the right of the composition that contains the equals sign. You see 2 in the field adjacent to it.

Now you can generate a graphical representation of the equation. Toward this end, first move the cursor to the top of the Cartesian plane. As you do so, the cursor turns into a horizontal line with arrows extending up and down. Press the left mouse button and pull the Cartesian plane upward until its top edge is even with the bottom of the composition area that contains your equation. Figure B.4 illustrates Visual Formula after you have extended the Cartesian plane.

Having extended the Cartesian plane, you are ready to generate the line. To accomplish this, locate and click on the Chart for Formula 1 button on the lower-right panel of the Visual Formula window. You see the line illustrated in Figure B.4.

Using Visual Formula

Use Visual Formula to implement a linear equation involving an absolute value. Toward this end, generate a graph that shifts the vertex of the graph to the left on the x axis 4 units. Here is the equation that accomplishes this task:

$$y = |4 + x|$$

To implement the equation, refer to Figure B.5 and use the following steps:

1. Double-click (| |Abs) from the menu bar (absolute value). Then click in the equation composition area to position the absolute value bars. Use the mouse cursor to pull the bars for the absolute value area far enough apart to accommodate two Value fields and a plus sign (see Figure B.5).

2. Select Value from the menu bar. Position the field just to the right of the left absolute value bar. Click in the field and type 4.

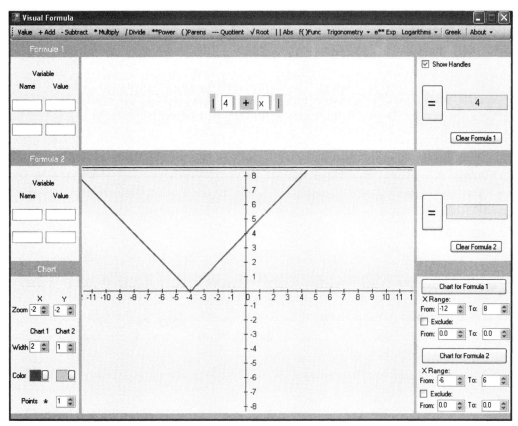

Figure B.5
Adding to the number inside the absolute value bars shifts the graph to the left.

3. Select Add from the menu bar and position the plus sign to the right of the Value field.

4. Select Value from the menu bar again and position the field after the plus sign and inside the absolute value bars. Click in the field and type *x*.

5. In the lower part of the Visual Formula window, move the cursor to the top of the Cartesian plane so that it turns into parallel bars. Pull the Cartesian plane up until it is even with the bottom of the top equation composition area.

6. In the lower-right panel, find the From and To fields for the X Range setting beneath the Chart for Formula 1 button. Click the To drop-down arrow and set the value to −12. Click the From drop-down arrow and set the value to 8.

7. In the lower-left panel, find the Zoom drop-down arrows for the X and Y field controls and set both fields to −2.

8. Under Chart 1, set the Chart 1 Width field to 2.

9. Click the Chart for Formula 1 button. You see the graph shown in Figure B.5.

To experiment, insert the following values in the field preceding the plus sign and observe the results: 2, 3, 5, 6. In each instance, the distance you shift the graph to the left on the x axis changes. To shift the graph so that its vertex moves to the right, use values of -2, -3, and -6. As you go, remember to click on the Chart for Formula 1 button to refresh the graph each time you change a value. Also, increase the value of the X Range To field to 12.

Parabolas

When you calculate values for a parabola, you use an exponent of an even value. The result is a graph that is symmetrical with respect to the y axis. A parabola crosses the y axis once, so if you employ an equation of the form $y = x^2 + c$, the value of c provides a translation value that is also the value of the y-intercept. As a translation value, the constant c moves the graph up or down the y axis. Figure B.6 provides a few examples of translation.

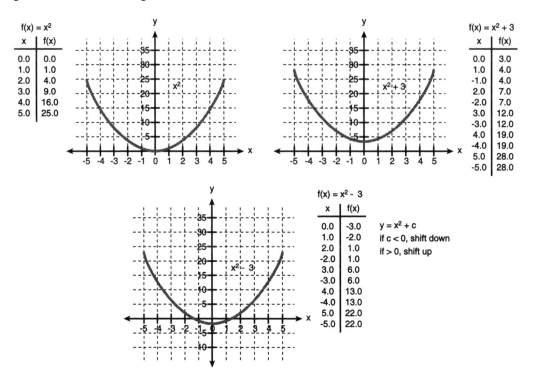

Figure B.6
Add a constant value to shift the graph up and down along the y axis.

Each parabola shown in Figure B.6 represents an equation that includes a constant for the y-intercept. In the first use of the equation, you can rewrite it as $x^2 + 0$. When the vertex rests on the coordinates $(0, 0)$, the y-intercept value is 0. The other two uses of the equation set the y-intercept at values greater than or less than zero. The first adds 3. The second subtracts 3.

The generalization then arises that if the value of the y-intercept exceeds 0, then the graph shifts upward. On the other hand, if the value of the y-intercept is less than 0, then the graph shifts downward. When the value of the y-intercept equals 0, then the vertex of the graph rests on the x axis.

To employ Visual Formula to implement a set of nonlinear equations that are shifted along the y axis, use these steps (refer to Figure B.7):

1. Select Value from the menu bar. To position the value field, click in the upper equation composition area. Type x in the Value field.

2. Select Power from the menu bar. Click to place the field for the exponent to the upper right of the Value field. Type 2 in the Exponent field.

3. Select Add from the menu bar. Then click to the right of the Value field to position the plus sign.

4. Select Value from the menu bar and then click to place the Value field after the plus sign. This is the y-intercept of the equation. To raise the vertex of the parabola 3 units above the x axis, type 3.

5. Now proceed to the lower-right panel and click the Chart Formula 1 button to generate the graph. As Figure B.7 illustrates, the vertex of the parabola that results rests above the x axis.

The y-intercept forced the top parabola in Figure B.7 to shift three units above the x axis. To generate the bottom parabola, perform the following steps:

1. Select Value from the menu bar. Then click in the lower equation composition area to position the Value field. Type x in the Value field.

2. Select Power from the menu bar. Position the field for the exponent to the upper right of the Value field. Type 2 in the Power field.

3. Select Subtract from the menu bar. To position the minus sign, click to the right of the Value field.

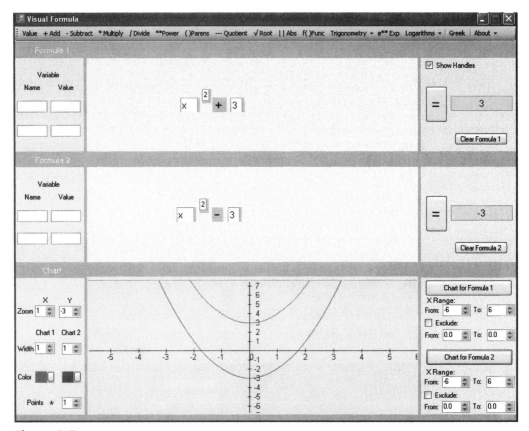

Figure B.7
Different *y*-intercept values shift the parabolas up and down the *y* axis.

4. Select Value from the menu bar. To position the Value field, click after the minus sign. To lower the vertex of the parabola 3 units below the *x* axis, type 3.

5. In the lower-right panel, click the Chart Formula 2 button to generate the graph. As Figure B.7 illustrates, the vertex of the graph that appears rests three units below the *x* axis.

Parallel Lines

The general form of the line-slope-intercept equation is $y = mx + b$. In this equation, *m* describes the slope of the equation, and *b* provides the value of the *y*-intercept. Given that a set of equations possesses the same slope, then if you vary only the value of *b*, you end up with a set of parallel lines.

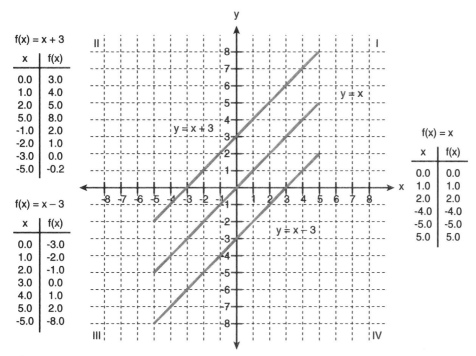

$f(x) = x + 3$

x	f(x)
0.0	3.0
1.0	4.0
2.0	5.0
5.0	8.0
-1.0	2.0
-2.0	1.0
-3.0	0.0
-5.0	-0.2

$f(x) = x - 3$

x	f(x)
0.0	-3.0
1.0	-2.0
2.0	-1.0
3.0	0.0
4.0	1.0
5.0	2.0
-5.0	-8.0

$f(x) = x$

x	f(x)
0.0	0.0
1.0	1.0
2.0	2.0
-4.0	-4.0
-5.0	-5.0
5.0	5.0

Figure B.8
The value of the y-intercept raises or lowers the line on the y axis.

Figure B.8 illustrates the graphs of three lines. The middle line crosses the origin of the Cartesian plane. You could rewrite it as $y = x + 0$. The other two lines include positive and negative values for the y-intercept. The top line provides a y-intercept of 3. The lower line provides a y-intercept value of -3. A generalization emerges from the work of these intercepts. If the intercept value is less than 0, then the line crosses the origin. If it is greater than 0, then it is above the origin. If it is less than 0, then it is below the origin. Whatever the y-intercept value, as long as the slopes remain the same, the lines remain parallel.

You can create parallel lines if you set the slope of the line to 1. In this instance, the equation assumes the form $y = x + b$, because the slope, m, equals 1. To use Visual Formula to generate a set of lines with slopes set to 1 but y-intercept definitions set at distinct values, follow these steps (refer to Figure B.9):

1. Select Value from the menu bar. Then click in the upper equation composition area to position the Value field. Type x in the Value field.

2. Select Add from the menu bar. Then click to the right of the Value field to position the plus sign.

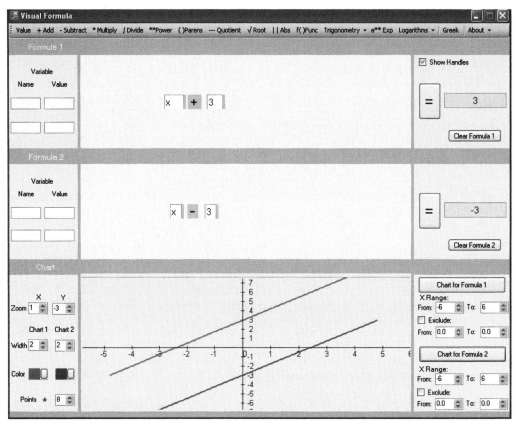

Figure B.9
Use *y*-intercept settings to generate parallel lines.

3. Select Value from the menu bar. To position the Value field, click to the right of the plus sign. This is the *y*-intercept of the equation. To raise the *y*-intercept 3 units above the *x* axis, type 3 in the field.

4. Now proceed to the lower-right panel and click the Chart Formula 1 button to generate the graph. As Figure B.9 illustrates, the line that results intersects the *y* axis above the *x* axis.

In Figure B.9, you created a line that intercepts the *y* axis 3 units above the *x* axis. To create a line that intercepts the *y* axis 3 units below the x axis, use the following steps:

1. Select Value from the menu bar. Then click in the lower equation composition area to position the Value field. Type x in the Value field.

2. Select Subtract from the menu bar. Then click to the right of the Value field to position the minus sign.

3. Select Value from the menu bar. To position the Value field, click after the minus sign. To set the y-intercept 3 units below the x axis, type 3 in this field.

4. To generate the graph of the line, in the lower-right panel, click the Chart Formula 2 button. As Figure B.9 illustrates, the resulting graph crosses the y axis below the x axis.

Note

The examples of how to use Visual Formula that appear in this appendix are derived from examples given in *Beginning Pre-Calculus for Game Developers,* by John Flynt and Boris Meltreger (Thomson Course PTR, 2006). See that book for many more examples of how to use Visual Formula.

INDEX

License Agreement/Notice of Limited Warranty